practical gardener

BEDDING PLANTS

MARTIN FISH

First published in 2004 by HarperCollins*Publishers*

77–85 Fulham Palace Road, London, W6 8JB

The Collins website address is:

www.collins.co.uk

Text by Martin Fish; copyright © HarperCollins*Publishers*

Artworks and design © HarperCollins*Publishers*

Photography by Tim Sandall and Martin Fish

Cover photography by Tim Sandall

Photographic props: Coolings Nurseries, Rushmore Hill,
Knockholt, Kent, TN14 7NN, www.coolings.co.uk and Martin & Jill
Fish, Meadowfield Gardens

Design and editorial: Focus Publishing, Sevenoaks, Kent

Project editor: Guy Croton

Editor: Vanessa Townsend

Project co-ordinator: Caroline Watson

Design & illustration: David Etherington

For HarperCollins

Senior managing editor: Angela Newton

Design manager: Luke Griffin

Editor: Alastair Laing

Editorial assistant: Lisa John

Production: Chris Gurney

A CIP catalogue record for this book is available from the
British Library

ISBN 0007164068

Colour reproduction by Colourscan

Printed and bound in Italy by L.E.G.O.

 practical gardener

BEDDING PLANTS

Contents

Introduction

Bedding plants are a large, varied group of plants for use in beds, borders, baskets and containers, and they provide seasonal colour throughout the year.

There are no particular rules as to what defines a bedding plant, although generally they are planted to provide colour and interest for one season at a time. Traditionally, Lobelia and Salvia were the mainstays of summer bedding schemes, and wallflowers (Erysimum) for spring flowers, but over the years many different types of plant have been used with great effect. Annuals, biennials, perennials, corms and tubers can all be used together and grown for either their flowers or attractive foliage – or a combination of both.

The use of bedding plants is a very simple and guaranteed way of making all gardens, whether large or small, look vibrant and appealing. Bedding plants can also be used with great success on patios and balconies. By changing colour schemes or the style of planting, a garden can be made to look very different for each season. Modern gardening trends tend towards instant colour, which is something you can certainly achieve with bedding plants. Plants can be bought in flower to give immediate effect in borders or containers.

It was during the nineteenth century that bedding plants gained popularity, although annual flowering plants were grown in gardens prior to that. People of that era very quickly realized the potential of bedding plants, creating elaborate designs in public parks. Their popularity soon spread to large private houses and stately homes, where vast numbers of bedding plants were planted to form intricate designs and coats of arms. By the early twentieth century, bedding plants were at their peak, and there was a great deal of competition between head gardeners to produce the most exciting and colourful displays. This enthusiasm soon filtered down to small-scale home gardeners, and planting out formal bedding schemes twice a year became the norm in many gardens.

During the 1970s and 1980s, bedding plants were not as popular as in the past, mainly due to changing gardening trends together with the cost and labour required to plant large bedding schemes. In recent years, however, interest in bedding plants has increased greatly both in the private and public sector, compelling seed companies and plant breeders to work very hard in order to meet demand for new and interesting plants.

Traditional mixed bedding schemes are once more very popular with gardeners

How to Use This Book

This book is divided into three parts. The opening chapters guide you through all areas of garden practice, from assessing your site, through planting and general care of bedding plants to propagation techniques. A comprehensive plant directory follows, with individual entries on over 200 of the most commonly available bedding plants, listed in alphabetical order. All the most colourful and popular flowers are included, covering many different styles of gardening and uses. The final section of the book covers plant problems. Troubleshooting pages allow you to diagnose the likely cause of any problems affecting your bedding plants, and a directory of pests and diseases offers detailed advice on how to solve them.

latin name of the plant genus, followed by its **common name**

detailed descriptions give specific advice on care for each plant, including pruning and pests and diseases

alphabetical tabs on the side of the page, colour-coded to help you quickly find the plant you want

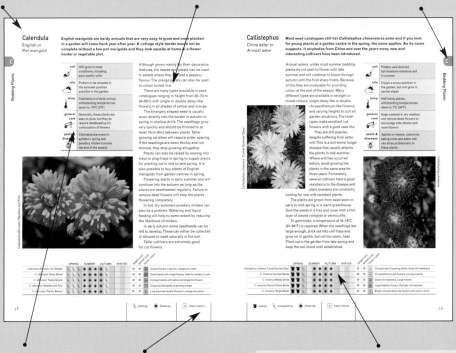

care charts provide an at-a-glance summary of the plant's specific needs

a key at the bottom of the page explains what each symbol means

variety charts list recommended varieties for most genera of bedding plants or the best individual species. These display key information to help you choose your ideal plant, showing:

- when the plant is in flower during the year
- the time to sow, plant or transplant for the best results
- the height and spread of the plants in centimetres
- the minimum temperature the plant will withstand
- the plant's watering and light/shade requirements
- a rough approximation of the flower colour
- additional comments from the author

Assessing Your Garden

All gardens are different and before you plant, it pays to assess the various conditions that might affect what you can grow. The fact that growing conditions can vary, even in very small gardens, need not be negative – it offers more scope for a wider range of plants to be used.

If you intend to raise your own plants, care needs to be given to the location of a greenhouse or cold frame. In spring, when many plants are being started from seed or cuttings, maximum light is needed for strong growth. Avoid positioning a greenhouse or cold frame in heavy shade. Ideally, it should receive sun for most of the day (see Equipment for Growing, page 15).

Even if you intend to plant in containers, the amount of sun, shade or wind in the garden needs to be taken into account. Assessing the different conditions around your garden is very simple and only takes a short time.

Aspect

All plants need light to grow and some need more than others. Generally, bedding plants prefer good light, which means being in sun for a good part of the day. Check where the sun rises, where it is at mid-day and where it sets in the evening. Remember also that during the winter months the sun is much lower in the sky and even a low hedge or fence can cast a long shadow across the garden. During the winter, when the weather is frosty, borders in shade may not thaw out at all during the day; although this may not kill plants, it will slow down growth and reduce flowering.

A site in full sun for most of the day is ideal for plants such as petunias and geraniums (Pelargonium). In shady parts of the garden, the popular busy Lizzie (Impatiens) will thrive and flower profusely all summer long.

Wind

Wind can cause a great deal of damage to young plants by drying out the leaves. In severe cases, this wind scorch can kill.

Growing conditions must be compatible when combining plants

In most areas there is usually a prevailing wind direction and this should be noted. Filtering the wind by planting a few trees or shrubs on the windward side of the garden may be all that is needed to reduce wind speed. This method is more effective than a solid barrier, which can cause turbulence around the plants.

In coastal or hilly places it may not be possible to reduce wind speed as much, so thought should be given to the choice of plants. Pick low growing plants that are less likely to be battered by the wind. Have a look at what type of plants are growing well in nearby gardens.

Occasionally, especially during the winter months, cold, biting winds come from a different direction and these can be very damaging. In this situation, a temporary windbreak of fine garden mesh or fabric fleece can be erected to protect the plants.

Passages and paths between buildings can cause problems by funnelling the wind, so avoid tender or tall plants in these areas. The use of a few shrubs or netting will help to filter the wind in this situation.

Soil

The majority of bedding plants will grow quite happily in most types of soil, providing you carry out some basic soil improvements where needed. Ideal soil drains freely in wet weather and retains moisture and nutrients in dry weather. Unfortunately, such soil conditions are rare. The two extremes are clay, which is wet and sticky in the winter, and sand, which dries out very quickly in the summer. Both of these soils can be improved over just a

> **TIP**
>
> Choose where you position various bedding plants carefully. Plants growing in heavy shade will often grow tall and leggy, and produce fewer flowers than those which are grown in a sunny position.

couple of seasons by adding bulky organic matter. Not only will your plants benefit from these improvements, it will become much easier to cultivate the soil.

Drainage

Plants need water to grow, but too much water around the roots will lead to the roots rotting off. Too little water will make the plants die from drought.

Digging in clay soils can be difficult at most times of the year. In winter the wet soil is very heavy, while in the summer it tends to dry out and bake hard. Adding organic matter will open up the structure of the soil, letting in more air and allowing water to drain more freely. Adding horticultural grit will also help water drainage.

Sandy soils are much easier to dig over, even in the winter after heavy rainfall. However, due to the rapid draining properties of sand, the soil soon becomes dry in the summer months. As the water drains through the sandy soil, valuable nutrients are lost. The addition of organic matter on an annual basis will help to retain moisture and, as the organic matter breaks down to form humus, more nutrients will remain in the soil.

Regardless of the type of soil, organic matter is beneficial. As well as improving drainage and water holding capacity, the activity of soil micro-organisms will increase, and the fertility of the soil will improve.

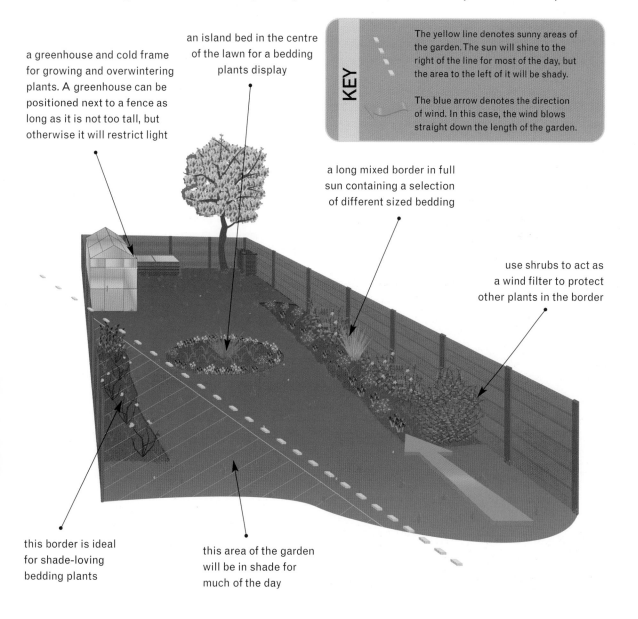

KEY

The yellow line denotes sunny areas of the garden. The sun will shine to the right of the line for most of the day, but the area to the left of it will be shady.

The blue arrow denotes the direction of wind. In this case, the wind blows straight down the length of the garden.

a greenhouse and cold frame for growing and overwintering plants. A greenhouse can be positioned next to a fence as long as it is not too tall, but otherwise it will restrict light

an island bed in the centre of the lawn for a bedding plants display

a long mixed border in full sun containing a selection of different sized bedding

use shrubs to act as a wind filter to protect other plants in the border

this border is ideal for shade-loving bedding plants

this area of the garden will be in shade for much of the day

Types of Bedding Plants

There are three main types of plant used for bedding purposes: annuals, biennials and perennials. However, this does not mean they need to planted in three distinct groups. They can all be mixed together to create interesting and colourful displays.

Annuals

These are plants that are raised from seed, produce flowers and then die in one season. For use in the garden they fall into two categories: hardy annuals and half-hardy annuals.

Hardy annuals can withstand frost and include plants such as the Californian poppy (*Eschscholzia californica*) and love-in-a-mist (*Nigella damascena*). Half-hardy annuals are tender and planted out when the danger of spring frosts has passed. These include plants such as French marigold (*Tagetes patula*) and the tobacco plant (*Nicotiana alata*). Many bedding plants, although technically perennials, are grown as half-hardy

A bed block planted with mixed Tagetes in yellows and oranges

annuals from seed each spring. Petunia and antirrhinum are examples, the former being frost-sensitive and the latter frost-hardy.

Biennials

This group of plants takes two growing seasons to complete their life cycle. During the first season they make vegetative growth and in the second they produce flowers and seed. The majority are hardy and can be overwintered outside. Biennials used as bedding plants include wallflower (*Erysimum cheiri*) and sweet Williams (*Dianthus barbatus*).

Perennials

A perennial lives for more than two years and most will live much longer. The perennials used in bedding displays are very often tender perennials, such as geranium (*Pelargonium zonale*) or Abutilon. They can be grown outside during the summer, but require frost protection in winter. Another group of perennials are grown from tubers or rhizomes and these also need frost protection. Dahlias and some begonias produce tubers that act as a food store while the plant is dormant during winter. Cannas grow from a fleshy rhizome – a modified underground stem that also acts as a food store. All of these plants die down in the autumn and re-grow in spring.

Bedding plant uses

When planning which bedding plants to grow or buy, it pays to have some idea of where they will be planted in your beds or borders. For this reason we can divide bedding plants into three groups. The suggestions are intended only as a guideline and some plants that are used as main bedding may be planted as edging plants in larger displays. The aim is to try and keep the different groups of plants in scale with the bed or garden.

[A] Edging plants These are low growing plants that are usually planted around the edge of a bed or the front of a border. Various plants can be used,

TIP
You do not have to conform to one of the traditional bedding styles. It is great fun experimenting with plants to create different effects in your garden. Hardy annuals, half-hardy annuals and perennials can all be mixed together.

such as lobelia, ageratum and impatiens. Normally, you would not want the edging plants to grow much taller than 20cm (8in) in height. However, taller edging plants could be used with larger main-bedding plants, or if the bed itself is very large overall.

[B] Dot plants To give extra height to the planting, dot plants or standards can be used. A dot plant is a taller plant, often architectural in habit, which will add extra interest to the planting. Abutilon, Canna and Cordyline are all suitable as dot plants. A standard,

This simple scheme features all three main types of bedding: main, edging and dot plants

A

B

C

such as a fuchsia or geranium, is a plant that has been grown on a single stem, and again will add height to the display.

[C] Main-bedding The majority of the planting in the bed will comprise of these plants. They should grow taller than the edging plants and can range in height between 25–60cm (10–24in). Plants such as petunias, bedding dahlias, cosmos and geraniums (Pelargonium) can be used. Whether you prefer the main-bedding plants to be a single colour or mixed will obviously depend on your personal taste.

Block planting

This method involves just one type of plant, mass planted in a block. There are no edging, main-bedding or dot plants, just a single block of plants either in one colour or mixed. You can use almost any type of plant from very low growing ones to tall plants. This method of planting is extremely useful in making a bold, spectacular statement in the garden.

Once your bedding scheme is established, don't worry if you are not happy with your particular choice of bedding scheme. After all, beds often only last for one year and you can easily change the scheme for the following season.

Seasonal Bedding

It is possible to have bedding plants in the garden or containers all year round. This involves planting twice a year in succession. The two main times of the year when bedding plants flower are summer and spring, although many plants will provide interest and colour during autumn and winter.

Summer bedding

This is the most popular form of bedding as it remains colourful for several months. Young plants are normally raised under cover and planted out in late spring when the danger of frost has passed. They will continue to flower until the first autumn frost. Some plants, such as *Nemesia strumosa*, are short lived and usually by mid-summer they are past their best. Whereas plants such as aster (*Callistephus chinensis*) bloom from mid-summer onwards. The range of plants for use as summer bedding is huge and there is something suitable for every taste and situation.

Spring bedding

This group of plants may cause confusion because it is sometimes referred to as winter bedding. They are usually planted after the summer plants have been removed in early autumn, in order to have time to establish before the onset of winter. Some plants, such as winter pansies (Viola), will produce flowers in the autumn and through the winter if the weather is mild, but most flowers are borne in spring, hence spring bedding. Other plants such as forget-me-nots (Myosotis) and wallflowers (Erysimum) only flower in spring, but still need to be planted in the autumn.

Some pansies (Viola) will flower throughout the autumn

Wallflowers (Erysimum) produce colourful spring bedding displays

A mixed display of Bellis brightens up the drab months of winter

Bedding styles

The style in which you arrange bedding plants depends greatly on the effect you are trying to create. Some gardens lend themselves to formal designs while others are less suitable; for example, a formal, angular bed in an informal garden with soft curves might look badly out of place. Consequently, it is important to think about what style of bedding suits your garden best. This also applies to containers, which can be very structured or form a mass of flowering plants growing into each other.

Modern bedding schemes often take on both styles and although the shape of the beds may be formal, the planting within will look informal. This style of bedding is becoming more popular and many local authorities are planting very interesting and innovative schemes that can be copied on a smaller scale in our gardens.

Formal bedding This is the type of bedding that you would normally see in a public park with geometrical or symmetrical designs. Within the bed there will be edging, main-bedding and dot plants arranged in a formal pattern. Many people also plant formal bedding in their own gardens on a much smaller scale by creating a bed or several beds in a lawn.

Informal bedding Many gardeners prefer informal bedding in their own gardens. Plants are not arranged in definite patterns, but can instead be mixed or planted in groups between other plants, such as herbaceous perennials or shrubs. Informal bedding is ideal for filling gaps in borders where extra seasonal colour is needed. Hardy annuals planted in drifts of colour are ideal for creating an informal display.

Tropical bedding For something different during the summer try creating a planting scheme with a tropical look. To create a stunning effect, use a selection of houseplants such as weeping fig (*Ficus benjamina*) and umbrella plant (Schefflera) with plants that have large leaves like canna and banana (Musa) and a mixture of hot, vibrant flowering plants. This style of planting can easily be done in small or large containers.

Carpet bedding This is very labour-intensive and so rarely done in the garden – you are more likely to see it in a public park. Low-growing plants are bedded out very closely together to form patterns or to create letters. Very often this type of bedding is done to commemorate a special event, but it would be easy to scale down if you wanted to do something similar in your garden.

Choosing & Buying Plants

Once you have decided to plant bedding plants in the garden or in containers, the next decision to make is whether to grow your own plants from seed, cuttings or plugs, or buy plants ready grown.

Growing your own plants

The main advantage of growing your own plants should be the pleasure you get from raising young plants. There is something very satisfying about sowing tiny seeds into compost and watching delicate seedlings emerge a few days later. It can also work out considerably cheaper if you are planning to plant several containers or a large area of bedding plants. The choice of varieties is much greater when you purchase seed from a seed company, which means you can grow exactly what you want and be able to time the crop according to your timescale.

The initial outlay of equipment (greenhouse, propagator, trays and pots, for example) prevents some people from growing their own plants. There is also a time element involved – in order to grow plants you need to check them on a daily basis.

Buying your own plants

The convenience of being able to pop in to a nursery or garden centre to buy plants ready for going straight in the soil is very appealing to many gardeners. Indeed, growing your own plants from scratch may not be possible if you have limited space in your garden.

Avoid buying plants with pale, weak, limp foliage

Good quality plants should have healthy, bushy foliage

TIP

It used to be thought bad practice to buy bedding plants in flower as it caused a check in growth when planted out. However, plants growing in cell trays do not suffer from root disturbance when planted out and can be bought in flower.

Buying plants from garden centres and nurseries means you are confined to the range of plants available, which is limited compared to what you are able to grow yourself. Buying a large amount of bedding plants can also be very expensive.

Choosing bedding plants

When purchasing bedding plants, ensure that they are of good quality and good value for money. All too often, sub-standard plants are being sold and these should be avoided at all times. Be prepared to spend some time when choosing plants and buy only those you are happy with.

Good plants to buy:
- Plants that have healthy green foliage that is unmarked
- Plants that are bushy and compact
- Plants that still have some growing room left in the pot or tray
- Plants with plenty of flower buds still to open

Plants to avoid:
- Plants that are tall and leggy
- Plants with compost that is very dry
- Plants that are hungry, with pale, weak foliage
- Plants that are showing signs of disease

Equipment for Growing

If you do want to grow your own bedding plants you will need a certain amount of space and equipment to get started. You can begin with the basics and gradually add more each year. The cost of getting started will repay itself quickly once you produce your own plants.

Greenhouse

In areas where frosts occur in spring, half-hardy annuals and tender perennials will need to be raised indoors. A frost-free greenhouse with a constant air temperature of 10°C (50°F) is ideal. Site it out of any shade to take maximum advantage of spring sunshine. Heat for early spring can be supplied by gas, electricity or paraffin.

If a greenhouse is not an option, many plants can be raised successfully on a windowsill or in a conservatory.

Propagator

Whether you are growing in a greenhouse or on a windowsill, a propagator is invaluable. There are many types of heated ones available to suit all situations. A propagator will provide optimum conditions for seeds that need a germination temperature warmer than the ambient air temperature. The electric heating element is built into the base of the propagator to supply gentle heat of around 15–21°C (60–70°F), which is ideal for most seeds.

A propagator is also ideal for rooting many cuttings and starting corms and tubers into growth.

Cold frame

During spring a cold frame is ideal for giving plants extra protection from the cold and wet. If you do not have a greenhouse and intend to raise some plants in the house, a cold frame will prove invaluable when the plants grow too large or numerous for the windowsill. It is also ideal for hardening off plants in spring before they are planted out (see page 19). A cold frame requires much less space than a greenhouse, making it ideal for small gardens.

Trays and pots

Nowadays, most pots and trays are made from durable plastic to allow them to be washed and used again, although some gardeners still like to use terracotta for sowing and taking cuttings. A selection of various sized pots ranging from 9–15cm (3½-6in) will suffice for most sowing and potting needs. Seed trays in different sizes can be used to transplant seedlings into, stand pots in or for sowing larger quantities of seed.

Cell or plug trays are very practical as they allow you to sow and grow plants without the need to prick out the seedlings. They can also be used for cuttings. Pots made from compressed peat or fibre allow you to plant out without removing the pot. The roots simply grow through the sides and into the soil and the pots simply rot away.

Miscellaneous equipment

Various other pieces of equipment will make life much easier when growing plants.
- A small sieve will make covering seeds with a thin layer of compost much easier.
- A plastic or wooden dibber can be used to make small holes and to prick out seedlings into larger trays.
- Labels and a waterproof pen or pencil are vital to make sure plants are correctly labelled while being grown.

Compost

Many types of compost are available for growing plants. For bedding plants, most gardeners use soilless compost, which is based on peat, coir or a mixture of bark and green waste. Peat-based composts are environmentally, unsound, although peat-free alternatives are now readily available. Lightweight, multipurpose compost is ideal for sowing seeds, taking cuttings and growing young plants.

Compost additives Two materials that can be added to compost are vermiculite and perlite. Perlite is a crushed mineral expanded by heat and vermiculite is a mica-like mineral expanded to 20 times its size. When mixed with compost, both will help improve drainage and aeration. They are often mixed with compost for rooting cuttings. Vermiculite can also be used to cover seeds after sowing.

Pots and cell trays are vital for seed growing

Growing Bedding Plants from Seed

There is great satisfaction to be gained from raising your own plants from seed and, providing you have the basic equipment and materials needed for the job, you should get good results. Whether sowing indoors or outdoors, seeds all need the same basic requirements in order to germinate. When given the correct temperature, air and moisture, most seeds will germinate without too many problems.

Wherever you sow seeds, it is worth spending a little time to do the job properly in order to give the seeds the best possible start. It is not a job that should be rushed and by paying attention to detail you will be rewarded with healthy seedlings.

When sowing indoors the temperature can be controlled to suit the seeds' requirements, whereas outdoors you have little or no control over the growing conditions. Check seed packets for growing temperatures.

Sowing indoors

The majority of half-hardy annuals, some biennials, hardy annuals and perennials used as bedding plants can be grown under cover. The ideal situation is a greenhouse, although a bright windowsill is fine if a greenhouse is not available or not possible due to space restrictions.

Seeds tend to be sown either in pots or trays. This will really depend on the size of the seeds and the amount of plants you intend to grow. The contents of the seed packet will also determine the size of the container and many seed companies now give an indication to the number of seeds in a packet.

Broadcast sowing

This is a technique where seeds are sown evenly over the surface of the compost, rather than in rows. The seeds can be gently scattered directly from the packet or sprinkled by finger and thumb over the compost. Both ways are perfectly acceptable and so

> **TIP**
> Very small, dust-like seeds such as those of Begonia and Lobelia do not need covering. To make sure they are in contact with moist compost, use a presser board to lightly push them into the surface of the compost.

it is best to opt for the method that you find most comfortable. The important thing is to ensure that the seeds are distributed evenly.

Sowing in containers

Over-fill the tray with seed sowing or multipurpose compost and using your hand or a straight edge strike off the compost level with the top of the tray.

The compost needs to be firmed lightly because if it is left loose it will dry out very quickly. This can be done using a small presser board that is pressed down approximately 10–15mm (½–¾in) to create a firm,

A  B

C  D

level surface that should still be slightly spongy to touch [A].

Sow the seeds evenly and thinly on the compost making sure that all the surface is used [B]. Seeds should not be sown so close that they are touching, as this can result in the seedlings growing tall and drawn.

Most seeds, except for very small ones, should be covered with a fine layer of sieved compost or vermiculite [C]. As a guide, the thickness of the covering should be roughly twice the diameter of the seed.

Finally, give the seeds a watering using a spray or fine rose attached to a watering can [D].

Sowing in plug trays

If the seeds you are sowing are large enough to be handled individually it is well worth considering sowing them into a plug tray. Smaller seeds can also be sown this way, although for ease of sowing a small pinch of

seed is usually sown to each cell. As the seedlings grow they can be thinned to leave just one per cell. The main advantage of this method is that the young plants can be transplanted without any root disturbance.

Simply fill the tray with fine compost, because coarse compost tends to block the cells. Level the compost off with your hand and give the plug tray a tap on the bench to settle the compost. Use a dibber to make a shallow hole in each cell and drop a seed or pinch of seed into it. Brush over the surface of the tray by hand with a little more compost to fill the holes and cover the seed.

Watering

Once the seeds have been sown they will need watering straight away to moisten the compost and to start the germination process. There are two ways in which the seedlings can be watered: from over head and from below.

Watering from above is best done with a watering can fitted with a fine rose. Start pouring the can away from the tray and only when in full flow bring it across the pots and trays. Finish watering away from the containers to avoid any large drips that would disturb the surface.

Alternatively, the containers of seed can be stood in a bowl of shallow water for ten minutes or so to allow water to soak up into the compost.

Germination conditions

Most seeds sown under cover will germinate in a temperature between 15–21°C (60–70°F) and a small electric propagator is ideal for this. For indoor use, narrow propagators that fit on a windowsill can be used. If the temperature is constantly warm or the seeds do not require high temperatures to germinate, the trays

can be placed in an unheated propagator, covered with a clear lid, placed in a polythene bag or covered with cling film. This will help to prevent the surface of the compost from drying out and maintain moisture around the seeds, which is vital for germination.

As soon as the seeds germinate remove the cover. Keep the compost moist and grow the seedlings on in bright light, but not direct sunshine, until they are ready to prick out (transplant).

Sowing outdoors

The bedding plants that are started off outside in the soil are hardy annuals and some types can be sown in the autumn and overwintered. All hardy annuals can be sown in spring. Much will depend on the severity of the winter or the type of soil. For autumn-sown hardy annuals to grow well, the soil should be well-drained and light. Wet, heavy clay does not provide ideal conditions and in this case sowing is best done in spring

SEED GERMINATION TEMPERATURES

All seeds have an optimum temperature for fast germination, but when growing several different types of plant from seed it is not always possible to give them all the exact temperature. The temperature range mentioned in Germination conditions (left) is fine for most bedding plants, even though a few, such as geraniums (Pelargonium) and busy Lizzie (Impatiens), prefer it slightly warmer. These seeds will still germinate at 15–21°C (60–70°F), but may take a few days longer to come through.

However, some seed, such as primula, need cooler conditions to germinate and if too warm will not grow.

Seed packets will show temperature requirements, the time to sow and any special conditions that are needed, so always read them first.

when the soil is drying out and warming up. Sowing in autumn will give the plants a head start in spring and earlier flowers, although for convenience most people tend to sow in spring.

Soil preparation

Once you have decided where to grow your annuals, the site should be cleared of any perennial weeds by forking them out or by using a weedkiller based on Glyphosate, which kills the whole of the weed, including the roots. Annuals do not require a very rich soil, otherwise they tend to produce lush growth at the expense of flowers, so there is no need to dig in large amounts of manure or compost. However, if the soil is poorly drained or you have heavy clay, digging in some manure or compost and grit will help to improve the soil. This is best done in autumn to allow time for the soil to settle and breakdown over the winter. In spring, the soil should be crumbly and easy to rake.

Preparation and sowing outdoors

To prepare a seed bed, choose a dry day and tread over the area to firm the ground. Add a general fertilizer to the soil and rake the surface to produce a fine seedbed [A].

SOWING HARDY ANNUALS

Hardy annuals are usually grown in groups of several different types, with taller plants towards the back of the border. When the ground has been prepared for sowing, the area for each block of plants can be marked out with a thin line of sand. For a natural effect the blocks or drifts can be curved. When the drills are made in each drift they should be approximately 15–30cm (6–12in) apart, depending on the eventual height of the plants. The direction of the drills can be altered in each drift, again to give a more natural effect.

The easiest way to grow and maintain hardy annuals is to sow them in shallow drills or furrows. Use a trowel, back of the rake or stick to scratch out the drill approximately 6–12mm (¼–½in). A tight garden line or measuring stick can be used as a guide for marking out the drill [B].

Sow the seeds thinly and evenly along the row either from the packet or from the palm of your hand [C]. If there are not many seeds in the packet, sow a few every 10cm (4in) as this is what they will be thinned out to at a later date.

Cover over the seeds by drawing soil across the drill with your hand or with a rake, being careful not to disturb the seeds in the drill [D]. Mark the drill with a label, so you can remember what type of seeds you have sown while they begin growing.

Now that the hardy annuals are in place in the bed, keep a close eye on them as they germinate and start to develop. You may need to protect the young seedlings from the ravages of slugs and snails, for example.

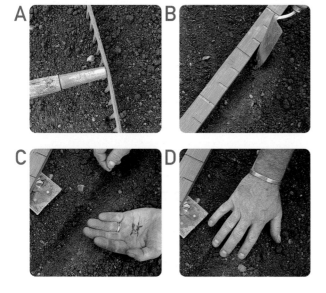

Growing Bedding Plants from Plugs & Seedlings

Another successful way of growing bedding plants is to buy small pots of seedlings or young plants grown in plug trays. These are produced by specialist nurseries and sold through garden centres or by mail order. Each year the range of plants available seems to become larger than ever before. This is a convenient way of growing plants and it is ideal if you do not have the conditions or the space to germinate seed at home. Growing bedding plants in this way will also save time and you will be able to buy the exact number of plants needed for the garden.

The disadvantage lies in the fact that it can work out slightly more expensive, especially if you are growing lots of plants. One way around this is to grow the easy plants from seed, such as marigolds (Tagetes), and buy the more difficult to germinate plants, such as begonias.

To grow bedding plants in spring from seedlings and plug plants, you will need somewhere that is frost free and light. A greenhouse is perfect, although a conservatory or windowsill can also be used. If the plants are purchased in mid to late spring, very little heat will be needed and in mild areas a cold frame may be sufficient to grow on the plants.

Pricking out

This is the term used to transplant seedlings from the container where they were sown into a larger one. If left in the original container for too long, the seedlings would grow tall and leggy as they compete for light and become more prone to fungal diseases. Ideally, the seedlings should be pricked out as soon as they are large enough to handle and this is usually when they are at the two-leaf stage. The smaller the seedling, the less check in growth there will be.

Pricking out is exactly the same whether you have raised your own seedlings or bought them. For most bedding plants, seed trays, cell trays or small pots can be used to grow them on. These should be filled with compost similar to the one they were sown in, although multipurpose compost is suitable for most bedding plants. Fill the tray or pot with compost, level it off by hand and give the container a tap to settle the compost.

Pricking out seedlings

Carefully ease out a seedling from the container by loosening the compost with a dibber or stick and try to keep plenty of compost around the roots. Only hold the seedling by its seed leaves, never the stem as this can cause bruising [A].

Using the dibber, make a hole in the compost and lower the roots into it so that the seed leaves are just above the compost level [B]. Use your finger or dibber to gently firm the compost around the seedling.

As soon as the seedlings are pricked out they should be watered using a can with a fine rose so as not to flatten the seedlings [C]. The compost should be kept moist, but not wet.

Growing on plug plants

Ideally, after the seedlings have been pricked out they should be grown on for a few days in a similar temperature to the one they were germinated at to

Three weeks after potting on, plants should be established

help them settle in. The temperature can then be lowered to a minimum night temperature of 10–12°C (50–55°F), which is suitable for most bedding plants. During the day, in sunny weather, the greenhouse should be ventilated to prevent it from getting too hot, because large fluctuations in temperature are not good for young plants.

Plug plants are available in several different sizes from individual plugs roughly 1cm (½in) in diameter to jumbo plugs up to 5cm (2in) across. Net pots also fall into this category. These are usually a plastic mesh pot filled with compost in which a cutting is rooted or seedling transplanted. When bought to be grown on, they are simply potted complete with the pot, as the roots will grow through the mesh into the new compost.

The advantage of buying plants grown in plugs or net pots is to save time. When you buy them they are already several weeks old and when potted on, will grow and quickly establish. In a matter of weeks you will have plants ready to use in the garden or in containers.

How to pot

The size of the plug or net pot will determine how to pot them up. Small plugs can be transplanted with a dibber in a similar way to pricking out. Fill the cell tray or pot with compost, level off by hand and make a hole to accommodate the plug [A] and gently firm in.

With larger plugs or net pots it is easier to half fill the plant pot with compost, position the plug in the centre and fill in around with compost ensuring the plant is not too deep or sticking out of the pot [B]. A light firming or a sharp tap on the bench will settle the compost. The pots should then be watered and the plants kept frost-free.

Hardening off

This is a term used to describe the process where plants that have been grown in a warm, protected environment are gradually acclimatized to outdoor conditions. Plants taken from a warm greenhouse and planted outside are likely to suffer a check in growth or even be killed by the sudden change of temperature.

As the plants mature, the temperature they are being grown in should be reduced until only frost protection is given. Next, place the pots or trays of plants in a cold frame. For the first few days, keep the cover closed at night and then leave the cover open, unless a frost is forecast. After about two to three weeks, the plants should be fully acclimatized to being outside.

ACCLIMATIZING YOUNG PLANTS

During the hardening off period listen to your local weather forecast and, if a frost is forecast, protect your bedding plants by closing the frame or by draping some horticultural fleece over them. This will give a couple of degrees protection.

As plants are hardened off their foliage may change colour. This is a natural process and there is no need to worry. An example of this is the half-hardy annual lobelia. During cool nights the green leaves gradually change to a bronze colour.

A  B

A cold frame is an excellent device for hardening off young plants

Planting Out

Once you have grown and hardened off your bedding plants, they will need to be planted out into the garden or containers. If you are planting out tender plants, this should be done only when the danger of frost has passed. Care should be taken when planting out in order to give the plants the best possible start.

Soil preparation

The success rate of bedding plants will depend partly on the soil they are growing in. This means preparing the soil before hand. If you plant both summer and spring bedding plants in your garden, the soil will have plants in it for most of the year and so all preparation will have to be done in between removing old plants and planting new ones. In soil that has been regularly cultivated, this preparation does not usually take very long, but is well worth doing as it makes planting easier and the plants will establish faster.

Over a period of time, organic matter will be lost from the soil, so it is a good idea to add some garden compost or well-rotted manure to the soil before planting in autumn. This will help to maintain healthy soil that retains moisture and nutrients.

Before planting

Fork the soil over, making sure any annual weeds are completely buried, but remove perennial ones, as these will regrow. Any lumps of soil can easily be broken down with the back of the fork [A].

Dig in organic material to improve the soil

To feed the bedding plants through the season, sprinkle a general fertilizer evenly on the soil, following the manufacturer's instructions [B].

Complete the soil preparations by raking the area over [C]. This will help to work the fertilizer into the soil and also create a firm, level surface to plant into [D].

Planting

There is something quite satisfying about planting out young bedding plants, whether you have grown them or bought them. It is the start of what will be a very colourful display over several months.

The planting technique is the same for bedding plants grown in plastic or polystyrene strips, cell trays or pots. The advantage of planting from cell trays and pots is that the plant roots are not disturbed at all, whereas plants in strips have to be gently teased apart, which does cause some root disturbance and the plants may take a little longer to establish.

Several hours before planting, water the plants to ensure the compost is moist. Plants growing in pots or cell trays should be gently removed and spaced out on the ground. Plants grown in trays or strips should be gently divided, making sure each plant has a good ball of compost around its roots. To prevent the roots from drying out, plant immediately.

A

B

C

D

TIP

If the border has a lawn at the side, it is also a good idea to trim the edges of the grass before planting. This not only makes the border look neat and tidy, but it is easier to do it before bedding plants are planted.

With a trowel, make a hole slightly larger than the rootball of the plant

TIP

If you want your bedding plants to follow the line of a path or lawn edge, use a string garden line or straight edge to make sure the first row of plants is in-line. All the other planting to the rear of the first row should be planted by eye, because if all the plants are in perfectly straight rows they will look like rows of soldiers.

How to set out the plants

The way to arrange the plants in your bed or border is entirely up to you. Hopefully, by the time planting comes along, you will have an idea of the effect you want to create.

However, when you set the plants out on the ground in readiness for planting, always start at the front of the border and work backwards. This helps avoid any uneven gaps at the front of the border when you have finished planting. It is also a good idea to set out and plant the edging plants first (see Types of Bedding Plants, page 8) to give a definite edge to the bed or border. The large-growing dot plants can then be positioned and planted, and finally the entire scheme can be finished off by filling the gaps with the main bedding plants.

Planting

Set out the bedding plants onto the ground. Edging plants are normally spaced around 15cm (6in) apart and main bedding plants 20–30cm (8–12in) apart, depending on the eventual size.

Make a hole with a trowel slightly larger than the rootball of the plant and position the plant so that the compost around the roots is just below the soil surface.

Fill in with soil and firm the soil around the roots with your fingers.

After planting, remove any footprints from the soil with the trowel or small fork and water each plant thoroughly around its base to give the roots and soil a soaking.

Thinning hardy annuals

Hardy annuals that have been sown directly into the border soil will need to be thinned when around 5cm (2in) tall. Even if you have sown the seed thinly in the first place, the chances are they will still be too close together to grow properly. If left to grow unthinned, you would get tall, leggy plants that are more liable to blow or fall over at a later date.

Thinning is simply a case of removing some of the seedlings to allow the remaining ones more growing room. One method of thinning a row of seedlings is to pull the spare seedlings out by hand. Normally weak, small seedlings are pulled out by hand, leaving the strongest one to grow on. However, when growing a mixed variety the small seedlings often produce a different coloured flower to the stronger seedlings, so in order to get a good flowering mixture, a selection of different sized seedlings should be allowed to grow on. Another method of thinning seedlings is to chop the spare ones out with a small hoe, but this gives less control of what to remove or leave.

The distance the final seedlings should be spaced apart will depend on the plant and its ultimate size. The spacing is usually given on the seed packet and varies between 10cm (4in) and 20cm (8in).

Bedding in containers

Bedding plants are used a great deal in all types of containers, such as pots, windowboxes and hanging baskets throughout the year. They are the perfect plants to use for seasonal colour and interest. Just a few well positioned containers can brighten up a dull patio and if you don't have a garden they are the ideal solution for adding colour to a balcony or patio.

Summer containers are usually planted in late spring after the danger of frost has passed and removed in autumn. These can be replaced with winter or spring containers that remain in position until the following spring; thus maintaining a display at all times.

Hanging baskets

Summer baskets are usually planted with annual bedding plants and tender perennials and trailing plants. They require regular watering and feeding to maintain a good flowering display all summer long.

Winter baskets are planted with a selection of hardy plants for both flower and foliage and are hung outside in the autumn after the summer baskets have finished, remaining outside until the following spring.

There are many designs of basket that can be used, including the traditional wire basket, ornate baskets made from woven stems, moulded plastic and even ones with a self-watering reservoir.

For all types of basket, soilless compost is preferable to keep the weight down. To help with watering and feeding in summer baskets, controlled-release fertilizer and water storing granules can be added at planting time (these can also be used in summer containers and windowboxes).

Containers and pots

The range of pots and containers available to gardeners nowadays is huge. They come in all shapes and sizes

Impatiens (busy Lizzies) are great plants for mixing in hanging baskets

Combine trailing plants like fuchsias and lobelias with foliage

and in various materials such as terracotta, wood, plastic and concrete.

For a successful display, avoid using very small containers, as they tend to dry out quickly in sunny weather. Good drainage is also essential for both summer and winter containers. To improve drainage, cover the drainage holes with pieces of broken clay pots or gravel before adding compost. For a display that will last for a season, soilless compost is fine, but for containers that are to be planted for several years always use a soil-based compost. For example, where you have large containers that have a few shrubs or conifers planted to give structure through the year. Seasonal bedding plants can be planted at the front of the container to give extra colour.

All containers need to be watered and fed with a balanced fertilizer to keep them in good condition.

Windowboxes

Windowboxes are an excellent way of adding interest to a building and can be seen from both outside and inside.

They need to be firmly secured to the building or windowsill with brackets. To minimise the weight, use soilless compost.

Just like containers and hanging baskets they can be planted with a selection of seasonal plants.

> **TIP**
>
> Wallflowers (Erysimum) can often be bought as bare-root plant in the autumn. These should be planted in exactly the same way. They may wilt a little after planting, but will soon pick up if the soil is kept moist.

Planting Combinations

When it comes to planting out your bedding scheme, there are no rules as to what plants you can use or where to plant them.

There are, of course, the very traditional designs, with plants in straight rows or circles to form definite shapes and patterns. Increasingly, bedding schemes are becoming more informal, but they are still structured and can take an equal amount of planning as a formal scheme. Some of the more interesting schemes are the ones that are completely different and innovative.

A common use of bedding plants is to use them to fill in spaces in a mixed border. They can be planted alongside herbaceous perennials and shrubs with great effect. This is a good way of adding extra interest and colour to a border. Very often there are times during the summer when borders lack flowers, but by adding a few annuals you can keep borders looking good for longer. In this situation it is often the taller growing or bushy annuals such as Cleome and dwarf sunflowers (Helianthus) that are planted, as they make excellent

gap fillers. Likewise, low-growing bedding plants such as petunias, impatiens and verbenas can be planted in groups at the front of a border.

Even if your garden is overflowing with perennials, you can always find a small space, which is perfect for two or three bedding plants.

Hardy annuals are also excellent plants as they can be sown directly between other plants or indeed used on their own in borders to give drifts of colour all summer long.

At the end of the day, of course, it is your garden and you can plant exactly what you want. It can be great fun experimenting with different colours, shapes and textures.

It is always worth trying different plant combinations to see how they work. In most cases you will be pleased with the results and if you are not, you can try something else the following year.

One thing that bedding plants offer is to give you the opportunity to alter the look of your garden on an annual basis without too much heavy work or expense. By changing the colour or shape of the plants that you use, the garden will take on a whole new appearance. This is particularly true when you use them in containers and hanging baskets on a patio or balcony.

Parks or garden centres are great places to visit to get inspiration for planting schemes

Colours

The main aim when planting bedding plants in your garden is to supply seasonal colour. The choice could be very bright or subtle colours – it is entirely up to you.

When choosing colour combinations it is worth remembering what effect you are trying to create. For example, if you have a cool, shady area that you want to look more appealing to sit out in, it is worth planting warm colours such as reds, oranges, yellows and purple shades. Alternatively, if you want to create a cool, calm area, then go for whites, silvers, soft pinks and light blues. Remember, also, that the colour does not come just from the flowers; the foliage of many plants can also be very attractive.

Many plants are available as single colours or a mixture of several colours that blend well together. Some people prefer a block of one colour, whereas others prefer mixed planting.

When it comes to mixing colours it is often advised that certain colours should not be mixed together. However, if done carefully most colours can be mixed successfully – although the end result may be loud as opposed to discreet. Once again, it comes down to personal choice.

Foliage

It is all too easy to forget foliage when planning what bedding plants to grow, but foliage size and colour does play an important role. If you want dramatic foliage, try plants such as the castor oil plant (Ricinus), with its large hand-shaped leaves, or cannas that have tall paddle-shaped leaves in various colours. These will form the main structure in a container or planting scheme and you can then fill in with smaller plants for extra colour and flowers. The use of plants with bold foliage can transform an area of bedding from a flat planting into a 3D effect. A good plant for this is *Nicotiana sylvestris*, which has large green leaves and white scented flowers. When mixed with other plants, it gives a feeling of movement as it sways in the breeze.

Delicate foliage such as grasses will also add texture and movement to the garden. These can be complemented with small flowers and plants with a fine leaf texture.

Getting ideas

If you are intending to put summer bedding plants in your garden for the first time or would like some fresh and new ideas of what plants are available and how best to arrange them, it pays to do a little research. This

The most effective mixed borders often comprise an eclectic mixture of form, foliage and colour

might be as simple as a visit to your local nursery or garden centre to see what they grow or having a chat with friends and neighbours to see what grows well in their gardens.

Garden shows are also a great source of inspiration and there you will often see bedding schemes used to great effect. Although these plantings will be too large for the average garden, you can scale them down or adapt them to your own situation. Local parks are another place that are well worth a visit. You will not only find very traditional planting schemes, but also many new planting ideas. Seed companies also have open days where customers and the general public can visit their trial fields. There you can see all that is new in the world of flowers and pick up a few possible ideas for your garden.

Planting ideas

There is no limit to the amount of ways that you can use bedding plants. Below are a few suggestions to give you some idea of how plants can be used together.

Planting scheme 1 In this informal planting, red Verbena and yellow French marigolds have been used very effectively to create a hot planting scheme. The plants are not in rows, which takes away the formality. Instead, they are planted in groups, which makes it much easier to blend the colours together. This method of planting is ideal for borders or filling gaps between permanent plants.

Planting scheme 1: creating an informal, hot border

Planting scheme 2 This summer bedding scheme is more formal and is planted roughly as a circular bed, although it could be adapted and planted in a border of any shape. Three heights of plants have been used to create a tiered effect. On the outside of the circle, low-growing Verbena has been used with a lovely mixture containing white, mauve and purple flowers.

The middle block of planting is slightly taller and uses *Salvia farinacea* 'Strata', which has bi-coloured flowers of light blue and silver. In the centre of the bed, height and texture have been achieved by using a white flowering Cleome. The colours of all the three different types of plants blend well together, and although this planting scheme is based on a formal design, it has a feeling of informality because of the choice of plants and the pastel colours.

Planting scheme 3 This simple but very effective planting scheme contains only one type of plant, French marigolds (Tagetes). They have been grouped in single colours of yellow, gold and orange to create a swirling movement around the garden by planting in a circular shape. This does away with corners and angles that can look very formal and the curves help your eye wander around the garden or lead you to a focal point. This type of design could be used in gardens large or small, and you could even create a similar style of planting in a large container. Different colours could also be used, such as pinks or purples of various shades. By changing the colour you could create a very different look and feel to the garden. You could also plant a round bed with a concentric circle that gets lighter or darker towards the centre for something a little different.

Planting scheme 2: a more formal, circular bed

Planting scheme 3: using only French marigolds

Planting scheme 6 Three different types of plants have been used to create this pink-themed scheme. At the front of the border is low-growing *Begonia semperflorens*. Mixed Dianthus dominates the middle of the arrangement and pink Cosmos have been included at the back of the border to provide height. The various shades all mix well together to create a tapestry, rather than a single block, of colour.

Planting scheme 4 Some of the most effective planting schemes are very simple, such as this one where two different colours of Ageratum are mixed together. To add extra height and form, large silver leaved perennials have been used as dot plants, but *Senecio cineraria* 'Silver Dust' would work just as well, as would *Tanacetum ptarmiciflorum* 'Silver Feather', with its finely divided bright silver foliage. This type of planting is very cool and relaxing, and could be used in many situations.

Planting scheme 5 Another traditional and very colourful summer bedding scheme that is ideal for when you want a bright splash of colour for several months. Blue Lobelia is used as edging plants with yellow French marigolds, succeeded by slightly taller plants and finally pink Cosmos at the centre of the scheme.

Planting scheme 7 This formal semi-circular bed is planted with a selection of mixed flowering and self-coloured plants. Dark blue Lobelia is used as the edging all the way around the bed. The second row of planting is with yellow French marigolds, which are slightly taller. Mixed flowering Nonstop begonias are used in the centre as the main block of planting. To add height to the bed, a single Canna has been used as a dot plant. The overall effect is a bright and colourful planting scheme.

27

Planting scheme 8: Cordyline blends well with begonias

Planting scheme 10 In borders where you want height, dahlias are a good choice and there are many different colours to choose from. They are both easy to grow and have a long flowering period. The rich red flowers of *Dahlia* 'Bishop of Llandaff' and their deep bronze foliage contrast well with the pale yellow daisy-like flowers and cut leaves of Argyranthemum. Both of these plants will flower well into the autumn.

Planting scheme 10: contrasting colours

Planting scheme 8 A simple but very effective scheme, using the warm colours of apricot and bronze. The main planting is with a mixture of Nonstop begonias in shades of apricot and pink. The dark leaved Cordyline, which also adds height and shape to the bed, highlights their shades. The colours all work really well together because of the sheer range of their variations. If single coloured begonias had been planted around the Cordyline, the effect would not be as good.

Planting scheme 9 In this planting scheme, tall growing orange African marigolds and white flowering Cosmos have been mixed together to provide masses of flowers all summer long. The colours complement each other and the feathery foliage of the Cosmos helps to create an informal cottage garden feel.

Planting scheme 11 In this border, a block of deep pink *Begonia semperflorens* creates a bold impact and provides the main bedding display. The contrasting edging plants of *Senecio cineraria* 'Silver Dust' add a light coloured edging to the border that looks attractive, but also serves as a guide to anyone with impaired vision by marking the edge of the border.

Planting scheme 9: complementary colours

Planting scheme 11: making a bold impact

Creative displays with spring bedding

For a spring flowering display, wallflowers (Erysimum) take some beating, especially if you want to plant a large area. They can be planted in groups of single colours for a formal look or as mixed colours for an informal cottage style garden. They look very good when inter-planted with tulips that flower in late spring and add extra height to the planting.

Winter flowering pansies are also extremely reliable for providing colour over a long period. They can be planted as blocks of single colours or as a mixture.

Myosotis also works well when planted with other spring flowering plants or on its own. It is available in several colours, although blue is the most popular.

Containers

Bedding plants are the perfect choice for containers, windowboxes, wall mangers and hanging baskets. With regular watering and feeding they will provide a long and colourful display for several months. Both summer and spring flowering plants can be used in containers to maintain colour and interest all year round.

Most of the different types of bedding plants that are used in the garden can be used in containers, from low-growing plants such as Lobelia to tall growing dot plants such as Canna. As long as the pot is large enough and in scale with the plants you intend to use, there are no limits as to what you can plant.

There are various ways containers can be arranged and, just like bedding in the garden, the choice of plants comes down to personal preference.

One way is to plant a selection of several different plants in one container. This creates a very colourful mixture of flowers and foliage shapes. Another method is to use just one type of plant in a single pot or container. The plants can be mixed flowering or a single colour to provide a block of colour. You can have lots of fun mixing plants together and experimenting with different plants in containers for varying effects.

The wall manger (bottom right) is planted with just mixed impatiens and no other plants. It is very easy to plant up in late spring and is guaranteed to produce masses of flowers all summer long. Impatiens are ideal for containers that get very little sun; in fact, the wall manger pictured is in shade until late afternoon and, as can be seen, the plants thrive.

Simple planting schemes in containers can also look very effective where only one or two types of plants are used. Pink trailing Verbena and pink pelargoniums in a

Low-growing bedding plants surround a Cordyline in a pot

Trailing busy lizzies spill attractively out of wall mangers

pot with a purple Cordyline in the centre is a combination that works well (top right). In mild areas, the Cordyline can remain in the pot over winter and have spring flowering plants, such as pansies or Bellis, planted around it.

Care & Maintenance

Living things all need a certain amount of care and attention, and plants are no exception. The simple maintenance steps outlined over the next few pages will ensure your garden – and the bedding plants growing in it – remains healthy and looks its best.

Watering

All plants need water to survive and grow. In the case of summer bedding plants, it is important never to allow plants to dry out completely. This is even more important for plants growing in containers and hanging baskets, as they are often totally dependent on you for water.

Bedding planted in the autumn for winter and spring displays usually only needs watering just the once. This is immediately after planting in order to settle the roots, because at this time of year the soil is usually moist enough.

Watering summer bedding

Summer bedding plants growing in the ground are able to get their roots out into the soil to search for moisture. To help them establish, they should be thoroughly watered after planting to make sure the soil is moist around their roots. In dry weather they should be checked a few days after planting and if necessary watered again. In most cases the plants will have grown out into the surrounding soil after a couple of weeks and watering may not be required. If, however, the weather is very hot and dry, the plants may require occasional watering throughout the summer to prevent them from suffering from drought. Small numbers of plants can be watered with a watering can, but for larger areas a

hosepipe should be used. The aim is to moisten the soil around the roots to a depth of around 5–8cm (2–3in) and it is therefore better to water thoroughly once every week rather than spray over the plants on a daily basis. This tends to moisten only the surface of the soil and encourage the roots to grow up towards the moisture; as the soil dries out these surface roots are damaged.

Where possible water early in the morning or late in the evening to prevent water evaporation. Watering in sunny weather can also cause scorch marks on the flowers and leaves.

Watering in containers

Plants growing in containers need to be watered on a regular basis, especially hanging baskets, which can dry out very quickly in warm weather. This can be done with a watering can or hosepipe. The aim is to keep the compost in the basket or container moist at all times. With containers, fill the gap between the surface of the compost and the rim with water and allow it to soak in. Baskets are a little more difficult to water because you cannot see the top of the basket. If the plants wilt you are not watering enough and should apply more. A good tip is to feel the weight of the basket when it has been watered; it should be fairly heavy. If, when checking the basket, it feels light, then it really needs more watering.

Automatic watering

There are now many automatic watering systems that can easily be installed to water plants in the garden and in containers. Not only do they save time, they also save water.

Water well after planting to establish the roots

For beds and borders, a seep hose or porous pipe can also be used. This is attached to a tap and laid along the ground or it may be buried just below the soil surface. When the tap is on, water will seep very slowly from the pipe into the soil around the plants' roots.

Containers and hanging baskets can be watered by means of small-bore pipes and drip nozzles that are positioned in the containers or baskets. These are connected to a mains pipe and tap; when turned on, many baskets and containers will be watered at once.

Both types of system can be used with a timing device that is attached to the tap. Usually, these are battery operated and require no mains electricity. They can be programmed to water once or several times a day for short periods and are perfect for when you are away on holiday.

Feeding

To grow and flower well, plants need a balanced feed. When lacking in certain nutrients, plants will make poor stunted growth and produce fewer flowers.

Soil in good condition generally contains a good supply of nutrients, although to give bedding plants a good start it is advisable to apply a base dressing of general fertilizer at planting time.

Hoe large weeds regularly to prevent them from using up soil nutrients

Plants growing in containers need feeding more often. The fertilizer in most composts only lasts for around six weeks, after which time you need to supply additional nutrients for the plants. This can be done by incorporating slow-release fertilizer at planting time or by liquid feeding on a weekly basis.

General fertilizer

Various types of general fertilizer are available as granules, powder or pellets. All of them supply a balanced feed. A base dressing is sprinkled onto the surface of the soil before sowing and planting, and worked in with a fork or rake. Topdressing is the term used when plants growing in the soil are given an additional feed half way through the season. The fertilizer is carefully sprinkled on the soil between the plants and again worked into the surface with a rake or garden hoe. Both organic and inorganic types of general fertilizer are available.

Slow-release fertilizer

This type of fertilizer is mainly used in baskets and containers and is also called controlled-release fertilizer. It can be bought as granules or tablets of pellets glued together. Nutrients are gradually released from the granules over a period of several months to keep the plants fed all season long. The fertilizer is normally mixed in with the compost when the containers are planted up.

Liquid fertilizer

Many different types of liquid fertilizer are available as a general feed or to supply specific plant needs. For bedding plants, a feed with a high potash content is usually used to encourage flowering. They are available as concentrated liquid or soluble powder that is added to water. When liquid feeding it is important to feed on a regular basis as the feed is instantly available to the plants and doesn't remain in the compost or soil for long. Application is by watering can or through a hose end feeder that automatically dilutes the fertilizer to the correct strength.

Weeding

Perennial weeds are not usually a problem among bedding plants if the ground has been properly prepared ahead of planting. Annual weeds, however, will grow from seed as soon as the soil warms up in spring or when you start to water newly planted bedding plants.

These are always best dealt with as soon as possible. If allowed to mature and flower, they will produce more seed that will lie dormant in the soil for many years. Where plants are close together, weeding by hand is a good option and it is simply a case of pulling out the weed seedlings.

Where there is a little more room between the plants, a Dutch or push hoe is ideal for removing the weeds. Choose a fine, sunny day to do the hoeing when the surface of the soil is fairly dry. Slide the blade of the hoe along the soil surface and chop off the weeds, which should wilt and die in the sunshine. Annual weeds only tend to be a problem for three or four weeks after planting and as the bedding plants grow and fill in to cover the ground, weeds will be smothered and not be able to grow due to lack of light.

Weeds are not normally a problem in containers that have been filled with multipurpose or potting compost, but if the odd weed does pop up between the plants it can easily be pulled out.

Deadheading

Most annuals and bedding plants will benefit from having their dead flowerheads removed. Not only does this keep the plants looking neat and tidy, it also prolongs the flowering period. Annuals only live for one season and their aim is to produce seed in order for the species to continue. If you allow seed pods to form, the plant thinks it has done its job and will not produce

Deadheading will prolong the flowering period

further flowers. By removing the flowers as soon as they fade, the plant will continue to produce more and more flowers.

The easiest way to deadhead is to pinch off the dead blooms with your finger and thumb or cut them off with a pair of scissors or secateurs.

Overwintering

Many plants that are used as bedding plants are tender perennials and can be overwintered in frost-free conditions either as rooted cuttings (see Propagation &

Move tender plants into a greenhouse over winter

Care of Perennial Bedding Plants, page 34) or established plants. The latter will require more room, but many people prefer to keep the whole plant and use it as a houseplant through the winter months. Plants such as pelargoniums, fuchsias and osteospermums can be lifted from the ground or containers in autumn, potted into as small a pot as possible and used indoors, where they will continue to flower for several more weeks or even months.

Alternatively, the plants can be grown on as stock plants in a greenhouse and used for propagation material the following spring. In this situation they should be kept cool but frost-free until early spring, when the temperature can be increased to encourage new shoots.

TIP

When composting old bedding plants, be sure to mix the material in with grass cuttings and general household waste, such as vegetable matter. This will help to ensure more effective decomposition and better compost in the long run.

Composting

At the end of the season, old bedding plants should be pulled out of the ground or from their containers and composted. Most types have reasonably soft stems and will soon break down when added to a compost heap or bin. Plants with tougher stems, such as dahlias or sunflowers, can be passed through a garden shredder before being added to the compost heap. This not only saves valuable landfill sites but also allows you to make your own compost that can be added back to the garden to help improve the soil for the following season.

The compost that is made from garden waste is intended as a soil conditioner and not as a medium for raising seeds and growing plants.

Other plants that can be easily overwintered are tuberous begonia, cannas and dahlias, which are lifted in autumn, cut down and stored over the winter months in peat or a peat-free material that is just moist. If the tubers or rhizomes are kept too dry they can dehydrate and die.

Saving seeds

If you intend to save some of your own seed, seedheads can be allowed to develop on some plants towards the end of the growing season, when deadheading is not as important. Growing plants from seed you have saved yourself is not only great fun, but will conserve money. Saving your own seed is simple, as long as you know what can and cannot be saved. One group of plants that will not grow true from saved seed are F1 hybrids. These are plants that are produced as a result of crossing two specific parent plants to create a hybrid. When seed is collected from an F1 hybrid the resultant plants may bear no resemblance to the original ones. This doesn't mean they will not be useable. They may well be, but you cannot be certain what they will grow like. Non-hybrid or open pollinated plants will usually come true from seeds and these are the ones to save.

Remove the seedheads when they have started to ripen but before they split open. Place them in a paper bag or on a tray in a warm airy place to finish ripening the seeds. After a couple of weeks when the seed pods have shed their seed, remove or gently blow away the chaff and store the seeds in envelopes or small jars until sowing time.

Propagation & Care of Perennial Bedding Plants

As already mentioned, many perennial bedding plants can be overwintered for the following season and in most cases it is possible to propagate these plants to increase their numbers.

Cuttings

Tender perennials that are used in summer displays are often increased from cuttings taken in early autumn, although they can also be taken in spring from over-wintered stock plants. One reason cuttings are taken in autumn is to save space; you can get many rooted cuttings in a tray into the space that would be occupied by one large plant in a pot.

The cuttings can be taken from plants growing in the garden during late summer and early autumn. At this time of the year they will root very quickly with fewer failures.

The length of the cutting taken will depend on the plant being propagated, but generally they are between 5–7.5cm (2–3in) in length.

Mixing 50:50 multipurpose compost and vermiculite together makes an ideal mixture for rooting cuttings. After inserting the cuttings into the pot they should be watered and placed in a greenhouse or on a windowsill. Rooting usually takes around three weeks and after a few more weeks, when the root system is established, the cuttings can be potted individually into 9cm (3½in) pots.

How to take cuttings

Select a cutting from a healthy stem and trim it just below a leaf (node). Remove the leaves from the lower half of the stem, leaving just two or three leaves at the top [A].

Dip the base of the cutting into hormone rooting compound and insert around the edge of a small plant pot filled with cutting compost [B].

Plants that can be increased by cuttings include pelargoniums, fuchsias, osteospermums, diascias, felicias, argyranthemums, New Guinea impatiens, and most basket and container plants.

A

B

Tubers & rhizomes

Many tender perennials can be started into growth in spring from tubers and rhizomes bought from garden centres. These are dormant storage roots and stems of plants, such as begonias, dahlias and cannas.

Although planting can be done directly into the garden or into containers in late spring, starting them off in smaller pots first will give the plants a head start.

Tubers Dahlias produce a thick, fleshy root called a root tuber that acts as a food store. In spring, the tuber starts into growth and new shoots grow from dormant buds around the base of the old stem.

When new dahlia tubers are bought they are usually very dry and are best

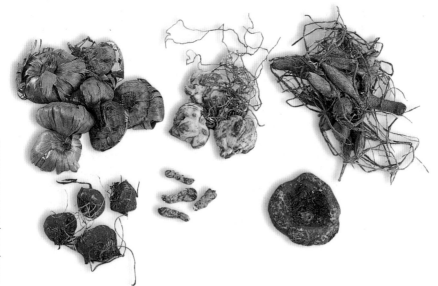

Tubers, bulbs, corms and rhizomes

Fill around dahlia tubers so that only the tops are visible

TIP Avoid storing tubers or corms too early in the autumn as it means they will have to be stored for longer. The shorter the storage period, the less chance of rot setting in.

potted in mid-spring to start them into growth. Pot the tuber so that the top is just visible, and keep moist and frost free. When planting directly into the garden, there should be 5cm (2in) of soil above the tuber. Tubers started in pots can be planted out after the danger of frost has passed.

Some begonias are grown from stem tubers – a modified, swollen stem that acts as a food store. When purchased they look very dry and often have no visual signs of life. When potted and kept warm, they will produce new shoots. To pot a begonia tuber, almost fill a pot with compost and place the tuber on the surface. Push it slightly into the compost so that the top of the tuber remains clearly visible.

Rhizomes A rhizome is an underground stem that has growth buds along it. Many plants such as cannas, that are ideal in tropical displays or as dot plants, grow from a rhizome. Again, these are best when started into

Begonia tubers should be pushed in, leaving only the top visible

growth in a greenhouse or large windowsill. The rhizomes are potted and kept moist. Very often the fat growth buds can be seen and these should be just below the surface of the compost. Each year the rhizome will increase in size and to propagate a canna you simply divide the clump. This can often be done by pulling off a piece of root complete with growth bud, or a knife can be used to slice through the root.

Overwintering

At the end of the season, the tuber or rhizome will need to be lifted for winter storage. In mild areas where there is little frost, dahlias and cannas can be safely left in the soil, but where frosts occur it is best to lift the roots. This is normally done in autumn when the first of the season's frosts has blackened the foliage. The roots are dug up and the stems cut back almost to the root.

Dust with a fungicide such as sulphur to protect against rots and moulds and store in large pots or else deep trays of peat or a peat substitute in a frost-free place. This should be on the dry side of moist to prevent the roots from drying out too much. Begonias are treated in much the same way, although many gardeners prefer to store the tubers in paper bags in a cool place.

Through the winter check the stored roots occasionally. In the case of begonias, if the tubers look very dry and shrivelled, they can be soaked in water for 15 minutes to re-hydrate them before being dried off and placed back into store.

Bedding Plants

The choice of bedding plants is huge and you only have to thumb through a few seed catalogues to see just how many different types of plants can be used.

Gardeners have grown most of the plants listed on the following pages for many years as part of bedding plant displays. They are guaranteed to provide seasonal colour, either in the garden or in containers.

Many of the cultivars chosen are reliable and well known to gardeners, although many recent introductions have also been included in the variety charts in this book. Plant breeders are continuously introducing new and exciting cultivars, many of which have improved flowering, growth uniformity or weather resistance. However, older cultivars that have been around for many years should not be forgotten, as they have stood the test of time.

Also included are several plants that would not normally be associated with bedding schemes. As gardeners strive for something different in the borders, more and more plants are used, often with great effect. Grasses are a good example of this trend and, when mixed with flowering bedding plants, they can look very effective. Gardening should be fun and enjoyable and experimenting with new plants and planting combinations should always be encouraged.

Details of colour, height and spread are provided for each variety of plant covered, as well as basic growing and cultivation instructions to make growing the plants as easy as possible.

Hopefully, the selection of plants that follow will not only help you to plan and grow your own bedding plants, but will also give you some inspiration to experiment and create a beautiful garden.

Abutilon

Flowering maple
or Indian maple

These tender perennials originate from sub-tropical regions of Africa, Asia, Australia and the USA, and have become a popular plant for use in summer containers and as dot plants in bedding schemes. As part of a tropical border they look striking.

Abutilons can either be grown as a standard plant with a single stem or as a bush. Most are not hardy and require frost protection, although a few species can be grown as large shrubs or small trees outside in mild areas where winter frosts are not severe.

It is the shape of their leaves that gives them their common names. Their deeply cut, lobed leaves resemble a maple leaf and many varieties also have attractive mottled or variegated foliage which is colourful in itself. The flowers tend to be bell-shaped and hang like lanterns. Their colours range from white, yellow, orange through to red.

Most abutilons are propagated from cuttings taken in spring or early autumn,

Abutilon 'Bella Mixed'

although with care cuttings can be taken throughout the year. In winter, established plants of tender varieties should be kept in light, frost-free conditions and kept just moist. In cool conditions the leaves may drop, but if grown in a warmer atmosphere they usually retain their leaves through the winter. Eventually the plants can grow to be large, but they do respond to

soil	Needs well-drained soil outside and good quality compost in pots
site	Prefers to be sited in a sunny position out of the wind
temp	Needs to be given winter frost protection – minimum 7°C (45°F)
general care	Pinch out tips of the plant for a more bushy appearance. Provide liquid feed in summer
pests & diseases	Outdoors, generally free from disease; can be prone to whitefly, red spider mites and mealy bug under glass

being pruned in spring just as they start into growth.

Several seed companies offer Abutilon seeds, which can be grown quite easily from a spring sowing at a temperature of 18°C (64°F). These plants all have green foliage, but they do have very colourful and showy flowers resembling large paper blooms. The seed-raised plants are also perennials and if given protection during the winter will live for many years as container specimens.

	SPRING	SUMMER	AUTUMN	WINTER	height (cm)	spread (cm)	flower colour	
Abutilon 'Bella'					50	40	+	Long flowering, pastel colours
A. 'Souvenir de Bonn'					180	150		Cream/green variegated leaves. Can grow much smaller
A. pictum 'Thompsonii'					180	150		Orange flushed flowers and mottled leaves

 sowing   *transplanting*   *flowering*   + *many colours*

Ageratum
Floss flower

The half-hardy ageratums make ideal edging plants for the border or else in containers and hanging baskets. They produce mounds of small, fluffy flowers for several months throughout the summer.

Cultivars of *Ageratum houstonianum* are used for summer bedding. They are mainly compact plants, although there are a few taller growing specimens. The blue flowering types are still the most popular plants to buy, but you can also get pink and white flowers as well as the many shades of blue and mauve. Unfortunately, in cool, damp summers the flowers of pink and white cultivars are prone to discolouring fairly quickly.

Ageratum is grown from seed that is sown in mid-spring in warm conditions. The seed is sown thinly on the surface of compost and should be covered with a light covering of compost or vermiculite. A temperature of approximately 18°C (64°F) or slightly warmer is ideal for germinating the seeds.

After pricking out the small seedlings, the young plants should be grown on in

soil	Enjoys any reasonable garden soil that retains moisture in summer
site	Prefers to be positioned in full sun, but will grow in partial shade
temp	This plant is not particularly hardy and will be damaged below 1°C (34°F)
general care	Deadhead to encourage more flowers to appear and apply a liquid feed in mid-summer
pests & diseases	Mainly trouble free from pests and diseases, but can suffer from foot rot on heavy soils

warmth and good light. The plants are naturally compact and form a dense mound of foliage. It is very important that the plants are properly hardened-off before they are planted into the garden, as they are very sensitive to a sudden change of temperature. One night of frost is all that is needed to damage or kill the plants.

Occasionally, you may find plants offered for sale in garden centres that have a dark area or bronzing on the leaves. This is normal and an indication that the plants have been hardened off.

Ageratum is a plant that does benefit from being deadheaded on a regular basis to keep a continuous supply of flowers. If the faded flowers are not removed they shrivel and turn brown, and stop the production of new flower buds.

Ageratum houstianum 'Blue Danube'

	SPRING	SUMMER	AUTUMN	WINTER	height (cm)	spread (cm)	flower colour	
Ageratum houstonianum 'Blue Champion'	sowing / transplanting	flowering			15	20		Compact plants, very reliable
A. houstonianum 'Blue Danube'	sowing / transplanting	flowering			15	30		Early flowering
A. houstonianum 'Blue Mink'	sowing / transplanting	flowering			30	30		Strong growing and open habit
A. houstonianum 'Hawaii Mixed'	sowing / transplanting	flowering			15	15		Pastel coloured flowers on compact plants

 sowing   transplanting   flowering

Agrostemma
Corn cockle

A hardy annual suitable for growing in a cottage-garden border, between shrubs or to fill gaps in mixed borders. The growth is lax and the plants may need to be supported in windy areas. The large five-petalled flowers in shades of pink and white are silk-like and produced on the tips of the slender stems from early to late summer.

Agrostemma grows naturally as a wild flower on stony slopes and cultivated land in southern Europe, the Mediterranean and west Asia. To grow well they need a sunny position and good drainage. Wet soils and heavy shade should be avoided at all times.

The seeds of Agrostemma can be sown directly into the border or started off in plug trays under cover. If sowing outdoors, avoid very rich, fertile soil as this encourages tall growth and fewer flowers. Sowing can be done in autumn or early spring. Autumn sown plants are hardy and will flower earlier than spring sown plants, although they will also finish flowering earlier in late summer.

Where garden soil has a lot of clay, it is always best to sow in spring when the soil is warming up and drying out.

If sowing under glass, sow very thinly and keep the plants as cool as possible until they are large enough to plant out. They grow quickly and if not planted out while small will soon grow leggy and spoil in trays.

Agrostemma githago 'Ocean Pearl'

soil	Agrostemma thrives on well-drained, stoney and poor soil
site	Grows best situated in a position in the full sun in a sheltered spot
temp	These plants are fully hardy, surviving temperatures down to -15°C (5°F)
general care	Deadhead these plants, but leave some seed pods if you want Agrostemma to self-seed
pests & diseases	Generally easy to grow and trouble free, with no particular problems from pests and diseases

Agrostemma is a very easy plant to grow and will often seed itself and grow all around the garden, but it is not invasive like some other plants.

The flowers can be used as cut flowers and they are excellent plants for attracting bees and other pollinating insects into the garden.

Agrostemma githago 'Pink Pearl'

	SPRING	SUMMER	AUTUMN	WINTER	height (cm)	spread (cm)	flower colour	
Agrostemma githago 'Ocean Pearl'					90	45		Dark speckles in centre of flower
A. githago 'Pink Pearl'					90	45		Masses of flowers
A. githago 'Rose of Heaven'					80	40		Easy to grow

 planting　 flowering

Amaranthus

Love-lies-
bleeding *or*
Tassel flower *or*
Chinese spinach

Amaranthus are half-hardy annuals that come from temperate and tropical regions around the world. They make excellent summer bedding plants and are ideal for borders or beds where you want some extra height and colour. They are also very good when used as dot plants for creating a tropical border. The plants are strong growing, self supporting and come in various forms.

Some plants produce long hanging tassels up to 60cm (2ft) in length in green, yellow and red, and other plants produce stiff, upright tassels. Both types make excellent cut flowers and dried flowers, and are sought after by flower arrangers. Other amaranthus are grown mainly for their bright decorative foliage and these plants tend to be used as dot plants in bedding schemes, planted to create a block of colour or in the centre of large containers.

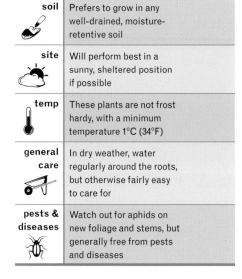

soil	Prefers to grow in any well-drained, moisture-retentive soil
site	Will perform best in a sunny, sheltered position if possible
temp	These plants are not frost hardy, with a minimum temperature 1°C (34°F)
general care	In dry weather, water regularly around the roots, but otherwise fairly easy to care for
pests & diseases	Watch out for aphids on new foliage and stems, but generally free from pests and diseases

The plants are half-hardy annuals and are sown under glass during early to mid-spring at about 20°C (68°F) and grown on in trays or small pots. The plants grow quickly, so avoid sowing too early in the season to prevent the plants from growing long and leggy. When growing in a greenhouse, try to keep the temperature as cool as possible. This will help the plants stay bushy and compact, as will pinching out the growing tips. Planting out is done in late spring or after the danger of frost has passed.

Seed can also be sown directly into the garden in late spring, but this is not as successful as raising the plants in a greenhouse and the plants will be much later coming into flower.

Amaranthus caudatus

	SPRING	SUMMER	AUTUMN	WINTER	height (cm)	spread (cm)	flower colour	
Amaranthus caudatus 'Love-lies-bleeding'	🪣🪣 ⚘	⚘ ● ● ●	●		100	50	▨	Bushy habit, long tassels
A. caudatus 'Magic Fountains'	🪣🪣 ⚘	⚘ ● ● ●	●		120	60	▨	Good colour mix and easy to grow
A. cruentus 'Plentitude'	🪣🪣 ⚘	⚘ ● ● ●	●		200	50	▨	Tall with bushy habit
A. tricolour 'Joseph's Coat'	🪣🪣 ⚘	⚘ ● ● ●	●		75	45	▢	Red and yellow foliage

 sowing   *transplanting*   ● *flowering*

Anagallis

Pimpernel *or* Poor man's weather glass

This very colourful, low growing plant is becoming more and more popular each year. It comes from the Mediterranean and western Europe and is related to the weed, scarlet pimpernel. However, the flowers on the cultivated forms are much more decorative. The most popular colours are blue, although other colours including orange are also available.

The cultivars used for summer bedding plants tend to make low growing plants with mid-green leaves. The saucer-shaped flowers are produced on long stalks during the summer. Flowering will often continue into the autumn and until the first frosts.

Anagallis monellii 'Blue Pimpernel'

Anagallis makes a very good container or basket plant where it will trail over the sides, although it can be grown in beds and borders in a sunny position. It is easy to grow and will flower until early autumn. The flowers are small, but produced in large numbers. Due to the fact that its flowers open in sunny weather it has been given the common name of poor man's weather glass.

Although some anagallis are short-lived perennials, for bedding plants they are all best treated as half-hardy annuals and raised under glass in spring. The seed should be sown into pots or small trays and germinated at around 18°C (64°F). The seedlings are best grown on in cool conditions and planted out when the danger of frost has passed.

Through the summer keep the plants watered in dry weather and fed with a liquid fertilizer.

At the end of the summer, short cuttings can be taken in a propagator and over-wintered until the following spring. However, as they are very easily raised from seed it hardly seems worth propagating from cuttings.

soil	Multipurpose compost in containers or moisture-retentive soil outside
site	Performs best when grown in the sunniest position in the garden
temp	These plants are hardy down to a minimum temperature of 1°C (34°F)
general care	Easy to care for. Keep Anagallis well watered and fed during the summer months
pests & diseases	Prone to aphid damage, but apart from this, generally trouble free from pests and diseases

	SPRING	SUMMER	AUTUMN	WINTER	height (cm)	spread (cm)	flower colour	
Anagallis arvenis var. *caerulea* 'Gentian Blue'	🪣🪣 🥄	● ● ● ●	●		20	15		Good for containers or annual ground cover
A. monellii 'Blue Pimpernel'	🪣🪣 🥄	● ● ● ●	●		25	15		Excellent in baskets and containers

 sowing   transplanting   flowering

Anchusa
Alkanet *or*
Summer
forget-me-not

Anchusa is perhaps best known as a perennial flowering plant used in herbaceous borders, although there are several annual and biennial forms that are used as summer bedding plants. The annual forms are much smaller than their perennial cousins and form neat, compact plants.

If you want anchusas as bedding plants, they are not widely available to buy in spring from garden centres, but most seed companies sell the seed, which is easy to grow.

The seeds can be sown directly into the border in mid-spring into shallow drills. As the seedlings grow they are thinned to allow space to grow. Alternatively, and perhaps the best way to raise plants, is to sow the seeds indoors in small pots or trays and grow on before planting out into the garden.

This is an ideal plant to grow in an unheated greenhouse, as the seed doesn't need to be very warm to germinate – 13°C–15°C (55°F–59°F) is sufficient.

Anchusa is related to borage and the flowers tend to be blue, although a very attractive mixed form is available that produces pink, white and lavender flowers. The small saucer-shaped flowers borne in large numbers attract bees and the leaves and stems are covered in bristly hairs.

Anchusa azurea 'Loddon Royalist'

soil	Likes to be planted in any moist, but well-drained fertile soil
site	Performs best when grown in the sunniest position in the garden
temp	Will withstand some frost. Hardy down to temperatures of -2°C (28°F)
general care	Water well in dry weather and deadhead regularly or the plant will stop flowering
pests & diseases	Prone to powdery mildew. Spray with fungicide as soon as white spots appear on leaves

The marine-blue flowers of *A. capensis* 'Blue Angel' work well when planted with silver foliage or white flowers to create a 'cool' effect. They can also be planted in containers and windowboxes.

The plants are generally easy to grow, but during the summer keep them watered in dry weather and remove faded flowers on a regular basis.

	SPRING	SUMMER	AUTUMN	WINTER	height (cm)	spread (cm)	flower colour
Anchusa azurea 'Loddon Royalist'					90	60	Self-supporting plant
Anchusa capensis 'Blue Angel'					20	15	Compact habit

 sowing   transplanting   flowering

Antirrhinum
Snapdragon

Antirrhinum majus is possibly one of the most recognisable bedding plants due to its flowers that open like a mouth when gently squeezed. It is a short-lived perennial that is grown as a half-hardy annual. Plants that are not removed from the garden in autumn will usually survive the winter and flower again for a second season, but the best flowers are always on young plants.

Seed catalogues carry a wide selection of antirrhinums that range in height from 15cm–90cm (6–36in). Trailing types are also available that are particularly good when used in hanging baskets and containers.

When growing from seed, sowing should be done in late winter or early spring. Sow the small seeds thinly onto a pot of compost and do not cover the seeds. A temperature of around 18–20°C (64–68°F) is needed for germination. Do not overwater the compost as damping-off can be a problem in the early stages.

Some gardeners prefer to use soil-based compost to sow the seeds and grow on to try and prevent damping-off. Once the seedlings have been pricked out and are established in trays or pots, grow on in cool conditions or a cold frame. Pinching out the growing point will encourage the plant to bush out and produce more flower spikes.

Some older cultivars are prone to rust, a fungal disease that coats the leaves in orange/brown spots, however most new cultivars have good resistance to the disease.

Tall growing cultivars can be used as cut flowers in the home. Dwarf types can be used as main bedding or edging plants.

Antirrhinum majus 'Hobbit'

soil	Likes to be planted in any reasonable, well-drained garden soil
site	These plants perform at their best when grown in a sunny position
temp	Protect young plants from frost. Established plants often survive down to -5°C (23°F)
general care	Remove flower spikes as flowers fade. Otherwise, little general care is necessary
pests & diseases	Rust is a problem, but new varieties have good resistance. Powdery mildew can be a problem in hot weather

Antirrhinum majus

	SPRING	SUMMER	AUTUMN	WINTER	height (cm)	spread (cm)	flower colour	
Antirrhinum majus Concept 'Pink'	🪣 ✂ ✂	● ● ● ●	●		45	30	▨	Strong growing hybrid
A. majus 'Dancing Flame'	🪣 ✂ ✂	● ● ● ●	●		45	30	▨	Attractive variegated foliage
A. majus 'Hobbit'	🪣 ✂ ✂	● ● ● ●	●		20	20	+	Unusual bell-like flowers; compact plants
A. majus 'Luminaire'	🪣 ✂ ✂	● ● ● ●	●		15	40	+	Excellent in baskets
A.majus 'Pearly Queen'	🪣 ✂ ✂	● ● ● ●	●		20	20	+	Good in containers; bi-coloured flowers
A majus 'Sonnet' Series	🪣 ✂ ✂	● ● ● ●	●		60	40	+	Good rain resistance

 sowing   *transplanting*   *flowering*   + *many colours*

Arctotis
African daisy

Arctotis come from dry, stony regions of South Africa, and to grow well in gardens, they need a hot, sunny position with good drainage. In wet soils or shade they will struggle to grow and flower well. They are particularly good when positioned in a gravel garden or in pots on a sunny patio where the reflective heat suits them.

The modern cultivars available in seed catalogues have been bred for use in bedding displays and have a longer flowering period. The flowers have stronger stems and remain open all day, whereas the older strains used to close their flowers during the afternoon or in cloudy, dull weather.

Arctotis x hybrida 'Flame'

The silver-green cut foliage contrasts well with the large daisy-like flowers that are available in a wide range of pastel and bright colours. The blooms have long stalks and can be used as cut flowers, but they only last for a short while.

Seed is sown in early spring indoors with a temperature of 16–18°C (61–64°F). The seedlings should be pricked out individually and then grown on in small pots to prevent further root disturbance, and given gentle heat. After hardening off the plants can safely be transplanted into the beds or into containers where they will flower.

Cuttings can also be taken from established plants in late summer and overwintered in a light, frost-free place. The plants should be kept just moist in their pots because if they become too wet the roots tend to rot.

Outside in the border, Arctotis is treated as an annual and looks excellent when planted as part of a tropical border with other 'hot' colours.

In a greenhouse or conservatory they can be treated as pot-grown perennials, where they will also have an extended flowering season.

Arctotis can be troubled by aphids and leaf miners, so keep a watchful eye out for these pests, and remove before they become infested.

soil	Any reasonable garden soil that retains moisture, but which drains freely
site	These plants prefer to be grown in as sunny a position as possible
temp	Arctosis are frost tender. Plants may be damaged below 5°C (41°F)
general care	Deadhead regularly to encourage more flowers. Keep roots moist but not wet
pests & diseases	Aphids and leaf miners are the main problem, but otherwise fairly trouble free from pests and diseases

	SPRING	SUMMER	AUTUMN	WINTER	height (cm)	spread (cm)	flower colour
Arctotis x hybrida 'Flame'	🪣🪣 ✂	✂ ● ● ●			45	30	Vibrant coloured flowers
A. x hybrida 'Harlequin'	🪣🪣 ✂	✂ ● ● ●			45	30	＋ Attractive flowers and foliage
A. x hybrida 'Special Hybrids Mixed'	🪣🪣 ✂	✂ ● ● ●			45	30	＋ Good colour mix

🪣 *sowing* ✂ *transplanting* ● *flowering* ＋ *many colours*

Argyranthemum
Marguerite

Argyranthemums produce daisy-like flowers and are ideal for growing in containers or in a mixed summer border, where they mix very well with other daisy-flowered plants. They love a sunny position and when deadheaded and fed will flower from late spring through to autumn.

Many different colours are available such as white, pink and yellow, and new cultivars are being introduced in response to the plant's popularity as a patio plant. Several of the new cultivars are compact and ideal for pots and windowboxes. They are evergreen sub-shrubs and in frost-free areas will grow outside all year round. In frost-prone areas the plants need to be given protection from the cold and excessive moisture around their roots.

Container-grown plants can be brought into a conservatory or greenhouse in the autumn where they will continue to flower for several more weeks.

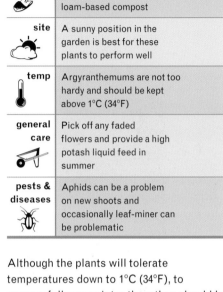

soil	Well drained. Container plants grow well in a loam-based compost
site	A sunny position in the garden is best for these plants to perform well
temp	Argyranthemums are not too hardy and should be kept above 1°C (34°F)
general care	Pick off any faded flowers and provide a high potash liquid feed in summer
pests & diseases	Aphids can be a problem on new shoots and occasionally leaf-miner can be problematic

Although the plants will tolerate temperatures down to 1°C (34°F), to successfully overwinter them they should be kept at around 5°C (40°F) or slightly warmer.

To keep established plants bushy and compact they can be lightly pruned in spring just as they start into growth.

The plants are propagated from short cuttings taken in spring or late summer. The later ones will produce bushy plants for the following season.

Standard argyranthemums on a single stem are also becoming very popular for growing in the centre of a large container or as dot plants in a bedding scheme. These can be grown for several seasons if kept frost-free over the winter months, paying particular attention to the main stem of the plant, which is susceptible to the cold.

Argyranthemum frutescens

	SPRING	SUMMER	AUTUMN	WINTER	height (cm)	spread (cm)	flower colour	
Argyranthemum frutescens	🝐 🝐	● ● ● ●	● ●		70	60		Bushy plants with yellow centre to flowers
A. 'Butterfly'	🝐 🝐	● ● ● ●	● ●		60	45		Bright flowers
A. 'Petite Pink'	🝐 🝐	● ● ● ●	● ●		30	30		Compact, dome shaped plant

🝐 *planting* ● *flowering*

Bassia

Summer cyperus
or Burning bush

Only one type of Bassia is generally available from seed (*Bassia scoparia*). Not all seed catalogues sell it, so you may have to search a little to find it. It used to be called Kochia, which is what it may still be listed under by some seed companies. It is a half-hardy annual that originates from southern Europe where it grows in light soils.

Bassia is not grown for its flowers, which are small and inconspicuous, but for its light-green feathery foliage that turns a deep red or purple in the late summer and early autumn. As a dot plant as part of a bedding scheme it is extremely useful, but it also looks good when planted in a

group between other tall bedding plants or perennials as part of a mixed border, or on its own in large containers.

It can even be used to form a low summer hedge to divide different areas of the garden.

It is a fast growing plant, and if regularly watered and fed will soon reach a height of at least 60cm (24in), forming a dense dome-shaped bush.

The plants are raised from seed sown in early or mid-spring in a greenhouse. Sow the seeds in a temperature of roughly 16–18°C (61–64°F) thinly on the surface of compost and leave them uncovered. When the seedlings are large enough, prick them out into cell trays or small pots and grow on in gentle heat. Plant them out after the danger of frost has passed.

Young plants of burning bush can sometimes be found in nurseries and garden centres in spring ready for planting out, but you may have to search around for them.

soil	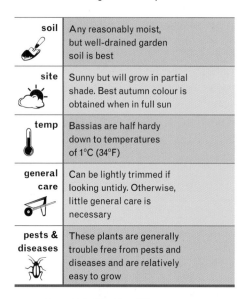	Any reasonably moist, but well-drained garden soil is best
site		Sunny but will grow in partial shade. Best autumn colour is obtained when in full sun
temp		Bassias are half hardy down to temperatures of 1°C (34°F)
general care		Can be lightly trimmed if looking untidy. Otherwise, little general care is necessary
pests & diseases		These plants are generally trouble free from pests and diseases and are relatively easy to grow

Bassia scoparia

Begonia

All begonias are very tender perennials and will provide a colourful display all summer long. They can be used in bedding schemes, containers, windowboxes and hanging baskets, and come in a wide range of colours. The two groups mainly used for bedding are the fibrous rooted plants and tuberous ones.

Begonia semperflorens and its cultivars are reliable and produce masses of small flowers in several colours, such as white, pink and red. Their foliage is either glossy dark green or bronze. They tend to be used as massed bedding, but are also excellent in containers.

They are grown from seed that needs to be started very early in the season. The dust-like seed is sown onto the surface of compost and not covered. The germination temperature should be between 20–25°C (68–77°F) with a humid atmosphere. Even then seed can take up to three weeks to germinate. For this reason many people prefer to buy seedlings or small plug plants and grow them on in gentle heat. These are readily available from garden centres and mail order companies.

Although grown as half-hardy annuals, the fibrous begonias are perennials and can be lifted from the garden in early autumn and grown as a conservatory or house plant throughout the winter.

Tuberous begonias have larger flowers in white, pink, yellow, red and

Begonia semperflorens 'Olympia Red'

soil	Any well-drained, moisture-retentive garden soil is fine for begonias
site	These plants perform best in a sunny position or partial shade.
temp	Begonias are tender and will only withstand temperatures down to 5°C (41°F)
general care	Need to be well fed in summer. Remove dead flowers from larger flowering types
pests & diseases	Vine weevils are a problem on tuberous types. Powdery mildew and grey mould can also affect begonias

Begonia tuberhybrida Nonstop Series

several unusual bi-colours. They grow from a dormant tuber that is started into growth in the warmth in early spring. New shoots grow to form a plant that can be upright or trailing, depending on the variety. In the autumn the plant naturally dies down and the tubers can be dried off and stored in a frost-free place until early spring.

Many of the tuberous types can be bought as dormant tubers from garden centres or mail order companies, although several types such as the 'Nonstop' and 'Illumination' Series can be grown from seed that is sown in late winter. Seedlings and plug plants of these types are also readily available in early spring for growing on.

All begonias produce both male and female flowers on the same plant. With the larger flowering tuberous begonias, the smaller female flowers are produced underneath the much larger showy male flowers. By removing these smaller, female flowers, you will encourage more flowers to be produced on the plant.

It is also a good idea to allow tuberous begonias, both upright and trailing types, to die down naturally in the autumn if you wish to save the tubers for the following year. Only when the stems have yellowed and started to dry off should they be removed.

The longer the growing season and the shorter the dormant season, the less chance there is of rots forming on the dormant tubers when kept over winter.

Begonia 'Illumination Rose'

Begonia 'Champagne'

	SPRING	SUMMER	AUTUMN	WINTER	height (cm)	spread (cm)	flower colour	
Begonia 'Champagne'	🪴 ✂	● ● ●			90	45	☐	Pendulous, may require support
B. pendula Illumination Series	🪴 ✂ ✂	● ● ●		🪴	30	45	+	Double flowers, trailing habit
B. pendula Sensation Series	🪴 ✂ ✂	● ● ●		🪴	30	45	+	Double flowers, trailing habit
B. semperflorens Ambassador Series	🪴 ✂ ✂	● ● ●		🪴	20	20	+	Green leaves, early flowering
B. semperflorens Devil Series	🪴 ✂ ✂	● ● ●		🪴	20	20	+	Bronze glossy foliage
B. semperflorens Olympia Series	🪴 ✂ ✂	● ● ●		🪴	20	20	+	Green and dark foliage
B. semperflorens Senator Series	🪴 ✂ ✂	● ● ●		🪴	20	20	+	Bronze foliage, compact habit
B. tuberhybrida Fortune Series	🪴 ✂ ✂	● ● ●		🪴	25	25	+	Upright habit, early flowering
B. tuberhybrida Nonstop Series	🪴 ✂ ✂	● ● ●		🪴	30	30	+	Upright habit, double flowers
B. tuberhybrida Picotee Series	🪴 ✂ ✂	● ● ●		🪴	40	40	+	Double, bi-coloured flowers

 🪴 *sowing*　✂ *transplanting*　● *flowering*　+ *many colours*

Bellis
Daisy

This is a hardy perennial that is grown as a biennial to flower in spring. It is very closely related to the common daisy that grows in lawns, although the cultivars have much larger and showier flowers that can be either single or double in white, pink or red.

Bellis looks good when planted with other spring flowering plants such as forget-me-not (Myosotis), wallflowers (Erysimum) and tulips. On its own it also looks stunning when planted as a large block in a border. Daisies can also be used in spring flowering containers and windowboxes.

The plants can be easily raised from seed sown in trays in mid-summer. A greenhouse or cold frame can be used to germinate the seeds, but no artificial heat is required. The seedlings should be pricked out into trays or small pots and grown on outside in a sheltered spot until the autumn when they can be planted into containers or into flower beds.

Occasionally, a few flowers are produced in late winter, but the main flowering time is from early spring and will continue until early summer, although the plants are normally removed in late spring to make way for summer bedding plants.

The plants are perennials and can be saved for the following year or planted into a mixed border, but mostly they are disposed of

soil	Moist garden soil, as long as it is not waterlogged in winter
site	Happy positioned in a sunny site, but will grow in partial shade
temp	These are hardy plants, withstanding temperatures down to -15°C (5°F)
general care	Remove any dead flowers regularly to prevent the plants from seeding, but otherwise easy to care for
pests & diseases	Rust can sometimes be a problem in the foliage, but generally trouble free from pests and diseases

and grown fresh each year. Bellis will seed itself in the garden, so it is best to remove the plants before the seedheads mature, or deadhead on a regular basis.

Young green plants of Bellis can be found in garden centres in autumn or in flower in the spring.

Bellis perennis Tasso Series

Bellis perennis 'Habanera'

	SPRING	SUMMER	AUTUMN	WINTER	height (cm)	spread (cm)	flower colour	
Bellis perennis 'Habanera'	● ● ●	🪣 🪣	✂ ✂ ✂		20	20		Fully double, large flowers
B. perennis 'Goliath Mixed'	● ● ●	🪣 🪣	✂ ✂ ✂		20	20		Giant spiky flowers
B. perennis 'Medicis Mixed'	● ● ●	🪣 🪣	✂ ✂ ✂		15	15		Pompom-like flowers
B. perennis 'Strawberries & Cream'	● ● ●	🪣 🪣	✂ ✂ ✂		20	20		Flowers change colour as they open
B. perennis Tasso Series	● ● ●	🪣 🪣	✂ ✂ ✂		20	20	+	Compact plants, pompom flowers

 sowing   *transplanting*   *flowering* + *many colours*

Beta
Beet *or* Beetroot

This plant is gaining in popularity and is very useful where dark contrasting foliage is wanted. It looks stunning when planted with pink flowering plants or next to silver foliage. It is a type of vegetable beetroot and is still grown in some ornamental vegetable gardens for both its dark coloured foliage and edible root.

The seed can be sown directly into the border in spring along shallow drills. As the seedlings emerge they should be thinned to leave approximately 15cm (6in) between plants.

Direct sowing is perhaps the best way to grow beet, although it can also be raised in plug trays in a cold frame. This method is useful where you want just a few plants between other types of plant. Sow one seed per cell and keep the tray in a cool greenhouse or cold frame. When the seedlings have four or five healthy looking leaves they can be planted out into the garden, being careful not to disturb the roots.

Occasionally, beetroot will produce a tall flower spike, especially if the weather has been hot and dry. As the plant is being grown for its leaves, these flower spikes should be cut off as soon as they appear.

Beta vulgaris 'Bull's Blood'

soil	Enjoys a rich, light, moisture-retentive soil, but grows in most cultivated soils
site	Prefers to be in a position in the full sun or partial shade
temp	Frost hardy, but foliage will be damaged in very cold weather
general care	Keep well watered in dry weather to prevent the plants from flowering (bolting)
pests & diseases	Generally trouble free, although in hot, dry weather powdery mildew may attack the foliage

Although grown mainly for decorative reasons, some of the red-leaved beets produce swollen roots that can also be eaten. The young leaves can be used as well in salads, where they add a splash of colour.

The plants will stand in the garden until autumn and if the weather is mild they will continue to look good until the frost cuts back the foliage in winter.

They can also be planted in containers with great effect.

Watch out for powdery mildew forming during periods of hot, dry weather.

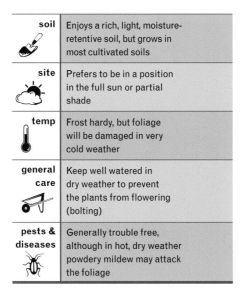

	SPRING	SUMMER	AUTUMN	WINTER	height (cm)	spread (cm)	foliage colour	
Beta vulgaris 'Bull's Blood'	🪣 ✂	● ● ●	🌰 🌰		30	25	■	Dark red foliage
B. vulgaris 'MacGregor's Favourite'	🪣 ✂	● ● ●	🌰 🌰		25	25	■	Glossy red leaves

 sowing   transplanting   flowering 🌰 harvest

Bidens

The bidens that we use in bedding schemes or in containers is a short-lived tender perennial, but tends to be grown as a half-hardy annual. It produces a spreading plant with ferny foliage and lovely golden yellow flowers at the end of the stems and side shoots.

Bidens is mainly used in hanging baskets and containers, although when planted in a bed or border it will spread to form a carpet of foliage and flowers. When used in hanging baskets it does grow quite vigorously and produce a large plant.

The buttercup yellow flowers contrast well with oranges and reds to form a vivid display. Seed is readily available in catalogues and should be sown in early spring in a temperature of 15–18°C (59–64°F). When large enough to handle, the small seedlings with delicate foliage can be grown on in small pots or cell trays in gentle heat. To encourage bushy plants, keep pinching out the growing points as the plants grow. This will delay flowering for a short while, but the end result will be a better plant.

Planting out into the garden or containers is done in late spring.

At the end of the growing season, cuttings from bidens can be taken and overwintered for the following season, but as the plants are so easy to raise from seed, it is just as easy to start afresh each spring. In fact, bidens will often self-seed itself in the garden, showing just how easy it is to germinate.

Commercially, some cultivars are produced by cuttings taken from stock plants during the spring. These plants are mainly sold through garden centres and some are more compact than the seed-raised plants.

soil	Well drained soil in the garden. In containers, any quality compost
site	Prefers a position in the full sun to perform at its best
temp	These plants are half hardy, withstanding temperatures only down to 1°C (34°F)
general care	Deadhead these plants regularly and pinch back shoots to encourage more side shoots
pests & diseases	Generally trouble free from pests and diseases, but aphids can be a problem on young plants

Bidens ferulifolia

	SPRING	SUMMER	AUTUMN	WINTER	height (cm)	spread (cm)	flower colour	
Bidens ferulifolia 'Golden Eye'	🪣🪣✎	✹✹✹✹✹			30	60		Easy to grow, masses of flowers
B. ferulifolia 'Golden Goddess'	🪣🪣✎	✹✹✹✹✹			30	60		Easy to grow, good trailing habit

🪣 sowing   ✎ transplanting   ✹ flowering

Brachyscome

Brachyscome is a group of annuals that come from Australasia and are useful for planting in hanging baskets, windowboxes or as a low growing plant for a summer bedding display. Cultivars of the half-hardy annual *B. iberidifolia* are available with flowers in blue, white and pink and are easily raised from seed sown in spring.

Brachyscome are bushy or spreading plants with soft, feathery, grey-green leaves and slightly fragrant daisy-like flowers through the summer. Cultivars of the perennial *B. angustifolia* are also available as cutting-raised plants from garden centres in spring and summer.

They bear mauve or pink flowers from late spring to late summer. These plants can withstand some frost and will survive outside where the winters are mild, but where hard frosts occur, the plants should be given

soil	Well-drained soil but moisture retentive. Compost in containers
site	These plants prefer to be grown in the full sun for the best results
temp	Seed-raised plants only down to 1°C (34°F); others down to -5°C (23°F)
general care	Deadhead these plants regularly and feed during summer to prolong flowering
pests & diseases	Slugs and snails can be a problem, but otherwise fairly trouble free from pests and diseases

protection during the winter or propagated from cuttings in late summer.

For seed-raised types, the seed is sown in late winter or early spring. This will give a flowering plant by late spring. The small seeds should be sown thinly in a tray and lightly covered with sieved compost before being placed in a germination temperature of around 18°C (64°F). When the seedlings are large enough they can be pricked out into small pots and grown on in gentle heat. Avoid hot conditions as the plants are more likely to rot than when they are grown cool.

Although the plants are naturally bushy, pinching out the growing tips will benefit the plants.

Harden the plants off in spring and plant out when the danger of frost has passed.

Brachyscome iberidifolia 'Bravo Mixed'

	SPRING	SUMMER	AUTUMN	WINTER	height (cm)	spread (cm)	flower colour	
Brachyscome angustifolia 'Mauve Delight'	transplant	flowering			000	000		Perennial, not fully hardy
B. iberidifolia 'Blue Star'	sowing / transplant	flowering		sowing	30	30		Star-shaped flowers, excellent in pots
B. iberidifolia 'Bravo Mixed'	sowing / transplant	flowering		sowing	25	30		Compact habit, good colour mix
B. iberidifolia 'Purple Splendour'	sowing / transplant	flowering		sowing	30	30		Masses of vibrant flowers
B. iberidifolia 'White Splendour'	sowing / transplant	flowering		sowing	30	30		Dark centre to flowers

 sowing   transplanting   flowering

Brassica

These ornamental cabbages and kales with their brightly coloured leaves are becoming more popular for use during the autumn and winter to add colour to containers and beds. They are closely related to cabbages and broccoli grown in vegetable gardens; the leaves of the ornamental plants are edible, but not as tasty!

The foliage will start to change colour from the centre of the rosette of leaves outwards as autumn approaches and the nights turn cooler. Planting out is normally done after summer bedding plants have been removed in mid-autumn. Garden centres often sell the plants all through the winter and early spring for anyone wishing to add instant colour to the garden.

Although biennials they are grown as hardy annuals and will stand through the winter. For best results, seed should be sown from early summer onwards and not before. Sow a single seed to each cell of a plug tray and keep them cool and moist at all times. During the summer, a greenhouse may be too hot, so stand the trays outside in a sheltered position. The young seedlings can be transplanted into pots for growing on. Ideally, use a pot with a 10cm (4in) diameter to allow room for the plants to develop fully. Again, keep the plants in a cool position and well watered at all times.

Just like garden cabbages, the ornamental forms are susceptible to several pests and diseases. The main pest during summer is caterpillars with their tell-tale holes in the leaves.

Brassica oleracea 'Northern Lights'

Brassica oleracea 'Pink Beauty'

soil	These plants enjoy any fertile, well-drained garden soil
site	Prefers to be grown in the full sun but will grow in partial shade
temp	Brassicas are frost hardy plants down to temperatures of -15°C (5°F)
general care	These plants are easy to grow. Performs best in soils that are neutral or slightly alkaline
pests & diseases	Aphids, caterpillars, slugs and snails, pigeons and clubroot can all be problematic to brassicas

	SPRING	SUMMER	AUTUMN	WINTER	height (cm)	spread (cm)	foliage colour	
Brassica oleracea 'Nagoya'		🪣🪣 ✂	✂		20	35		Uniform habit, good cold resistance
B. oleracea 'Northern Lights Mixed'		🪣🪣 ✂	✂		23	40		Tight rosettes and frilled leaves
B. oleracea 'Pink Beauty'		🪣🪣 ✂	✂		20	35		Frilled leaved type

🪣 sowing   ✂ transplanting

Briza

Quaking grass *or*
Pearl grass

Ornamental grasses are now being used more as part of summer bedding schemes and although they do not produce colourful flowers, their seedheads add movement and texture to a group of plants. They look particularly good when planted in drifts between flowering plants.

Briza is one type of grass that is grown for its ornamental panicles of pearly or purple-brown spikelets that dangle on thread-like stalks and dance around in the wind. The seedheads look good in the garden until well into autumn or even early winter.

Both types will self-seed around the garden, but spare seedlings can easily be controlled by hoeing.

The annual type, *Briza maxima*, comes from the Mediterranean and can be sown into trays in spring and planted out at a later date, although for the best results the seed should be sown directly into the border. If sown in short drills, weeding will be easier and when the seedlings are a few centimetres tall they can be thinned to 10cm (4in) between each plant. This allows room for the plant to develop.

The mature plant is erect and tufted with attractive oval-shaped seed heads in tall spikes that rustle in the breeze.

B. media is a perennial grass that originates from parts of Europe and Siberia. It forms a dense tuft of blue-green leaves. They are ideal for including in a mixed border and will complement bedding plants that are used to fill gaps in the border. The nodding heart-shape seedheads are green with a purple tint to start with and gradually turn straw colour. Seed is also sown in spring, or mature plants can be lifted and divided in mid-spring.

The flowerheads of both types can be dried and are very popular with flower arrangers.

Briza maxima

Briza media

soil	Annual brizas prefers well-drained soil, perennial will grow in most soils
site	These plants perform best when grown in sun or partial shade
temp	Both types are hardy down to temperatures of -15°C (5°F)
general care	These plants are relatively easy to grow. Will seed into border soil. Little general care necessary
pests & diseases	These plants are particularly trouble free from many pests and diseases and are fairly easy to grow

	SPRING	SUMMER	AUTUMN	WINTER	height (cm)	spread (cm)	flower colour	
Briza maxima	🌱 🌱	● ● ●	●		60	45		Graceful nodding heads
B. media	🌱 🌱	● ● ●	●		75	60		Taller growing perennial grass

🌱 planting   ● flowering

Brugmansia
Angel's trumpet

Angels' trumpets are grown for their large, often scented, tubular or trumpet-shaped flowers that hang from the plant. There is often confusion over the naming of these plants and several are still listed in seed catalogues under their synonym of Datura. However, Datura still exists as a genus and has several interesting cultivars suitable for bedding schemes (see Datura, page 76).

Brugmansias are tender, shrubby perennials and can be grown as conservatory plants during the winter months and brought into the garden as dot plants during the summer. They are ideal for adding height to a bed and giving a tropical feel to the planting scheme.

Many Brugmansia can be grown from seed sown in early spring in a greenhouse with a temperature of 16–18°C (61–64°F). Seedlings should be grown on in warm conditions and gradually potted up into larger pots as they grow.

Cuttings can also be taken in late spring and late summer. These root easily in a propagator when kept warm and moist.

During the winter, if the plants are in a conservatory or greenhouse below 10°C (50°F) the compost should be kept just moist. At cool temperatures the plants may drop their foliage, but will regrow in spring when temperatures increase. When grown warm over winter the plants remain evergreen and continue to flower into late autumn.

Although the plants may reach a height of 3m (10ft) or more, they can be pruned to maintain a smaller size.

All parts of the plants are toxic if eaten.

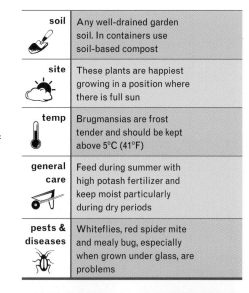

soil	Any well-drained garden soil. In containers use soil-based compost
site	These plants are happiest growing in a position where there is full sun
temp	Brugmansias are frost tender and should be kept above 5°C (41°F)
general care	Feed during summer with high potash fertilizer and keep moist particularly during dry periods
pests & diseases	Whiteflies, red spider mite and mealy bug, especially when grown under glass, are problems

Brugmansia x candida 'Variegata'

Brugmansia versicolor

	SPRING	SUMMER	AUTUMN	WINTER	height (cm)	spread (cm)	flower colour	
Brugmansia x candida 'Variegata'					250	150	☐	Long scented, trumpet-shaped flowers
B. versicolor					180	100	▨	Flowers can be 40cm (16in) long

 transplanting   flowering

Bupleurum

Thorow-wax

An unusual plant, with flowers that look like euphorbia and leaves that resemble eucalyptus. Bupleurum is not grown extensively as a bedding plant, but is ideal for informal bedding schemes or where you want to fill some gaps between shrubs and perennials. The type grown for bedding purposes is a hardy annual and comes from south Europe and central Asia.

Although grown as an annual, in mild areas Bupleurum may survive the winter and grow as a short-lived perennial. However, after a couple of years the quality of the plant will deteriorate and look straggly and woody at the base. For this reason it is best to start with new plants each spring from seed.

In light, sandy soil it will often self-seed itself each year. If you wish to prevent this from happening, remove the dead flowerheads before seed is produced.

The plants are bushy with yellow stems and oval or rounded glaucous to mid-green leaves. In summer, yellow bracts

soil	Likes a well-drained soil, but will grow in most garden soils
site	These plants are happy growing in either full sun or partial shade
temp	Fairly frost hardy. Will withstand temperatures down to -5°C (23°F)
general care	Very easy to grow and will last well into autumn. Deadhead if you do not want it to self-seed
pests & diseases	Relatively trouble free. Does not have any particular problems from any pests or diseases

develop that are surrounded by tiny star-shaped yellow-green flowers that last for several months.

The seeds can be sown where the plants are to flower during the spring and thinned out as they grow. Alternatively, they can be sown into plug trays and grown on before planting out in mid to late-spring. This prevents the roots from being disturbed when planting out and promotes faster establishment.

The taller growing *Bupleurum rotundifolium* produces flattish umbels on tall erect stems and can be used as cut flowers during the summer months. It also looks good when grown with other tall growing plants, such as cleome or *Nicotiana sylvestris* towards the back of a border to add height.

Bupleurum rotundifolium 'Green Gold'

	SPRING	SUMMER	AUTUMN	WINTER	height (cm)	spread (cm)	flower colour	
Bupleurum rotundifolium 'Green Gold'	🌱🌱🌱	● ● ● ●	●		45	30		Bushy habit
B. rotundifolium 'Griffiti'	🌱🌱🌱	● ● ● ●	●		80	45		Good for cut flowers

 planting ● flowering

Calceolaria

Slipper flower *or* Pouch flower

Calceolarias used to be a common sight in public parks during the summer months, but nowadays they are not planted as widely. They are a very versatile group of plants and, despite their exotic appearance, they are quite hardy.

There are many different types of Calceolaria that can be used as house plants, in rock gardens or as bedding plants. The one usually used for bedding is *C. integrifolia*, which originates from Chile. It is a half-hardy perennial that is grown as an annual from seed. The stems are covered in soft hairs and the leaves lightly wrinkled. The pouch-shaped flowers are yellow, although many hybrids with different coloured flowers have been developed from the original species.

Slipper flowers can be used in containers, hanging baskets or bedded out into beds and borders. They can also be grown in small pots to decorate a greenhouse or conservatory in spring and autumn.

For bedding, the fine seed should be sown in early spring onto the surface of compost. Germinate at around 18°C (64°F) and keep the surface of the compost moist. Prick out into pots or trays and grow on in a cool greenhouse until the plants are large enough to harden off.

Calceolarias soon grow tall and leggy in warm conditions, so keep them cool. A cold frame that offers frost protection will be

fine once the seedlings are established in their pot or tray. If the plants start to look drawn and tall, pinch out their growing points to encourage side shoots.

Bed out into the garden or plant in containers from late spring onwards.

Calceolaria integrifolia 'Sunshine'

soil	Enjoys most garden soils that are reasonably well drained
site	Likes a sunny, sheltered position, but will grow in partial shade
temp	These plants are half-hardy, withstanding temperatures down to 1°C (34°F)
general care	Can take up to three weeks to germinate. Feed and deadhead to prolong flowering once established
pests & diseases	In the greenhouse aphids can be a problem; when planted out slugs and snails are attracted to them

	SPRING	SUMMER	AUTUMN	WINTER	height (cm)	spread (cm)	flower colour	
Calceolaria x *hybrida* Sunset Series	🪣🪣 ✂	● ● ●			20	20		Attractive bi-coloured flowers on compact plants
C. integrifolia 'Sunshine'	🪣🪣 ✂	● ● ●			30	30		Masses of bright flowers

 sowing   *transplanting*   *flowering*

Calendula

English or Pot marigold

English marigolds are hardy annuals that are very easy to grow and once planted in a garden will come back year after year. A cottage style border would not be complete without a few pot marigolds and they look equally at home in a flower border or vegetable plot.

soil	Will grow in most conditions, including poor quality soils
site	Prefers to be situated in the sunniest position possible in the garden
temp	Calendula is a hardy annual, withstanding temperatures down to -15°C (5°F)
general care	Generally, these plants are easy to grow, but they do require deadheading for continuation of flowers
pests & diseases	Calendula are prone to aphids in spring and powdery mildew towards the end of the season

Calendula officinalis 'Needles and Pins'

Although grown mainly for their decorative features, the leaves and petals can be used in salads where they will add a peppery flavour. The orange petals can also be used to colour boiled rice.

There are many types available in seed catalogues ranging in height from 20–75cm (8–30in) with single or double daisy-like flowers in all shades of yellow and orange.

The strangely shaped seed is usually sown directly into the border in autumn or spring in shallow drills. The seedlings grow very quickly and should be thinned to at least 15cm (6in) between plants. Taller growing varieties will require wider spacing. If the seedlings are sown thickly and not thinned, they stop growing altogether.

Plants can also be raised by sowing into trays or plug-trays in spring to supply plants for planting out in mid to late spring. It is also possible to buy plants of English marigolds from garden centres in spring.

Flowering starts in early summer and will continue into the autumn as long as the plants are deadheaded regularly. Failure to remove dead flowers will stop the plants flowering completely.

In hot, dry summers powdery mildew can also be a problem. Watering and liquid feeding will help to some extent by reducing the likelihood of mildew.

In early autumn some seedheads can be left to develop. These can either be collected or allowed to seed naturally in the soil.

Taller cultivars are extremely good for cut flowers.

	SPRING	SUMMER	AUTUMN	WINTER	height (cm)	spread (cm)	flower colour	
Calendula officinalis 'Art Shades'	🌱🌱🌱	●●●	●●		60	60	+	Double flowers in apricot, orange and cream
C. officinalis 'Daisy Mixed'	🌱🌱🌱	●●●	●●		20	20	+	Dwarf plants with single flowers. Ideal for borders or pots
C. officinalis 'Fiesta Gitana'	🌱🌱🌱	●●●	●●		30	30	+	Compact plants with yellow and tangerine flowers
C. officinalis 'Needles and Pins'	🌱🌱🌱	●●●	●●		45	30		Unique quilled petals of glowing orange
C. officinalis 'Pacific Beauty'	🌱🌱🌱	●●●	●●		60	45	+	Long stemmed double flowers in orange and yellow

🌱 *planting*   ● *flowering*   + *many colours*

Callistephus

China aster *or* Annual aster

Most seed catalogues still list *Callistephus chinensis* as aster and if you look for young plants at a garden centre in the spring, the same applies. As its name suggests, it originates from China and over the years many new and interesting cultivars have been introduced.

Annual asters, unlike most summer bedding plants do not start to flower until late summer and will continue to bloom through autumn until the first sharp frosts. Because of this they are invaluable for providing colour at the end of the season. Many different types are available in straight or mixed colours, single daisy-like or double chrysanthemum-like flowers, and varying heights to suit all garden situations. The taller types make excellent cut flowers with a good vase life.

They are still popular, despite suffering from aster wilt. This is a soil-borne fungal disease that usually attacks the plants in mid-summer. Where wilt has occurred before, avoid growing the plants in the same area for three years. Fortunately, several cultivars have a good resistance to the disease and plant breeders are constantly looking for new wilt-resistant plants.

The plants are grown from seed sown in early to mid-spring in a warm greenhouse. Sow the seeds in a tray and cover with a thin layer of sieved compost or vermiculite.

To germinate, a temperature of 16–18°C (61–64°F) is required. When the seedlings are large enough, prick out into cell trays and grow on in gentle, but not too warm, heat. Plant out in the garden from late spring and keep the soil moist until established.

Callistephus chinensis 'Comet Summer Days'

soil	Prefers well-drained but moisture-retentive soil in summer
site	Enjoys a sunny position in the garden, but will grow in partial shade
temp	Half-hardy plants, withstanding temperatures down to 1°C (34°F)
general care	Keep watered in dry weather and remove dead flowers to encourage side shoots and more flowers
pests & diseases	Aphids on leaves, cutworms eating roots and aster wilt can all be problematic to these plants

Callistephus chinensis

	SPRING	SUMMER	AUTUMN	WINTER	height (cm)	spread (cm)	flower colour	
Callistephus chinensis 'Comet Summer Days'	sow sow transplant	flower flower	flower flower		20	20	+	Compact early flowering plants. Good wilt resistance
C. chinensis Duchess Series	sow sow transplant	flower flower	flower flower		60	30	+	Chrysanthemum-like flowers, curving inwards
C. chinensis Milady Series	sow sow transplant	flower flower	flower flower		30	25	+	Good wilt resistance. Large flowers
C. chinensis Ostrich Plume Series	sow sow transplant	flower flower	flower flower		60	30	+	Large feathery flowers. Partially wilt resistant
C. chinensis 'Single Mixed'	sow sow transplant	flower flower	flower flower		60	30	+	Bright coloured daisy-like flowers with yellow centre

 sowing   transplanting   flowering   + many colours

Canna
Indian shot plant

Cannas are wonderful plants to grow as part of a summer bedding scheme, where they add a lush and tropical feel. They are tender perennials producing large paddle-shaped leaves and attractive colourful flowers on tall stems.

Most types are grown from roots purchased in early spring. The roots are potted and started into growth in warm conditions. The plants grow quickly and can be planted out or potted into larger containers after the danger of frosts has passed.

Several seed companies also sell a seed mixture that contains a selection of different coloured cannas. Seed sown in early spring will produce a flowering plant in its first season, although the plants will improve in their second year. The round, hard seeds are fairly easy to germinate when given warm, moist conditions, although soaking the seed in tepid water for 24 hours before sowing will help speed up germination. With a seed mixture you do not know what colours you will get until they flower, but that makes growing them even more exciting. Seed is also much cheaper if you want several plants.

Cannas can be grown in the open ground or in containers. The plants do need to be protected during the winter, although in mild areas where there is little frost they will survive outside. In frosty areas the plants need to be lifted in autumn when frost damages the foliage. Cut back the stems and leaves and pot the large root system into a pot or tray using compost or peat substitute. Overwinter in a cool place until growth starts in early spring.

Named cultivars of this plant are increased by dividing the roots in early spring.

Canna 'President'

Canna 'Durban'

soil	Grow in fertile, well-drained, moisture-retentive soil. Soil-based compost in pots
site	Prefers full sun, but grows in light shade. Purple foliage may turn green in shade
temp	Tender. Down to 1°C (34°F). Ideally, when over-wintering, keep around 5°C (41°F)
general care	Keep well watered when growing and feed regularly. Remove faded flowers to encourage new ones
pests & diseases	Slugs will attack in spring. Canna virus is becoming a growing problem in some areas

	SPRING	SUMMER	AUTUMN	WINTER	height (cm)	spread (cm)	flower colour	
Canna 'Ambassador'	🌱🌱🌱	✺ ✺ ✺			120	50		Green foliage
C. 'Durban'	🌱🌱🌱	✺ ✺ ✺			120	60		Dark variegated foliage
C. 'President'	🌱🌱🌱	✺ ✺ ✺			120	50		Blue-green foliage
C. 'Richard Wallace'	🌱🌱🌱	✺ ✺ ✺			150	50		Dark green foliage
C. indica Hybrids mixed	🪣🌱🌱	✺ ✺ ✺		🪣	100	50		Bronze or green foliage
C. indica 'Purpurea'	🌱🌱🌱	✺ ✺ ✺			180	60		Purple foliage

🪣 sowing   🌱 transplanting   ✺ flowering

Celosia
Cockscomb

Cockscomb are tender perennials that are usually grown as annuals for use in bedding schemes, containers or as conservatory plants. The Plumosa cultivars have plume-like feathery flowers that are the most popular for bedding out.

Several different types can be grown. *Celosia argentea* is divided into two groups, with the Plumosa cultivars being the favourite for bedding out. The Cristata cultivars have crested flowers rather like a cockscomb and can be used for bedding, but in wet conditions the flat flowerheads hold water which can cause rot to set in. For this reason plant either in containers or in a sheltered position and do not water from overhead.

Celosia spicata has slender flower spikes and can be used as part of a bedding scheme or for use as cut flowers.

All types are raised from seed sown in spring in a greenhouse. The fine seed should be sown into pots of compost and lightly covered with compost or vermiculite. Keep the compost moist and germinate in a temperature of approximately 18–22°C (64–72°F). If kept cool, germination will be very slow and erratic. Once the seedlings are large enough to handle, prick out into small pots of multipurpose compost and grow on in a temperature of at least 13°C (55°F) until established. The temperature can then gradually be lowered until the plants are ready to harden off.

soil	Likes a well-drained soil that is able to retain moisture
site	Prefers to be situated in a sunny position but with shelter
temp	Half-hardy plants, withstanding temperatures down to 1°C (34°F)
general care	Celosias need to be watered regularly in dry weather and given liquid fertilizer
pests & diseases	Prone to root rot in cool weather and fungal leaf spot. Aphids can also be a problem in greenhouses

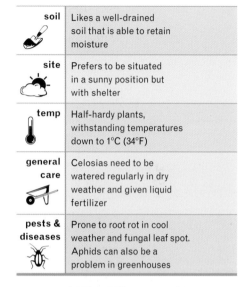

Celosia Century Series mixed

Try to avoid any checks in growth, as this will cause premature flowering and the plants will be stunted.

Plant out only when the danger of frost has passed and keep the plants moist until established in the soil. Plants in containers should be watered and fed regularly to keep them growing.

Celosia 'Century Fire'

	SPRING	SUMMER	AUTUMN	WINTER	height (cm)	spread (cm)	flower colour	
Celosia argentea Century Series		● ● ● ●	●			40	40	+	Good for bedding out
C. argentea Olympia Series		● ● ● ●	●			20	20	+	Dwarf plants with cockscomb flowers
C. spicata 'Flamingo Feather'		● ● ● ●	●			60	60		Strong stems, good cut flowers

🪣 *sowing*   ✂ *transplanting*   ● *flowering*   + *many colours*

Centaurea
Cornflower

The annual cornflower that is grown in gardens is a form of the wild cornflower that grows on cultivated farm land. The wild flower is blue and many of the named cultivars are also blue which is a lovely colour for a summer garden because of its cooling effect. Other colours such as white, pink and deep mauve are also available.

When planted with other hardy annuals such as English marigold (Calendula) and poppies (Papaver) you can create a very natural border. Grasses also look good mixed with cornflowers.

Various sizes are available from compact plants that can be grown in containers to taller types that are ideal in mixed borders and for summer cut flowers.

Cornflowers are very easy to raise from seed sown directly into the border. Plants can also be grown in containers, but as the plants do not like any root disturbance, it is better to sow them into the ground. Sow the seed into shallow drills and thin the young plants to approximately 15–25cm (6–10in) apart. The spacing will vary depending on the type being grown. The seed can also be mixed with other hardy annuals and broadcast thinly over the soil and lightly raked in. This gives a natural effect, but makes weeding more difficult. Cornflowers will self-seed themselves.

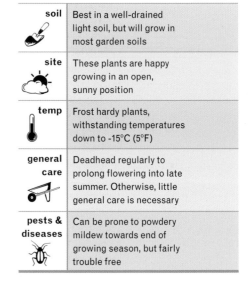

soil	Best in a well-drained light soil, but will grow in most garden soils
site	These plants are happy growing in an open, sunny position
temp	Frost hardy plants, withstanding temperatures down to -15°C (5°F)
general care	Deadhead regularly to prolong flowering into late summer. Otherwise, little general care is necessary
pests & diseases	Can be prone to powdery mildew towards end of growing season, but fairly trouble free

Seed can be sown in early autumn or spring. Autumn sown plants will grow larger than spring sown plants and will start to flower from late spring onwards. Spring sown plants will start to flower from mid-summer. As the plants do not naturally have a long flowering period, sowing in autumn and spring is a good way of extending the flowering period. Deadheading will also help to expand the flowering season by a few weeks.

Centaurea cyanus 'Blue Diadem'

	SPRING	SUMMER	AUTUMN	WINTER	height (cm)	spread (cm)	flower colour	
Centaurea cyanus 'Black Ball'	🌱 🌱	● ● ●	● ●	🌱		75	45	■	Double flowers. Good for cut flowers
C. cyanus 'Blue Diadem'	🌱 🌱	● ● ●	● ●	🌱		75	30	■	Double flowers
C cyanus 'Florence Mixed'	🌱 🌱	● ●	● ●	🌱		35	25	+	Compact plants, ideal for containers
C. cyanus 'Polka Dot'	🌱 🌱	● ● ●	●	🌱		45	30	+	Bushy plants and good colour range

🌱 *planting*　　● *flowering*　　+ *many colours*

Cerinthe

Honeywort *or* Wax flower

This is a plant that is being grown more and more for its lovely grey-green foliage, blue bracts and tubular flowers. It is grown as a hardy annual, although in mild areas the plants will often overwinter and grow as short-lived perennials.

Cerinthe looks extremely good when planted as part of a mixed border between perennials and shrubs or in a cottage border. The glaucous foliage and blue bracts look particularly stunning against orange flowers such as English marigolds (calendula) or yellow flowering bidens.

The plants are easily propagated in spring from seed that can be sown directly outside into a border. This method is suitable where the soil is light and well drained. In other types of soil it is advisable to sow the seeds in a greenhouse or coldframe. The seeds are large enough to handle individually and can be sown into plug trays filled with multipurpose compost. In gentle heat the seeds will germinate quickly and develop into sturdy plants. In mid to late spring plant out into the border. The stems are rather lax and will benefit from having the growing point pinched out. This will create a much

Cerinthe major 'Purpurascens'

soil	Likes a well-drained soil, preferably not heavy clay if sowing direct into soil
site	Prefers a sunny position, although will grow in partial shade
temp	Established seedlings will over-winter down to -5°C (23°F)
general care	Avoid wet soils and pinch out shoots to encourage side growths
pests & diseases	Generally trouble free, although aphids can attack young shoots, so keep an eye out for this

bushier plant. As the plant grows, the fleshy leaves develop white mottling which is perfectly normal and not a disease. Flowering starts from early summer until autumn depending on how early the seed was sown or whether the plants have been over-wintered.

Cerinthe will often self-sow itself and a flush of seedlings will appear in the autumn. In a mild winter the seedlings usually survive or you can lift a few, pot them up and grow them in a cold greenhouse or frame until the following spring when they can be planted out again.

	SPRING	SUMMER	AUTUMN	WINTER		height (cm)	spread (cm)	flower colour	
Cerinthe major 'Purpurascens'	🪴 ✂ ✂	● ● ● ●	●			60	45		Blue-green foliage and purple bracts
Cerinthe minor aurea 'Golden Bouquet'	🪴 ✂ ✂	● ● ● ●	●			45	30		Compact habit

 sowing   ✂ transplanting   ● flowering

Chrysanthemum

The annual chrysanthemum is a bushy, half-hardy annual that produces clusters of attractive flowers all summer long. They are easy to grow and fast growing, making them ideal for where you want to fill gaps in a border between shrubs. They are also perfect for adding height to an annual or informal border.

The flowers for bedding tend to be single, unlike the chrysanthemums sold by florists as cut flowers. Many have bright contrasting colours, whereas others are softer and produce pastel shades. Some types also have attractive finely cut, blue-green foliage.

The seed can be sown into shallow drills where the plants are to flower in late spring when the soil has warmed up and the danger of frost has passed. When the seedlings are large enough to handle, thin them out to approximately 15cm (6in) apart to allow them room to develop. Chrysanthemums sown this way will flower from mid to late summer until autumn.

They can also be started in a greenhouse and this is perhaps the best way to grow them as it will give a much

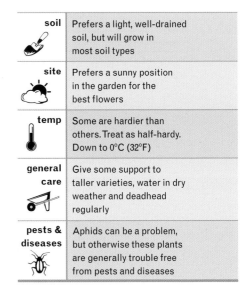

soil	Prefers a light, well-drained soil, but will grow in most soil types
site	Prefers a sunny position in the garden for the best flowers
temp	Some are hardier than others. Treat as half-hardy. Down to 0°C (32°F)
general care	Give some support to taller varieties, water in dry weather and deadhead regularly
pests & diseases	Aphids can be a problem, but otherwise these plants are generally trouble free from pests and diseases

longer flowering season. Sow the small seeds into a pot or tray of compost in early spring in a temperature of 16–18°C (61–68°F). Prick out the seedlings into cell trays and grow on the plants in cool conditions. Avoid hot conditions in the greenhouse as the plant grows quickly and soon spoils. A cold frame is ideal once the seedlings have been established in their cell tray.

After hardening off, they can be planted out into the garden in late spring where they will start to flower from early summer, and if deadheaded regularly will continue to produce flowers until early autumn.

Chrysanthemum carinatum 'Coconut Ice'

	SPRING	SUMMER	AUTUMN	WINTER	height (cm)	spread (cm)	flower colour	
Chrysanthemum carinatum 'Coconut Ice'	🪣🪣 🌱	● ● ● ●	●		45	30		Double flowers and good colour mix
C. carinatum 'Court Jesters'	🪣🪣 🌱	● ● ● ●	●		60	30	+	Single flowers with dark inner circle
C. carinatum 'German Flag'	🪣🪣 🌱	● ● ● ●	●		45	30		Single flowers with yellow circle and dark centre
C. multicaule 'Moonlight'	🪣🪣 🌱	● ● ● ●	●		25	20		Compact habit, ideal for containers
C. segetum 'Prado'	🪣🪣 🌱	● ● ● ●	●		45	30		Flowers have dark brown central discs

 sowing   *transplanting*   *flowering*   [+] *many colours*

Clarkia

Clarkia *or* Godetia

The genus Clarkia contains two attractive summer annuals. *Clarkia amoena* is listed in many seed catalogues under its old name of Godetia, which is also its common name. The other, *Clarkia unguiculata*, tends to be known by its genus name.

Both produce colourful flowers in mauves, pinks and reds all summer long. The Royal Bouquet Series of Clarkia are tall growing and make good cut flowers, as well as striking plants in a border. The double, frilly flowers are produced on tall spikes and look a little like hollyhocks, with each flower measuring up to 5cm (2in) across.

Godetia has fluted flowers that can be either single or double depending on the cultivar and are produced in large numbers at the tips of the shoots.

Clarkia and Godetia are easy to grow from seed. Neither type likes root disturbance and they are best sown directly into the border in spring. The seed should be sprinkled along a shallow drill and carefully covered over.

When the seedlings are 5cm (2in) tall thin them out to 15–30cm (6–12in) between plants. The final distance will depend on whether you are growing a dwarf or tall cultivar. Pinch out the tips of the seedlings to encourage side shoots to develop. This will delay flowering by a week or two, but each plant will be bushier and carry many more flowers.

In mild areas seed can also be sown in autumn. These plants will flower earlier the following season, but flowering will also finish sooner than in spring-sown plants.

Clarkia amoena 'Dwarf mixed'

soil	Prefers to be planted in a light well-drained soil, low in nutrients
site	A sunny position is best, although Clarkia will grow in partial shade
temp	Hardy annuals, withstanding temperatures down to -15°C (5°F)
general care	Avoid over feeding these plants, as this encourages growth at the expense of flowers
pests & diseases	Can be prone to root and stem rots on damp soils, but otherwise, fairly trouble free

	SPRING	SUMMER	AUTUMN	WINTER	height (cm)	spread (cm)	flower colour	
Clarkia amoena 'Azalea Flowered'		● ● ●			40	30	+	Frilled, double flowers
C. amoena 'Blood Red'		● ● ●			30	20		Single blooms with white centre
C. amoena 'Dwarf Mixed'		● ● ●			25	20	+	Upward fluted, cup-like flowers
C. amoena 'Summer Paradise'		● ● ●			30	20	+	Dwarf habit, with many dark colours
C. unguiculata 'Apple Blossom'		● ● ●			90	40		Masses of double flowers
C. unguiculata 'Choice Double Mixed'		● ● ●			45	30	+	Double flowers, good mix of colours
C. unguiculata 'Royal Bouquet Mixed'		● ● ●			60	30	+	Double flowers, good for cut flowers

 planting   flowering + many colours

Cleome
Spider flower

This unusual flower is guaranteed to brighten up any border and will help to create an exotic effect. The tall growing plants can be used as dot plants within a bedding scheme, planted in groups for mass effect or used as fillers between other plants such as perennials and shrubs.

Cleome originates from subtropical regions and it gets its common name from the flowers that have four petals with long stamens that are spider-like. The scented flowers are borne in white, pink and red on the ends of the tall stems from early summer until autumn. The attractive foliage has hand-shaped leaves, each with a spine at its base of the leaf stalk.

Despite the exotic appearance of this plant, it is extremely easy to grow from seed sown undercover. Sow the seeds into a tray of multipurpose compost in early spring and maintain a temperature of approximately 18–20°C (64–68°F) until the seeds start to germinate. Prick out into large cell trays or, better still, 9cm (3½in) plant pots and grow on in warm conditions with good light.

As the plants grow, space the pots to allow the plants room to develop. Pinching out the growing point will encourage a much bushier plant.

soil	Grows in most soils that are well-drained and retain moisture
site	These plants require a sunny position to flower well
temp	These are tender plants, only withstanding temperatures down to 5°C (41°F)
general care	Needs regular watering in dry weather, as well as liquid feeding to keep it looking its best
pests & diseases	Generally trouble free from pests and diseases, however aphids can attack, so keep a watchful eye out

Only when the plants are well established should they be hardened off in readiness for planting out. Plant out when the danger of frost has passed in late spring, as the plants are still tender at this stage. Keep the plants well watered for the first few weeks after planting until they start to make new growth.

The long flowering stems of Cleome can be used as cut flowers. As the flowers fade, prune off the stems to encourage new side growth and a bushier habit, and continued flowering.

Spider flowers may be attacked by aphids, which cause the plants to weaken. Look out for these pests on the leaves and buds, particularly when young, and deal with them immediately.

C. hassleriana 'Sparkler Lavender'

	SPRING	SUMMER	AUTUMN	WINTER	height (cm)	spread (cm)	flower colour	
Cleome hassleriana 'Colour Fountain'	🪣 ✄ ✄	✿ ✿ ✿	✿		120	60	+	Large flower heads and good colour mix
C. hassleriana 'Rose Queen'	🪣 ✄ ✄	✿ ✿ ✿	✿		120	60		Large flowers, tall plants
C. hassleriana 'Sparkler Lavender'	🪣 ✄ ✄	✿ ✿ ✿	✿		90	45		Compact habit, large flowers
C. hassleriana 'Violet Queen'	🪣 ✄ ✄	✿ ✿ ✿	✿		90	45		Compact plants, large flowers
C. hassleriana 'White Spider'	🪣 ✄ ✄	✿ ✿ ✿	✿		45	30		Dwarf, compact habit

 sowing   *transplanting*   🌼 *flowering*   + *many colours*

Consolida

Larkspur *or* Annual delphinium

Larkspur is a traditional cottage garden flower that is closely related to delphiniums and indeed looks very much like its perennial cousin. It is a hardy annual that originates from Europe where it grows in fallow fields. It is usually listed in seed catalogues under its common name of larkspur rather than its botanical name.

The plant is erect and produces several stems of mid-green ferny foliage which bear the flowers from mid-summer onwards. The flowering period is not very long, but the showy flowers more than make up for this.

There are several cultivars available, ranging from dwarf types to tall growing ones. The single or double flowers are produced in many shades of blue, pink or white and there are several cultivars that have unusual markings on the petals such as *Consolida ajacis* 'Frosted Skies' with its mauve and silver bi-coloured flowers.

Larkspur is easy to grow by sowing directly into the garden in autumn or spring. Autumn sown plants will overwinter without any problems. Once you have grown them in your garden, they will generally self-seed.

Consolida ajacis

Consolida ajacis

soil	Will be happy in any reasonably well-drained garden soil
site	These plants will perform their best when grown in a sunny position
temp	These are hardy annuals, withstanding temperatures down to -15°C (5°F)
general care	Cut off any faded flower spikes to encourage smaller side shoots to develop on the plant
pests & diseases	Can be prone to attacks by slugs and snails, and susceptible to powdery mildew in dry weather

It is also possible to raise plants by sowing into plug trays in early spring. The seed does not require much heat to germinate and a cold frame is ideal for this purpose. When the seedlings are 5–7.5cm (2–3in) tall they can be planted out into their flowering position.

Consolida ajacis 'Frosted Skies'

	SPRING	SUMMER	AUTUMN	WINTER	height (cm)	spread (cm)	flower colour	
Consolida ajacis 'Dwarf Double Mixed'	planting	flowering	planting		30	20	+	Compact plants with masses of flowers
C. ajacis 'Frosted Skies'	planting	flowering	planting		40	20		Semi double flowers with attractive colouring
C. ajacis 'Giant Imperial Mixed'	planting	flowering	planting		90	30	+	Bright colours on tall spikes
C. ajacis 'Kingsize Scarlet'	planting	planting	planting		100	30		Tall growing, ideal for cut flowers
C. ajacis 'Sublime Mixed'	planting	flowering	planting		90	30	+	Fully double flowers, strong stems

 planting   *flowering*   *many colours*

Convolvulus
Bindweed

Convolvulus tricolor is a hardy annual from southern Europe and North Africa that is an unusual and pretty plant and is one of the easiest plants to grow. It is not, however, the weed hated by so many gardeners. Ornamental bindweed is ideal for beginners and children, and also attracts beneficial insects such as hoverflies, making it popular with organic gardeners. It is a good plant to put under roses to help control aphids.

Convolvulus plants are bushy and do not need any support, forming a cushion of foliage and flowers about 40cm (16in) high. The flowers, which unfortunately last only a day, are however freely produced over a long period, giving a more prolonged display than many other hardy annuals.

It is important that the plants are thinned to at least 20cm (8in) apart, so each has room to develop and branch freely for the best display.

The flowers are funnel-shaped and typically deep blue with a white centre and bright golden eye, the three colours giving rise to the name 'tricolor'.

Convolvulus will grow in poor soil and prefers a sunny spot, but it will also grow in semi-shade as long as the plot gets sun for at least half the day. It is a good plant to combine with other, larger annuals such as flowering tobacco (Nicotiana), Cosmos and Lavatera. They can also be used to fill hanging baskets inexpensively. 'Blue Ensign' is the standard variety, but 'Royal Ensign' is more compact. 'Blue Flash' is even shorter at 15cm (6in). For a change, try a mixture of colours which will include pink and white flowers.

Seeds should be sown direct into the soil, where the plants are to flower in spring. They can also be sown in pots in the greenhouse at a temperature of 20°C (68°F). Put two seeds in each small pot and plant them out without disturbing the roots.

Convolvulus 'Blue Ensign mixed'

soil	Enjoys any well-drained soil. Grows particularly well in poor soils
site	These plants are happy growing in either full sun or partial shade
temp	These are frost-hardy, withstanding temperatures down to -15°C (5°F)
general care	Usually, these plants are easy to care for. Water in dry weather and remove dead flowerheads
pests & diseases	Generally trouble free from pests and diseases. Plants raised indoors can suffer from aphids, though

	SPRING	SUMMER	AUTUMN	WINTER	height (cm)	spread (cm)	flower colour	
Convolvulus tricolor 'Blue Ensign'	🌱🌱🌱	●●●	●		40	30	◼	Bushy, spreading habit
C. tricolor 'Dwarf Mixed'	🌱🌱🌱	●●●	●		40	30	◻	Bushy, spreading habit
C. tricolor 'Royal Ensign'	🌱🌱🌱	●●●	🌱		30	30	◼	Bushy, neat habit

 sowing   🌱 transplanting   ✺ flowering

Cordyline
Cabbage palm

Though cabbage palms are really long-lived trees, they are easily raised from seed and make an excellent dot plant in a bedding scheme. They also add an architectural quality to a garden design.

The most common form is *Cordyline australis* from New Zealand. In mild, coastal areas it becomes a branched tree and is commonly called Torbay palm. It will then regularly produce its large clusters of tiny, white, fragrant flowers. In colder gardens it is usually seen as a single-stemmed plant with a palm-like habit. In cold winters the top growth may be killed but the plant often produces new shoots from the trunk. It is a popular choice for growing in pots on patios but care should be taken to make sure the roots do not freeze or the plant may die.

The common green type and the purple-leaved cordyline are easy to grow from seed but as young plants they look like grass. Variegated cordylines must be bought as young plants and these often have dazzling foliage colours. They tend to be less hardy than the green and purple and are more expensive to buy.

Cordyline indivisa has broader foliage and looks more exotic, but it only thrives in mild areas where it is not too cold in winter. The large leaves are also more prone to wind damage, especially in winter, so it should be sited in a sheltered spot, either in sun or partial shade.

Cordyline australis 'Sundance'

Cordyline australis 'Atropurpurea'

soil	Enjoys any well-drained, moisture-retentive garden soil
site	Plant in a sunny position if possible. Good for coastal areas
temp	Mature plants are hardy in mild areas but protect plants below freezing
general care	Remove old foliage as it turns yellow and brown. Otherwise, generally easy to care for
pests & diseases	These plants are usually trouble free from problems caused by pests and diseases

Sow seeds in spring or summer at around 20°C (68°F). Summer sowings should be potted and overwintered in a greenhouse or coldframe for planting out the following year. Small plants are less hardy than older plants and care must be taken that they do not get waterlogged and frozen in winter.

	SPRING	SUMMER	AUTUMN	WINTER	height (cm)	spread (cm)	foliage colour	
Cordyline australis	🪴🪴 ✂✂				500	90		Foliage plant with a palm-like habit
C. australis 'Atropurpurea'	🪴🪴 ✂✂				500	90		Wine-purple foliage
C. australis 'Sundance'	🪴🪴 ✂✂				500	90		Green leaves with a red stripe
C. indivisa	🪴🪴 ✂✂				500	120		Exotic foliage plant with wider leaves

 sowing   transplanting   flowering

Coreopsis

Coreopsis are cheerful, sunny flowers and their daisy-like flowers are produced in masses all summer, especially if you take the time to deadhead the plants. In addition to the true annuals, the perennial 'Early Sunrise' and new 'Heliot' will flower in their first year from seed but differ in their habit, having lots of large leaves at the base rather than flowers.

The annuals are bushy plants with fine foliage and produce a cloud of bright, small flowers. The colours are in shades of yellow, orange and red and they associate well with marigolds, yellow cosmos and rudbeckia. The taller varieties are good for cutting.

'Seashells' has strange flowers with fluted, trumpet-shaped petals. It is much taller than most others and needs support or the plants can lean over. 'Tiger Flower' will give you a superb display of rather starry flowers in a mixture of gold and deep red shades. Each flower is striped and spotted in a contrasting colour and no two are identical. A more subdued effect is produced by 'Mahogany Midget' which has glorious, dark scarlet flowers that look effective next to yellow flowers or with bright red geraniums and salvias. The smaller Coreopsis can also be grown in patio pots and single plants in 15cm (6in) pots are attractive flowering plants for the greenhouse and conservatory.

Coreopsis grandiflora 'Heliot'

soil	Any reasonable well-drained, moisture-retentive garden soil
site	These plants perform at their best when grown in a sunny position
temp	Best treated as not hardy, withstanding temperatures down to 0°C (32°F)
general care	Little care, apart from watering in dry weather and deadhead regularly to encourage more flowers
pests & diseases	Protect young plants from slugs and snails, otherwise relatively trouble free from pests and diseases

The seed can be sown under glass in early spring in plug trays and planted out in late spring or sown outside in mid-spring where the plants are to flower. Sowing under glass in a temperature of 20°C (68°F) will give the best results and the earliest flowers.

Coreopsis tinctoria 'Seashells'

	SPRING	SUMMER	AUTUMN	WINTER	height (cm)	spread (cm)	flower colour	
Coreopsis grandiflora 'Heliot'	🪴🪴 ✂️✂️	● ● ● ●	●		50	30		Perennial, but can be grown as an annual
C. tinctoria 'Mahogany Midget'	🪴🪴 ✂️	● ● ● ●	●		30	20		Compact plants. Good in containers
C. tinctoria 'Seashells'	🪴🪴 ✂️	● ● ● ●	●		70	30		Tall plants with curious flowers
C. tinctoria 'Tiger flower'	🪴🪴 ✂️	● ● ● ●	●		25	20		The pretty flowers are speckled and striped

🪴 *sowing*   ✂️ *transplanting*   ● *flowering*

Cosmidium

This delicate annual grows wild in Texas but adapts well to wetter climates provided it is planted in full sun. It is far more delicate than Cosmos, and the stems and leaves are extremely thin and delicate, but the unusual flowers will brighten up a mixed border and are good for cutting. Each stem produces a golden yellow flower with a wide, central zone that is rich, chocolate brown.

This is not a plant for formal bedding because of its slender habit, but it is good to mix with less formal annuals and among perennials as a gap filler in borders. It is especially lovely planted among grasses and brown sedges, such as *Briza maxima* and *Carex comans*. These will help to prevent the stems from flopping over in more exposed gardens and in wet weather. If planted in large groups, it is best to push in some thin, branched twigs among the plants at planting time. Trim these to about 30cm (12in) high so they are hidden by the plants when in flower. These will support the plants and ensure a prettier display.

Cosmidium has large seeds and is easy to grow, but the thin seedlings are easily damaged when transplanting so it is better to sow two per cell in a plug tray. Sow the seeds in early to mid-spring using multipurpose compost. If both germinate, leave them both to develop. The seeds should be kept at around 20°C (68°F) to germinate and should be grown in full light in cool conditions. Harden off the plants in late spring before planting out.

soil	Any reasonable well-drained, moisture-retentive garden soil
site	These plants are happy in full sun and a sheltered position
temp	Cosmidium are not frost hardy plants, only withstanding 0°C (32°F)
general care	Easy to care for, but plants are slender and need support with twiggy branches
pests & diseases	Apart from aphids attacking young stems, these plants are relatively trouble free from pests and diseases

Cosmidium burridgeanum 'Phillipine'

	SPRING	SUMMER	AUTUMN	WINTER	height (cm)	spread (cm)	flower colour	
Cosmidium burridgeanum 'Brunette'	🪴🪴 ✂	● ● ● ●			50	15		Willowy, delicate plants with intriguing flowers
C. burridgeanum 'Phillipine'	🪴🪴 ✂	● ● ● ●			45	15		Pretty golden flowers with large brown centres

 sowing   *transplanting*   *flowering*

Cosmos

Annual Cosmos is perfect for gardeners who want fast results and something showy. Apart from the perennial chocolate cosmos (*Cosmos atrosanguineus*), only two species are widely grown. *Cosmos bipinnatus* is the most familiar. The oldest strain is 'Sensation Mixed' and this remains a popular choice for something substantial.

The plants are large and well-branched, and are especially useful for filling gaps between recently planted shrubs and herbaceous plants. Modern varieties have been produced that are shorter and more suited to bedding displays and even large containers; 'Gazebo Mixed' and the 'Sonata' series are especially popular. 'Sonata White' is often sold as a pot plant and is a good companion for most flowers, and as the basis for a white colour theme with tall *Nicotiana sylvestris* and lime green nicotiana and silver foliage.

Not many gardeners know the yellow and orange cosmos bred from *Cosmos sulphureus*, but these are bright, cheerful flowers with a slender habit and smaller flowers in shades of yellow, orange and red.

All cosmos have a long flowering season and the taller varieties are excellent for cut flowers.

Cosmos develop quickly from seed and can be sown in spring. Sow the seed in trays in a greenhouse at around 20°C (68°F). The seedlings are large and can be transplanted into individual small pots to produce large plants to set out in the garden in late spring. Seed can also be sown direct into the soil in late spring in sheltered areas, but these plants will be later flowering.

Cosmos bipinnatus 'Sonata Carmine'

Cosmos sulphureus 'Cosmic Orange'

soil	Any reasonable well-drained, moisture-retentive garden soil
site	These plants perform at their best in sunny spots in borders
temp	Cosmos are not frost hardy plants, only withstanding 0°C (32°F)
general care	Easy to care for and robust plants. Deadhead to prolong flowering into autumn
pests & diseases	Watch out for aphids on shoots. Slugs in spring on young plants can be a problem

	SPRING	SUMMER	AUTUMN	WINTER	height (cm)	spread (cm)	flower colour	
Cosmos bipinnatus 'Daydream'	🪴🪴 ✎	● ● ●	●		90	45	☐	Bushy plants with masses of pastel blooms
C. bipinnatus 'Gazebo Mixed'	🪴🪴 ✎	● ● ●	●		60	40	▨	Compact, bushy plants with large flowers
C. bipinnatus 'Sensation Mixed'	🪴🪴 ✎	● ● ●	●		120	50	▨	Taller than most and ideal for cutting
C. bipinnatus Sonata Series	🪴🪴 ✎	● ● ●	●		60	40	▨	Compact plants. Separate colours are often available
C. sulphureus 'Cosmic Orange'	🪴🪴 ✎	● ●	●		30	20	▨	Slender, bushy plants with vibrant flowers

🪴 *sowing*　　✎ *transplanting*　　● *flowering*

Cuphea

Cupheas are rather unusual plants with tubular flowers. A popular choice is _Cuphea ignea_, the cigar plant. As well as being planted in the open ground, this can be grown as a greenhouse plant or a flowering potplant as a curiosity. The small, tubular flowers are bright orange with a black and white tip, resembling a lit cigar. It is easy to grow from seed and there is a variegated form that is propagated by cuttings.

Cupheas are natives of central America and of the 250 species, only a handful of species are widely grown and even these are unusual. But they are pretty plants with bright and unusual flowers.

In recent years, _Cuphea llavea_ 'Tiny Mice' has become a popular plant, with its bright flowers in deep, furry purple and two red petals that look like ears. It has a loose, branching habit and flowers all summer. It can be planted in the open ground, but it grows best in a sheltered position and is perfect for large patio pots and hanging baskets. It combines well with yellow,

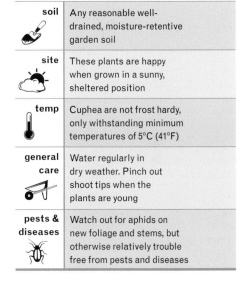

soil	Any reasonable well-drained, moisture-retentive garden soil
site	These plants are happy when grown in a sunny, sheltered position
temp	Cuphea are not frost hardy, only withstanding minimum temperatures of 5°C (41°F)
general care	Water regularly in dry weather. Pinch out shoot tips when the plants are young
pests & diseases	Watch out for aphids on new foliage and stems, but otherwise relatively trouble free from pests and diseases

Cuphea llavea 'Tiny Mice'

orange and red flowers, and looks especially good with deep indigo-blue flowers such as dark lobelia.

Although 'Tiny Mice' is propagated mainly from cuttings, _Cuphea llavea_ 'Summer Melody' is grown from seed. It is similar in habit but has flowers with five petals in a range of pink and crimson colours. It is suitable for sunny, sheltered borders and is tall enough to compete with _Cosmos_ 'Sonata', which shares a similar colour range.

Cupheas are easy to raise from seed, which should be sown in early spring in a greenhouse at a temperature of 20°C (68°F). The seeds are large enough to handle singly and these can be space-sown on trays or sown in plug trays. The plants can be put outside in late spring.

	SPRING	SUMMER	AUTUMN	WINTER	height (cm)	spread (cm)	flower colour	
Cuphea ignea	🪣 ✂ ✂	● ● ● ●	● ●		30	25	▓	Fascinating, cigar-shaped blooms on neat plants
C. llavea 'Summer Melody'	🪣 ✂ ✂	● ● ● ●	● ●		30	250	▓	Bushy plants with pretty flowers
C. llavea 'Tiny Mice'	✂ ✂ ✂	● ● ● ●	●		40	40	▓	Curious flowers on lax plants

 sowing   transplanting   ● flowering

Dahlia

The Mexican dahlia has become one of the most popular garden flowers. The taller varieties are useful at the back of the border and for cutting, and the dwarf types will fill flower beds with a long season of colourful flowers throughout the summer.

The taller dahlias, such as *Dahlia* 'David Howard' and *D.* 'Bishop of Llandaff', are grown from tubers or bought in spring as young plants. The dwarf types are usually grown from seed, but these also produce tubers that can be lifted in autumn, stored in a frost-free place and replanted the following spring. In this way you can keep your favourites from a mixed batch of seedlings.

Dahlias prefer a sunny spot and rich soil. It benefits the plants if you can dig some garden compost into the soil before planting and give them liquid fertilizer and plenty of water throughout the summer. Full sun is especially important for those dahlias with dark or purple foliage, which do not develop their full colour in shady positions.

In addition to the seed-raised *D.* 'Aztec Jewels' and *D.* 'Diablo', *D.* 'David Howard' and *D.* 'Bishop of Llandaff' have dark leaves. These are especially desirable because the plants are interesting even before the flowers appear.

Most seed-raised dahlias have semi-double or double flowers but they cannot compare in form with the doubles grown

soil	Enjoys any well-drained, rich, moisture-retentive garden soil
site	Prefers to be situated in a position in the garden where it can get full sun
temp	Dahlias are not frost hardy, only surviving down to 5°C (41°F)
general care	Generally easy to care for. Water well in dry weather and remove dead flowers regularly
pests & diseases	Slugs and snails can be troublesome, and blackfly often attack new shoots, so keep an eye out for them

Dahlia 'Aztec Jewels'

from tubers. However, for general garden display the seed-raised types are ideal. An exception is *D.* 'Dandy' which has flowers of the collerette form. These have a row of large petals and a central ring of smaller petals, often of a contrasting colour.

Dahlias are easy to raise from seed and the plants develop quickly. Seed should not be sown before mid-spring, unless you have room to put seedlings into individual pots

Dahlia 'Rigoletto mixed'

before planting out in late spring. Because they develop so quickly, the frost would kill them if they were planted out too early. Sow the seeds thinly in trays at a temperature of 20°C (68°F). The seeds germinate quickly and should be transplanted into large-cell trays.

Tubers of named varieties are bought in spring and should be planted in pots in late early-spring in the greenhouse

Dahlia 'Bishop of Llandaff'

where they must be kept free from frost. When the shoots are about 10cm (4in) high they can be removed, with a small piece of the tuber, and rooted to make more plants. Alternatively, the tubers can be planted directly in the garden in mid-spring, about 10cm (4in) deep. If the shoots emerge before the danger of frost has passed, cover them with soil or straw.

Protect the young dahlias, after planting out, from slugs and snails which will devour the plants overnight. Keep plants watered in dry spells to maintain growth and remove dead flowers to keep the plant tidy and encourage more flowers.

	SPRING	SUMMER	AUTUMN	WINTER	height (cm)	spread (cm)	flower colour	
Dahlia 'Aztec Jewels'	🪣 ✂	● ● ● ●	● ● ● ●		30	20	+	Double flowers over bronze foliage
D. 'Bishop of Llandaff'	✂ ✂ ✂	● ● ● ●	● ● ● ●		120	70	■	Single flowers and dramatic purple leaves
D. 'David Howard'	✂ ✂ ✂	● ● ● ●	● ● ● ●		100	60	■	Ideal for the back of a border
D. 'Dandy'	🪣 ✂	● ● ● ●	● ● ● ●		60	30	+	Intriguing, collerette flowers
D. 'Diablo Mixed'	🪣 ✂	● ● ● ●	● ● ● ●		35	25	+	Double flowers and dark leaves
D. 'Figaro Mixed'	🪣 ✂	● ● ● ●	● ● ● ●		25	20	+	Semi-double and double flowers on compact plants
D. 'Figaro Orange Shades'	🪣 ✂	● ● ● ●	● ● ● ●		25	20	■	Vibrant flowers and green foliage
D. 'Redskin'	🪣 ✂	● ● ● ●	● ● ● ●		40	20	+	Wide range of flower colours over burgundy foliage

 🪣 *sowing*   ✂ *transplanting*   ● *flowering*   + *many colours*

Datura
Angels'
trumpets

Daturas are grown for their huge, fragrant flowers that are often most intensely scented at dusk. Grow them by patios, doors or windows where you can really appreciate their heady perfume. Unlike their perennial relatives, the brugmansias, the flowers of daturas are upright and the plants are usually annuals or treated as such.

They vary in height according to the variety but because they prefer a warm, sheltered spot, they are often best grown in containers of good compost. They will benefit from being given plenty of liquid fertilizer. Starved plants rarely flower. Remove faded flowers to prevent seed pods forming. *Datura inoxia* 'Ballerina Mixed' is the best for patio pots because the flowers are compact. The double flowers are held above the foliage and are cream, white or purple and white. *D.* 'Cherub' has double, cream flowers, rather like Cornish ice cream cones, also with a heady scent. *D. innoxia* is a big, spreading plant with jagged, velvet foliage and the 30cm (12in) long trumpet-shaped blooms open in the evening.

In the open garden they look best when planted with other exotic annuals

Datura innoxia 'Evening Fragrance'

soil	Datura is happiest in any garden soil that is rich and moist
site	Prefers to be situated in a sunny, sheltered spot out of strong wind
temp	These plants are not frost hardy – only down to a minimum of 5°C (41°F)
general care	Generally easy to care for. Supply plenty of water, especially during hot, dry weather, along with fertilizer
pests & diseases	Aphids, whitefly, red spider mite and caterpillars can all cause problems to these plants

such as cleomes, ricinus and amaranthus, and tender perennials such as cannas, bananas and lantanas.

Seed should be sown in early spring in a greenhouse at 20°C (68°F) and the seedlings transplanted into individual, small pots. They should be kept in the greenhouse until late spring when they can be planted out. Protect newly planted seedlings from slugs and snails, and keep them well watered.

	SPRING	SUMMER	AUTUMN	WINTER	height (cm)	spread (cm)	flower colour	
Datura innoxia 'Ballerina Mixed'	🪣 ✂ ✂	● ● ●	●		60	40		Good for pots and patios
D. innoxia 'Evening Fragrance'	🪣 ✂ ✂	● ● ●	●		80	100		Large, velvety, sprawling plants with exotic flowers
D. fastuosal 'Cherub'	🪣 ✂ ✂	● ● ●	●		120	60		Large, double, fragrant flowers

 sowing   transplanting   ● flowering

Dianthus

Carnation *or* Pinks *or* Sweet William

Dianthus include many of our favourite flowers such as carnations, alpine pinks and sweet Williams. These are biennials or perennials, but many can be grown as annuals. They are easy to raise and will give a lovely display of flowers in summer.

Sweet Williams (*Dianthus barbatus*) are usually grown as biennials; sown in summer, planted in their flowering positions in autumn and removed the following summer after flowering. But dwarf varieties such as 'Indian Carpet' and 'Noverna Purpurea' can be treated as annuals. They make an unusual, bright and fragrant edging around beds and to fill gaps on rock gardens. Cut off the flower clusters when they have faded to encourage more blooms to be produced.

Chinese pinks (*Dianthus chinensis*) are true annuals, raised from seed in spring. They are not strongly scented but have masses of colourful flowers. 'Baby Doll Mixed' is a traditional variety with enormous flowers on compact stems. There is a wide range of colours including many with contrasting eyes.

Dianthus prefers a well-drained, sunny spot and thrives on chalky soils. It looks especially lovely with cottage garden annuals, such as Nigella and larkspur, and with herbs such as lavender, rosemary and sage. It can also be planted in containers.

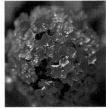

Dianthus barbatus 'Noverna Purpurea'

Seed should be sown in spring in the greenhouse at a temperature of 20°C (68°F), and grown on in trays until large enough to plant out in late spring. Though they should be kept free from frost when young, they will tolerate light frosts, so can be planted out before most other annuals.

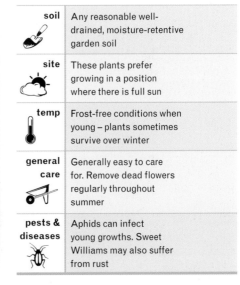

Dianthus barbatus cultivar

Dianthus 'Baby Doll Mixed'

soil	Any reasonable well-drained, moisture-retentive garden soil
site	These plants prefer growing in a position where there is full sun
temp	Frost-free conditions when young – plants sometimes survive over winter
general care	Generally easy to care for. Remove dead flowers regularly throughout summer
pests & diseases	Aphids can infect young growths. Sweet Williams may also suffer from rust

	SPRING	SUMMER	AUTUMN	WINTER	height (cm)	spread (cm)	flower colour	
Dianthis barbatus 'Indian Carpet'	transplanting	flowering			15	20		Dwarf, annual sweet William, good for edging
D. barbatus 'Noverna Purpurea'	transplanting	flowering			20	20		Can be grown as biennial or annual
D. chinensis 'Baby Doll Mixed'	sowing transplanting	flowering			15	15		Huge flowers on compact plants
D. chinensis 'Strawberry Parfait'	sowing transplanting	flowering			30	20		Small. Fringed flowers over a long season
D. chinensis 'Fire Carpet'	sowing transplanting	flowering			20	20		Easy and reliable
D. hybrida Diamond Series	transplanting	flowering			20	20		Compact plants, good for containers

 sowing   transplanting   flowering

Diascia
Twinspur

Diascias have become extremely popular container plants in the last decade, largely because of the many new, exciting varieties that have been bred. These, and many others, are grown from cuttings and treated as tender perennials, but others can be treated as annuals, sown in spring and discarded at the end of summer.

Diascias are short, spreading, bushy plants with a habit that makes them suitable for hanging baskets, windowboxes, patio pots and the front of borders. They also make a colourful addition to rockeries and gaps in crazy paving. They have a long flowering period and, if trimmed over after the first flush of flowers, will produce another flush of growth.

The flowers, usually in shades of salmon or rose pink, are carried on thin stems and create a colourful display. They are native to South Africa but come from mountain areas so do not need high temperatures or bright sun to thrive and they are useful for planting in partially shaded spots, though

soil	Any reasonable garden soil that retains moisture, but which drains freely
site	These plants are happy in full sun or partial shade – good for containers
temp	These plants are not frost hardy – minimum 1°C (34°F) when young
general care	Trim off flowered shoots to keep plants tidy. Otherwise, little general care is necessary
pests & diseases	Aphids can infest new shoots. Apart from this, relatively trouble free from pests and diseases

_D._ 'Red Delight' (Sun Chimes Series)

Diascia 'Coral Delight' (Sun Chimes Series)

flowering is always most profuse when in full sun. The unusual shades of the salmon-coloured varieties such as 'Apricot Queen' can be difficult to blend with other annuals but look good with blue flowers, cream Gazania and the yellow foliage of coleus and _Helichrysum petiolare_ 'Limelight'.

Seed should be sown in spring at a temperature of 20°C (68°F) in the greenhouse. The seedlings are tiny and delicate and must not be over-potted – at this stage they are prone to rotting if they are overwatered. Once established in their trays, they grow rapidly and can be planted out in the garden or containers in late spring Established plants will withstand light frost.

Named varieties are available in spring in garden centres that are grown from cuttings and these can be propagated from short cuttings in late summer or in spring.

	SPRING	SUMMER	AUTUMN	WINTER	height (cm)	spread (cm)	flower colour	
Diascia barberae 'Apricot Queen'	🪣🪣 ✂	●●●	●●		25	20		Unusual colour for baskets and containers
D. barberae 'Rose Queen'	🪣🪣 ✂	●●●	●●		30	20		Ideal for patio pots
_D._ Sun Chimes Series	✂ ✂ ✂	●●●	●●		20	20		Propagated by cuttings – buy plants in spring

 sowing   transplanting   ● flowering

Dimorphotheca

African daisy *or*
Star of the veldt *or*
Rain daisy

Dimorphothecas are sometimes mistakenly called osteospermums and both are South African plants that thrive in warm, sunny spots in the garden. Dimorphothecas are neat plants that branch at the base and produce upright plants of many stems with bright, daisy-like flowers. Flowers open in sunshine and close in wet and cloudy weather.

Dimorphotheca pluvialis (rain daisy) is one of the prettiest annuals. The glistening white blooms are enhanced by the deep, purplish blue centre. In contrast, *D. sinuata* has flowers that are typically orange and apricot shades, but most mixtures include yellow and white flowers.

The plants flower quickly from seed. They may need to be supported in windy gardens; if planted where there is some shade it is best to mix them with other bright annuals such as salvia, larkspur, Nigella and Californian poppies (Eschscholzia). They are good for

sunny, light soils and dry banks, but should not be planted in shady borders where they will be floppy and won't flower well.

The plants are half-hardy annuals and will not tolerate hard frosts, so they are usually sown in late mid-spring in a greenhouse at 20°C (68°F). The seedlings are quite big and can be transplanted into cell trays when large enough to handle. They should be grown in the greenhouse until transplanted in the garden in late spring. It is also possible to sow them in situ during late spring and early summer. Plants must be thinned to 15cm (6in) apart. Remove faded flowers to keep plants neat and extend the flowering period. Even so, they do not last as long as some other bedding plants and they will be one of the first annuals to be removed in late summer.

Dimorphotheca pluvialis 'Glistening White'

soil	Any reasonable garden soil that retains moisture, but which drains freely
site	These plants perform their best when positioned in the full sun
temp	Not frost hardy, only withstanding a minimum of 1°C (34°F)
general care	Keep free from weeds when plants are young. Otherwise, little general care is necessary
pests & diseases	Slugs and snails may attack plants and greenfly can affect young stems

	SPRING	SUMMER	AUTUMN	WINTER	height (cm)	spread (cm)	flower colour	
Dimorphotheca pluvialis 'Glistening White'		● ● ●			20	20	☐	Crisp. Clean, bright flowers
D. sinuata 'Flash of Orange'		● ● ●			30	20	▨	Dazzling colour in borders
D. sinuata 'Moonshine'		● ● ●			30	20	▥	Pastel shades on neat plants
D. sinuata 'New Hybrids'		● ● ●			30	20	▥	Bright range of colours
D. sinuata 'Out of Africa'		● ● ●			40	20	▥	Bright flowers, suitable for cutting

 sowing   transplanting   flowering

Dorotheanthus
Livingstone daisy

You may find this sparkling, half-hardy annual listed in catalogues as either *Dorotheanthus bellidiformis* **or its old name,** *Mesembryanthemum criniflorum.* **Whichever name you find it under, it is an excellent addition to your borders.**

Its succulent leaves and bright flowers that only open in sunny weather are a clue to its native home, South Africa, where it carpets the ground after rain moistens the soil, allowing the seeds to germinate. It grows quickly but also sets seed after a brief, dazzling display of flowers that completely obscure the foliage, so this may not be a good choice if you need a continuous show of blooms from early summer until first frosts.

Yet the flowers have a brightness and silky texture that endears them to gardeners, and they are ideal for filling gaps in rockeries which are often dull after the spring display. They thrive in gravel and can be planted in gaps in paving. Even the long, fleshy leaves are attractive and look as though they are dusted with ice or crystals.

Livingstone daisy grows best when planted in full sun in dry, sandy soil. It should

Dorotheanthus bellidiformis 'Magic Carpet'

be placed at the front of borders and will not do well when swamped by taller plants.

It is easily raised from seed, which should be sown in warmth in the greenhouse at a temperature of 20°C (68°F). The young seedlings are liable to damp-off (rot) if the compost is too wet or cold, so it is best to delay sowing until mid-spring unless you have perfect conditions. The seedlings are small and delicate, and must be transplanted with great care – it is best to transplant them in small groups. Keep them free from frost until they are planted out in the garden in late spring.

It is also possible to sow the dust-like seed in patches in the garden in late spring, but care must be taken to ensure that slugs do not devour the tiny seedlings.

soil	Prefers to be planted in most well-drained, but light garden soils
site	These plants are happy when situated in a position in the full sun
temp	Very tender, only withstanding temperatures to a minimum 5°C (41°F)
general care	Removing dead flowers regularly will extend the flowering season. Easy to care for
pests & diseases	Slugs and snails can be a problem when plants are put out in late spring, so watch out for these

	SPRING	SUMMER	AUTUMN	WINTER	height (cm)	spread (cm)	flower colour	
Dorotheanthus bellidiformis 'Apricot Tutu'					10	20		Soft orange colours. Low, spreading habit
D. bellidiformis 'Gelato Red Shades'					10	20		Low-growing annual; flowers are watermelon shades
D. bellidiformis 'Magic Carpet Mixed'					10	20		Low-growing, spreading habit
D. bellidiformis 'Sparkles'					10	20		Low, spreading habit

 sowing   transplanting flowering

Echium
Viper's bugloss

Echiums vary from tall perennials to small annuals and *Echium vulgare* is one of the easiest annuals you can grow. It is a hardy annual that grows wild throughout Europe and is especially useful for new gardens where something inexpensive is needed to fill large beds with colour.

The flowers, in shades of pink, blue and white, cover the bushy plants for many months and they attract bees and butterflies. Echium thrives in poor, sandy soils and also enjoys chalky soils. It usually self-seeds so that once you have planted it in the garden, it will reappear for many years to come.

Echium is an ideal plant for any cottage garden style and can be planted around early-flowering perennials such as aquilegias and poppies to cover any gaps that are left in mid-summer. It also looks good planted alongside lavender (Lavendula), Cistus, sage (*Salvia officinalis*) and other grey and silver-leaved plants that also enjoy the same dry, sunny positions.

Plants can be grown from seed that is sown in spring or in early autumn. In spring, sow the seeds in cells in the greenhouse at a temperature of approximately 20°C (68°F). As soon as the seedlings are established, they must be planted outside before they become potbound. It is better to sow the seeds

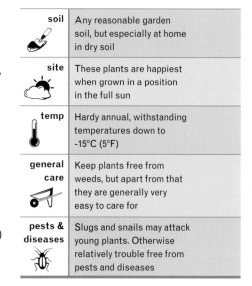

soil	Any reasonable garden soil, but especially at home in dry soil
site	These plants are happiest when grown in a position in the full sun
temp	Hardy annual, withstanding temperatures down to -15°C (5°F)
general care	Keep plants free from weeds, but apart from that they are generally very easy to care for
pests & diseases	Slugs and snails may attack young plants. Otherwise relatively trouble free from pests and diseases

outside in prepared, weed-free ground, in mid to late spring. Sow the seeds in shallow drills about 30cm (12in) apart and thin the seedlings to about 15cm (6in) between each plant.

Some of the most colourful displays are produced by sowing in autumn. Because echiums are hardy annuals, the young plants will survive the winter and bloom earlier, and, on larger plants, will even bloom the following summer. This technique is most successful if the plants are grown in any well-drained, light, sandy soil and also when the plants are kept free from competition from weeds.

Watch out for attacks by slugs and snails on the young plants. Try to offer as much protection as possible.

Be careful when handling echiums. The foliage is bristly and may cause irritation on sensitive skin.

Echium vulgare 'Blue Bedder'

	SPRING	SUMMER	AUTUMN	WINTER	height (cm)	spread (cm)	flower colour	
Echium vulgare 'Blue Bedder'	🌱 🌱 🌱	✺ ✺ ✺	🌱		30	30		Flowers age to bluish pink. Bushy habit
E. vulgare 'Dwarf Mixed'	🌱 🌱 🌱	✺ ✺ ✺	🌱		45	30		Flowers in purple, pink, lilac-blue or white. Bushy habit

 planting ✺ *flowering*

Eleusine coracana

Finger millet

This is a fascinating, unusual ornamental grass that is an extremely pretty addition to any garden. It also has its uses as a cut flower and can be dried for winter decoration. As a young plant it looks like any ordinary grass, but when it blooms, the strange shape of the green flowerheads provides a pleasant attraction to the garden.

The clusters of flowers are branched and look either like fingers or a claw, hence the name of the most common variety, 'Green Cat'. Plants are easy to grow but because of their subdued colouring it is best to plant alongside other flowers that are yellow, white or lime green. Suitable companions are lime green flowering tobacco (Nicotiana), white cosmos and busy Lizzies (Impatiens), yellow bidens and dahlias. Alternatively, use Eleusine as a

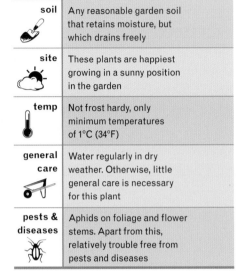

soil	Any reasonable garden soil that retains moisture, but which drains freely
site	These plants are happiest growing in a sunny position in the garden
temp	Not frost hardy, only minimum temperatures of 1°C (34°F)
general care	Water regularly in dry weather. Otherwise, little general care is necessary for this plant
pests & diseases	Aphids on foliage and flower stems. Apart from this, relatively trouble free from pests and diseases

Eleusine coracana 'Green Cat'

contrast to bright red salvias or geraniums (Pelargonium). Though the plants are not tall, they are bushy, filling up the border and should flower over several months.

Plants can be raised in the greenhouse in early to mid-spring or sown outside where they are to flower, also in mid-spring. In the greenhouse, sow at a temperature of approximately 20°C (68°F) in trays and transplant as soon as the seedlings are big enough to handle or, preferably, sow in large plug trays.

Sow a small pinch of seeds in each cell and allow them all to grow on, planting them out in late spring. It is important not to sow the seeds too early, because if the plants are allowed to become potbound in their cells the plants will flower prematurely and not develop their full size.

If growing Eleusine for cut flowers, sow in rows outside in the border in late spring and thin the seedlings to about 20cm (8in) apart as soon as they are fully established.

Erysimum
Wallflower

Wallflowers are the traditional companion to tulips in the spring garden. Though they do not flower as long as winter-flowering pansies, their display is bolder and they have an intoxicating fragrance. They are usually planted in formal beds but are useful for all sunny parts of the garden. The shorter varieties are suitable for containers.

Wallflowers are biennials and should be sown in early to mid-summer outside in the garden in drills. Transplant the seedlings when they are about 5cm (2in) tall and grow them on until they are transplanted into their flowering position in mid-autumn, when the summer flowers have been pulled up. It is important that the plants are bushy and well-grown when they are planted in order to ensure a good display in spring.

Wallflowers are related to cabbages and suffer from clubroot, a fungal disease that causes the roots to swell. Never buy wallflower plants with affected roots. It is easy to check the roots because the plants are usually sold in bunches with bare roots. As acid soils are more likely to encourage club root disease, it is worth applying lime to the soil before planting. It is also worth growing your own plants to avoid the risk of importing clubroot.

Traditional varieties are sown in summer and grow to about 45cm (18in) high but smaller types that are just as easy to grow are ideal for small and raised beds and should be planted slightly closer. The latest development is

Erysimum cheiri 'Blood Red'

soil	Any reasonable well-drained soil – preferably alkaline – will be fine
site	These plants are happy growing in a position where there is full sun
temp	Wallflowers are extremely hardy plants, withstanding winter temperatures
general care	Pinch out the tips of young plants to encourage a branching habit. Easy to care for
pests & diseases	Prone to clubroot disease on acid soils, but otherwise relatively trouble free from pests and diseases

'Vivaldi', which can be grown as an annual and will flower in about four months from sowing. It can be sown in spring or summer. Summer sowings will flower in autumn and the following spring.

Erysimum cheiri 'Fair Lady Mixed'

	SPRING	SUMMER	AUTUMN	WINTER	height (cm)	spread (cm)	flower colour	
Erysimum cheiri 'Blood Red'	● ● ● ✎		✎ ✎		45	25	▢	Traditional, fragrant variety
E. cheiri 'Cloth of Gold'	● ● ● ✎		✎ ✎		45	25	▢	Excellent, bright flowers and good fragrance
E. cheiri 'Fair Lady Mixed'	● ● ● ✎		✎ ✎		30	20	+	Exquisite range of subtle colours
E. cheiri 'Prince Mixed'	● ● ● ✎		✎ ✎		15	20	▢	Perfect for edging and window boxes
E. cheiri 'Tom Thumb'	● ● ● ✎		✎ ✎		20	20	+	Good for raised beds and exposed gardens
E. cheiri 'Vivaldi'	✎ ✎	● ● ●			30	20	+	Can be sown at any time, to flower after 4–5 months

 ✎ *planting* ● *flowering* + *many colours*

Eschscholzia
Californian poppy

A delightful, easy-to-grow, hardy annual that will provide colourful flowers during the summer months. The orange-yellow saucer-shaped flowers are followed by long, thin seed pods. The foliage is blue-green and ferny in texture. Many cultivars of Eschscholzia are available with red, yellow, cream, orange and pink flowers in single and double forms.

Eschscholzias are ideal where you want to create a natural or cottage-style border and they work well when planted with ornamental grasses to create a prairie effect. To open fully, the flowers need bright sun so avoid growing in a shady spot. Even on a dull day the flowers will close.

They also grow much better in poor, well-drained soil where there are few nutrients. In rich, fertile soils the plants will grow large and produce masses of growth, but flowers will be few and far between.

Grow the plants by sowing directly into the soil in spring or autumn. Sow the seed thinly along shallow drills and thin the seedlings to 15cm (6in) apart as they grow. Alternatively, the seed can be scattered over an area and gently raked in. This is a very good way of adding interest to a piece of waste land and usually the plants will self-seed and grow back the following year.

Eschscholzia californicum

soil	Any well-drained garden soil, which is low in nutrients
site	These plants are happy in a sunny position in the garden
temp	These are hardy annuals, withstanding temperatures down to -15°C (5°F)
general care	Eschscholzias dislike root disturbance. Remove any dead flowers to extend flowering season
pests & diseases	Generally these plants are trouble free from pests and diseases, although slugs and snails can be a problem

For bedding schemes, the seed can be sown into plug trays in a cold frame in spring and the young plants then grown on in small pots in cool conditions before being planted into the garden in the late spring.

To keep the plants flowering into late summer, pick off the cylindrical seed pods.

Eschscholzia californicum 'Dali'

	SPRING	SUMMER	AUTUMN	WINTER	height (cm)	spread (cm)	flower colour	
Eschscholzia californicum 'Appleblossom Rose'	🛠🛠🛠	●●●	🛠🛠		20	15		Frilly, double flowers on compact plants
E. californicum 'Dali'	🛠🛠🛠	●●●	🛠🛠		25	15		Compact with scarlet flowers
E. californicum 'Milkmaid'	🛠🛠🛠	●●●	🛠🛠		25	15		Fluted blooms and ferny foliage
E. californicum 'Monarch Art Shades'	🛠🛠🛠	●●●	🛠🛠		23	15	+	Semi double and single flowers
E. californicum Thai Silk Series	🛠🛠🛠	●●●	🛠🛠		20	15	+	Single or semi-double flowers

🛠 *planting*   ● *flowering*   + *many colours*

Fatsia

False castor oil plant

This exotic plant, with its glossy palmate leaves, is often sold in garden centres as a houseplant, where it grows very well. However, it is hardy and makes an excellent structural plant in the garden. Young specimens are perfect as dot plants in a tropical bedding scheme or for the centre of a large container.

Fatsias originate from Japan and South Korea, where they grow into large, evergreen shrubs or small trees. Fatsias will also grow large when given a sheltered position in the garden. The green form is the toughest and is totally hardy. The variegated form is not as hardy and needs a sheltered position or winter protection.

Fatsias are readily available at all times of the year, but to establish one in the garden you should plant in late spring or early summer to give the plant time to acclimatize and establish before the winter.

The green Fatsia can also be grown

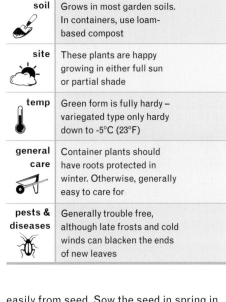

soil	Grows in most garden soils. In containers, use loam-based compost
site	These plants are happy growing in either full sun or partial shade
temp	Green form is fully hardy – variegated type only hardy down to -5°C (23°F)
general care	Container plants should have roots protected in winter. Otherwise, generally easy to care for
pests & diseases	Generally trouble free, although late frosts and cold winds can blacken the ends of new leaves

easily from seed. Sow the seed in spring in a tray of compost at a temperature of 20°C (68°F). Germination can take several weeks. When the seedlings start to develop their first true leaf, pot them individually into small pots and grow on in the greenhouse. Through the summer transplant fatsias into a larger pot and for the first winter keep the plants frost free. By the second season they will be large enough to use as dot plants or in outdoor containers.

The variegated form is propagated by removing suckers from around the base of the plant in spring. These root easily in a heated propagator.

When the plant is several years old it produces branched heads of white flowers in autumn.

If the plants get too large for their position they can be pruned in mid-spring.

Fatsia japonica 'Variegata'

	SPRING	SUMMER	AUTUMN	WINTER	height (cm)	spread (cm)	flower colour	
Fatsia japonica	🪣🪣 ✂				200	200		Large glossy hand-shaped leaves
Fatsia japonica 'Variegata'	✂ ✂				150	150		Variegated leaves, slower growing than the green form

 sowing   ✂ *transplanting*

Felicia
Blue daisy

Felicia is a very popular plant for use in hanging baskets and containers, although it can also be bedded out into the garden. It is grown for its daisy-like flowers that come in various shades of blue, purple, pink and white, many with a yellow centre. Several forms also have very attractive variegated foliage that contrasts well with the bright flowers.

soil	Any reasonable garden soil that is well-drained and fertile
site	Grows best when sited in a sunny position in the garden
temp	Tender, only to a minimum of 3°C (37°F). Annual forms down to 0°C (32°F)
general care	If overwintering perennial types, do not overwater. Otherwise, little general care is necessary
pests & diseases	Aphids and red spider mite can be a problem under glass, but relatively trouble free outside

Felicia amelloides 'Santa Anita'

The plants originate from South Africa and do require a sunny spot to flower well. Both annual and perennial types are available and flower from early summer until early autumn.

The annual *Felicia heterophylla* 'The Blues' is raised from seed sown in early to mid-spring in a greenhouse at a temperature of 18°C (64°F). As the seedlings grow they can be pricked out and grown on in small pots in gentle heat. Pinching their growing points out will encourage bushy plants.

In late spring, after being hardened off, they can be planted out in the garden or used in containers.

The perennial felicias such as *Felicia* 'Variegata', *F.* 'Read's White' and *F.* 'Santa Anita' are grown from cuttings and can be bought from garden centres in spring. They are mainly grown as annuals and are discarded in autumn, although with a little care container plants can be overwintered. Ideally, a winter temperature of 10°C (50°F) is needed to keep the plants ticking over and care should also be taken with watering. Try to keep the plants on the dry side as they have a tendency to rot off if cold and wet.

Cuttings can also be taken from these cultivars in late summer and overwintered for the following year. If kept in gentle heat and with the soil just moist, rooted cuttings usually overwinter without too many problems.

	SPRING	SUMMER	AUTUMN	WINTER	height (cm)	spread (cm)	flower colour	
Felicia amelloides 'Read's White'	🌱🌱🌱	● ● ● ●	●		30	30	⬜	Compact plant
F. amelloides 'Santa Anita'	🌱🌱🌱	● ● ● ●	●		30	30	▦	Large flowerheads
F. amelloides 'Variegata'	🌱🌱🌱	● ● ● ●	●		30	30	▦	Variegated foliage. Good in containers
F. heterophylla 'The Blues'	🪣🪣🌱	● ● ● ●	●		20	20	▦	Annual form with bushy habit and pastel colours

 sowing   transplanting   ● flowering

Festuca
Blue fescue

This is an ornamental grass that looks very good in many garden situations and is often planted with other grasses, herbaceous perennials, heathers and mixed borders. It also blends well with bedding plants to add movement and texture, as well as making an excellent container plant.

Festuca glauca is a hardy perennial grass that will live in the garden for many years. Plant it in its permanent position and add summer-flowering bedding plants around it. It goes very well with blue flowers such as Ageratum and Lobelia, as well as silver-leaved plants.

In containers it can be planted for year round interest and the seasonal bedding plants changed around it. In spring it looks good with blue and yellow pansies.

It is grown mainly for its tufted blue-green foliage, but it also produces flower spikes in mid-summer that remain on the plant into late autumn.

Plants are readily available at all times of the year, although it can also be easily raised from seed. This is a much cheaper alternative if you require many plants. Sow the seed into a tray in early spring. Gentle heat is needed for germination and a cold frame will do fine. As the seedlings grow, transplant them into small pots or cell-trays

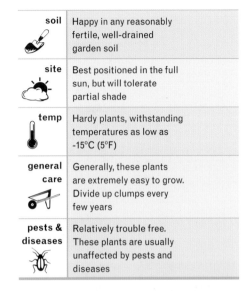

soil	Happy in any reasonably fertile, well-drained garden soil
site	Best positioned in the full sun, but will tolerate partial shade
temp	Hardy plants, withstanding temperatures as low as -15°C (5°F)
general care	Generally, these plants are extremely easy to grow. Divide up clumps every few years
pests & diseases	Relatively trouble free. These plants are usually unaffected by pests and diseases

Festuca glauca 'Blaufuchs'

and grow on. You could also sow a small pinch of seed into each cell of a plug tray to produce a clump rather than single seedlings. Seed-raised plants will be large enough to plant out in their second season.

Cultivars such as 'Azurii' are normally propagated by division. Lift established clumps in early spring, divide the clump into several smaller sections and re-plant.

Festuca glauca 'Azurii'

	SPRING	SUMMER	AUTUMN	WINTER	height (cm)	spread (cm)	flower colour	
Festuca glauca	sow sow transplant	● ● ●	● ● ●		30	25		Blue-green spikey foliage
Festuca glauca 'Azurii'	transplant transplant transplant	● ● ●	● ● ●		30	25		Attractive blue foliage
F. glauca 'Blaufuchs'	transplant transplant transplant	● ● ●	● ● ●		30	25		Bright blue leaves

 sowing   transplanting   ● flowering

Fuchsia

Fuchsias are such familiar garden plants it seems difficult to believe they are actually native to Central and South America. It was not until the 1820s that any effort was made to produce hybrids. There are about 100 species and from a few of these, many thousands of varieties have been produced. There is still potential for even more variation, but those available give us plenty of choice.

Fuchsia flowers typically hang down in pairs along the stems and each flower has a long tube and four sepals, that protect the flower in bud. The tube and sepals are usually the same colour. When the flower opens it reveals four petals, in a single flower or eight or more in doubles. These may be the same or a different colour. After the flower fades, if it has been pollinated, the seed pod at the base of the flower develops into a fleshy, edible fruit.

The flowers vary in size from just 1cm (½in) long to 6cm (2½in) or more but, in general, plants with small flowers tend to produce more of them. It also pays to remove the faded flowers and seedpods to prevent seed from being formed – this in turn encourages more flowers to develop.

Plant habit also varies. Some, such as *Fuchsia* 'Beacon', have a strong, upright, branching habit. This variety rarely needs pinching out or staking and the single

Fuchsia 'Swingtime'

Fuchsia 'Eva Boerg'

Fuchsia magellanica

soil	Any reasonable, well-drained, moisture-retentive garden soil
site	These plants are happy situated in full sun or partial shade
temp	Most fuchsias are not frost-hardy plants, surviving only down to a minimum 1°C (34°F)
general care	Generally very easy to care for. Water regularly in dry weather and pinch out growing tips
pests & diseases	Whitefly can be troublesome in greenhouses. Rust can infect plants in wet seasons; vine weevil in containers

flowers are abundant. *F.* 'Red Spider', *F.* 'Swingtime' and many others are trailing or basket types. They have naturally spreading stems and the flowers are best seen from below.

Fuchsias are relatively easy to grow from cuttings, which are taken in spring and late summer, and they are also rewarding when trained into standards.

Fuchsias are useful plants for semi-shaded parts of the garden. They dislike the hot, sunny conditions favoured by pelargoniums and they often flower best at the end of summer as temperatures start to drop. Fuchsias blend with many other plants, but in a shaded, summer bed they are natural companions for begonias, busy Lizzies and pansies. In less formal areas of the garden, small-flowered fuchsias look lovely planted alongside hostas and ferns.

Grow young plants in frost-free conditions in spring and plant out in late spring. Pinch out the growing tips of young plants. This will encourage bushiness and many more flowers.

Fuchsias vary in their hardiness. Some are sold as hardy fuchsias but much depends on your garden. Many fuchsias will survive outside in mild areas or if

Fuchsia 'Red Spider'

planted against a warm, sheltered wall. In average winters, even hardy fuchsias may be killed to ground level but they will send up shoots from below ground level in spring. The old stems can be cut back at this stage. A mulch of straw in autumn can help plants survive.

Because frost kills the stems above ground, standard plants and other large specimens must be protected from extremes of cold and should be kept in a frost-free greenhouse or garage – light is not necessary because fuchsias are deciduous plants.

Watch out for whitefly if kept over the winter months in a greenhouse, as well as vine weevils in container plants.

Fuchsia 'Snowcap'

Fuchsia 'Harry Grey'

	SPRING	SUMMER	AUTUMN	WINTER	height (cm)	spread (cm)	flower colour	
Fuchsia 'Beacon'	transplanting	flowering	flowering		80	45		Vigorous, single flowers. Upright habit
F. 'Blueberry Fizz'	transplanting	flowering	flowering		25	45		Trailing with double flowers
F. 'Carla Johnson'	transplanting	flowering	flowering		60	45		Single flowers. Upright habit
F. 'Claudia'	transplanting	flowering	flowering		60	45		Upright habit, large double flowers
F. 'Display'	transplanting	flowering	flowering		70	500		Vigorous, bushy plant. Masses of single flowers
F. 'Ellen White'	transplanting	flowering	flowering		25	45		Trailing habit, large double flowers
F. 'Eva Boerg'	transplanting	flowering	flowering		40	60		Reliable, trailing variety; masses of medium-sized blooms
F. 'Harry Grey'	transplanting	flowering	flowering		40	60		Trailing habit with double flowers
F. magellanica	transplanting	flowering	flowering		90	60		Can be grown permanently in sheltered borders
F. 'Red Spider'	transplanting	flowering	flowering		20	50		Elegant single flowers. Trailing habit
F. 'Snowcap'	transplanting	flowering	flowering		60	45		Semi double flowers, upright habit
F. 'Swingtime'	transplanting	flowering	flowering		50	60		Arching habit with large, double flowers

 sowing   transplanting   flowering

Gaillardia
Blanket flower

Gaillardias are often called blanket flowers because of the vibrant, usually red and yellow colours, reminiscent of Native American weavings that are made where these plants grow wild. They are hardy perennials but because they flower so quickly after sowing, and because they are short-lived plants, they are usually treated as annuals. If they survive the winter to bloom again the next year it is a bonus.

They are tough, rather hairy plants that form clumps of large, toothed leaves and the flowers are produced above these. The taller varieties such as *Gaillardia* 'Dazzler' are good for cutting because of the long stems, but the small types such as *G.* 'Kobold' can be used among regular bedding plants such as marigolds and geraniums where they will create a brilliant display of two-toned blooms.

They can also be used in mixed borders to fill gaps between shrubs or to provide late summer colour where perennials have finished flowering. The dwarf cultivars can also be grown in containers.

Each flower has a central, woolly, dark red centre and each petal is deep red at the base with bright golden tips.

Seed can be sown in summer in situ, in the open garden where they are to flower, but these plants will not flower until the following year. Therefore it is

soil	Any reasonable well-drained, moisture-retentive garden soil
site	These plants perform at their best when situated in the full sun
temp	Young plants need to be given protection from severe frosts
general care	Generally fairly easy to look after. Remove any dead flowers you find throughout summer
pests & diseases	Aphids on young stems. Avoid overwatering young plants. Mildew can be troublesome in late summer

best to sow the seed under glass in early spring. The seedlings will appear quickly in a temperature of around 20°C (68°F).

Transplant the seedlings into cell trays or small pots and grow them on in frost-free conditions. Because they tolerate light frosts, they are some of the first bedding plants that can be planted out in late spring. Watch out for aphids on young plants.

Gaillardia 'Kobold'

	SPRING	SUMMER	AUTUMN	WINTER	height (cm)	spread (cm)	flower colour	
Gaillardia 'Dazzler'	sowing transplanting	flowering			60	40		Tall plants with lots of flowers for cutting
G. 'Kobold'	sowing transplanting	flowering			30	30		Reliable, neat plants with masses of blooms
G. 'Indian Yellow'	sowing transplanting	flowering			60	40		Vibrant blooms for garden display and cutting

 sowing   transplanting   flowering

Gazania

On a hot, summer's day gazania flowers can be dazzling, surpassing in beauty and brilliance any marigold or pelargonium. But the following day, if it is wet and cloudy, the flowers of most varieties will remain closed for protection, and the border will be dull. It is this unreliability that prevents many from growing gazanias, but modern varieties have been bred to keep their flowers open in slightly overcast conditions.

The flowers combine brilliant colours and intricate patterns. Many have an olive green or black zone around the centre and others have stripes of contrasting colours. The

soil	Any reasonable, well-drained, moisture-retentive garden soil
site	These plants perform at their best when situated in the full sun
temp	Not frost-hardy plants – only enduring minimum temperature of 1°C (34°F)
general care	Easy to grow but plants must be positioned in full sun. Deadheading keeps plants looking tidy
pests & diseases	Can be affected by aphids attacking new foliage and flower stems, but otherwise fairly trouble free

Gazania 'Daybreak Red Stripe'

commonest colours are orange and yellow but mixtures also include brick red, mahogany and cream. Because they thrive in full sun they can be planted with most other orange and yellow annuals such as marigolds as well as pelargoniums and petunias. They are also suitable for patio pots if they are placed in full sun.

Gazanias are easily raised from seed and they flower within a few months. Sow the seeds in spring at a temperature of 20°C (68°F). The seedlings are quite large and can be easily transplanted into trays or cell trays, or individual, small pots where they can be grown on in cool conditions.

Plant out into the garden in late spring when the danger of frost has passed.

Remove faded blooms regularly. In mild areas, plants may survive the winter outside, especially in coastal regions.

Gazania F1 'Daybreak Tiger'

	SPRING	SUMMER	AUTUMN	WINTER	height (cm)	spread (cm)	flower colour	
Gazania Daybreak Series	sowing / transplanting / flowering	flowering			25	20	+	Reliable, flowering even in dull weather. Good colour range
G. Kiss Series		flowering			20	20	+	Bright flowers, many with dark, central zones
G. 'Sundance Mixed'		flowering			25	20		Large flowers, up to 15cm across; striped and zoned blooms
G. 'Tiger Mixture'		flowering			25	20		Large, vibrant flowers are striped with contrasting colours

 sowing   *transplanting*   *flowering*

Gypsophila
Baby's breath

Gypsophila elegans 'Monarch White'

Gypsophila is linked in the minds of most gardeners with sweet peas. Both are hardy annuals and while a bunch of Gypsophila may be dull, it is the ideal companion to a bunch of sweet peas.

There are both annual and perennial gypsophilas; the perennials can be difficult to grow unless the soil is well-drained in winter. The annual *Gypsophila elegans* is an easy plant to grow but it should be sown outdoors, where it is to grow, in mid- to late spring; seedlings dislike being transplanted.

The plants are bushy and make a tangled mass of stems, covered in a cloud of small white or pale pink flowers. Thin seedlings to about 15cm (6in) apart. Like other hardy annuals that are sown where they will flower, if they are too crowded, they will compete for space and water, and severely reduce the flowering period.

Gypsophila is good for cutting and you could sow a row in the vegetable garden for this purpose. The flowers will attract

soil	Any reasonable well-drained garden soil. These plants thrive in chalky soil
site	Gypsophila perform their best growing in a position in the full sun
temp	A hardy annual, enduring temperatures as low as -15°C (5°F)
general care	Generally these plants are extremely easy to care for. Water regularly in dry weather
pests & diseases	Aphids attacking new stems can prove troublesome. Plants may also rot in wet soils

beneficial insects that may help reduce pests on your vegetables. They can also be used in mixed flower borders among taller plants. Their fine foliage means they will not harm other plants. Mix them with hardy geraniums and other bushy herbaceous plants or alongside blue catmint (Nepeta) under pink or white roses. Another pretty combination would be Gypsophila sown under feathery, mauve *Thalictrum dipterocarpum*.

	SPRING	SUMMER	AUTUMN	WINTER	height (cm)	spread (cm)	flower colour	
Gypsophila elegans 'Covent Garden'	planting	flowering			60	45		Great clouds of white flowers
G. elegans 'Monarch White'	planting	flowering			45	45		White flowers above greyish leaves
G. elegans 'Rosea'	planting	flowering			60	45		Pretty alternative to the common white

 planting   *flowering*

Bedding Plants
G

Helianthus
Sunflower

Helianthus annuus 'Ring of Fire'

Helianthus annuus 'Teddy Bear'

Helianthus annuus 'Starburst Lemon Aura'

Sunflowers (*Helianthus annuus*) are often the first plants we ever grow, usually as children, because they are easy, dramatic and have some of the biggest flowers. As bedding plants they can be used as part of a tropical bed to add height and colour.

Sunflowers are native of Central America and it is easy to imagine that they were important to people that worshipped the sun – their large, showy flowers follow the sun. This makes it important to site them so that they are viewed from the sunny side or the flowers will obstinately face away from you!

In addition to the big yellow types, there are varieties with pale, cream flowers, deep, mahogany reds and even those with zoned flowers such as 'Music Box' and 'Ring of Fire'. Modern varieties have also been bred that are naturally bushy, so the flowering season is extended and you get a bunch of blooms on each plant. Pinch out the top bud when it forms to make a bushier plant. Dwarf sunflowers have also been developed. These can be bought as plants in flower, but it is better to grow your own. They are ideal for tubs and small borders. 'Pacino' has perfect, bright flowers on short plants and 'Teddy Bear' has intensely double blooms on knee-high plants.

Sunflowers are hardy annuals and can be sown where they are to bloom. They can also be sown in pots in spring in the greenhouse at 20°C (68°F). It is important that they are planted out while still small, or they end up becoming stunted.

soil	Any reasonable well-drained, moisture-retentive garden soil
site	These plants face the sun and should be protected from strong winds
temp	Not frost-hardy plants – only enduring minimum temperature of 1°C (34°F)
general care	Relatively easy to care for. Dig in plenty of garden compost and fertilizer for giant plants
pests & diseases	Generally free from pests and diseases. However, protect young plants from slugs and snails

	SPRING			SUMMER		AUTUMN		WINTER	height (cm)	spread (cm)	flower colour	
Helianthus annuus 'Music Box'	🪴 🪴 ✂		✂	● ●	● ●	● ●	●		100	45	▧	Branching plants with lots of blooms in a range of shades
H. annuus 'Pacino'	🪴 🪴 ✂		✂	● ●	● ●	● ●	●		40	20	▧	Compact plants with 12cm (4¾in) wide flowers
H. annuus 'Ring of Fire'	🪴 🪴 ✂		✂	● ●	● ●	● ●	●		120	45	▧	Pretty, zoned blooms, ideal for cutting
H. annuus 'Starburst Lemon Aura'	🪴 🪴 ✂		✂	● ●	● ●	● ●	●		180	60	▧	Double flowers on branched plants. Pollen free
H. annuus 'Teddy Bear'	🪴 🪴 ✂		✂	● ●	● ●	● ●	●		40	20	▧	Large, double flowers on short plants
H. annuus 'Velvet Queen'	🪴 🪴 ✂	✂		● ●	● ●	● ●	●		150	45	▧	Dusky blooms with chocolate centres

 🪴 sowing   ✂ transplanting   ● flowering

Helichrysum

Helichrysum is a popular trailing foliage plant that is used widely in baskets and containers, but can also be used in borders in summer. It is a perennial from South Africa that can be easily propagated from cuttings.

While the flowers are small and dull white, the foliage is a pretty complement to summer flowers. The plant has an arching habit and the long stems will sprawl out to cover the ground. The leaves are rounded and greyish green, but there are variegated varieties. *Helichrysum* 'Limelight' is probably the most popular, with its lime-green leaves, making it a pretty plant to combine with yellow flowers such as marigolds and yellow cosmos. It becomes

soil	Any reasonable well-drained, moisture-retentive garden soil
site	These plants are happy in sun or partial shade. Ideal for containers
temp	Not frost-hardy plants – only enduring minimum temperature of 5°C (41°F)
general care	Pinch out tips of young plants to encourage bushy growth. Otherwise, generally easy to care for
pests & diseases	Relatively free from pests and diseases. However, plants may get mildew in late summer

Helichrysum petiolare 'Variegatum'

bright yellow, though, when the plant is grown in full sun. However, if the sun is too bright and the soil too dry the leaves may scorch, so plant 'Limelight' in soil that is moist throughout summer.

Although its habit is naturally spreading, *H. petiolare* can be trained up canes to add height to borders and containers.

It is also useful for filling borders, along with vigorous, spreading bedding plants such as 'Wave' petunias and verbenas, and it is useful among low herbaceous plants in summer such as hostas.

Plants are frost-tender and must not be planted until the last frost has passed. In early autumn, take cuttings of sideshoots and root them in gritty compost. Keep them frost-free throughout winter. Alternatively keep a large plant in a pot in a greenhouse over winter and take cuttings in early spring.

	SPRING	SUMMER	AUTUMN	WINTER	height (cm)	spread (cm)	flower colour	
Helichrysum petiolare 'Bright Bikini'	✂ ✂ ✂	● ● ● ●	●		45	70	▣	Grey leaves
H. petiolare 'Limelight'	✂ ✂ ✂	● ● ● ●	●		45	70	▢	Golden foliage
H. petiolare 'Variegatum'	✂ ✂ ✂	● ● ● ●	●		45	70	▢	Green and grey foliage

 planting   ● flowering

Heliotropium

Heliotrope

Heliotrope is an old-fashioned plant that was a popular greenhouse ornament in the 19th century. Perhaps it is the purple colouring of the flowers that helps it retain its historical associations. Despite this, modern varieties, such as 'Marine', which are grown from seed and 'Nagano', which are bought as plants in spring, are gaining popularity because of their pretty flowers and wonderful fragrance.

Heliotrope is sometimes called cherry pie because of the sweet, fruity scent and this is best appreciated when the plants are grown where it is warm and sheltered.

Heliotrope is native to Peru and is a tender shrub. Plants can be kept for several years and in the past, plants were often trained as standards and kept in the greenhouse over winter.

If you are prepared to keep plants in this way there is a wide range of older varieties such as the purple *Heliotropium* 'Chatsworth' and the pinkish white *H.* 'White Lady', which have been selected and retained because of their exceptional fragrance.

H. 'Marine' has the advantage in that it can be raised from seed and will flower in the first year, so there is no need to keep plants over winter. 'Marine' also has exceptionally large heads of flowers and the plants do not need any special training or pinching.

The purple colouring of heliotrope makes it a perfect companion for pink and white flowers and silver foliage, but also a striking contrast with yellow flowers such as short African marigolds (Tagetes).

Seed should be sown in early spring in a temperature of 20°C (68°F). The young seedlings are sensitive to overwatering, so use a well-drained compost. Transplant them into cell trays to avoid further root disturbance. They can be planted into borders and containers after the last frost has passed.

An added benefit is that heliotrope attracts butterflies to the garden. However, the foliage can irritate both the skin and eyes, so take care when handling plants.

Heliotropium arborescens 'Nagano'

soil	Any reasonable well-drained, moisture-retentive garden soil
site	These plants are happy growing in a sunny, sheltered position
temp	Not frost-hardy plants – only enduring minimum temperature of 5°C (41°F)
general care	Water regularly in dry weather. Heliotropiums are ideal plants for patio containers
pests & diseases	Relatively trouble free. These plants are generally not prone to pests and diseases

	SPRING	SUMMER	AUTUMN	WINTER	height (cm)	spread (cm)	flower colour	
Heliotropium arborescens 'Marine'	🪣 🌱 🌱	● ● ● ●	● ● ● ●			45	45		Large heads of fragrant flowers. Will flower in first year
H. arborescens 'Nagano'	🌱 🌱 🌱	● ● ● ●	● ● ● ●			60	45		Modern variety. Large heads of fragrant flowers

 sowing   *transplanting*   *flowering*

Iberis
Candytuft

Candytuft is an old-fashioned, cottage garden favourite with a long season of flowers and a light, delicate fragrance. It is easily grown from seed, sown where the plants are to flower and it is surprising that it is largely ignored by gardeners today, who are often tempted by more unusual plants.

Although there are perennial candytufts, such as *Iberis sempervirens*, that are grown on the rock garden, the most common species are *I. amara* and *I. umbellata*. The species *I. amara* is taller than most and has long spikes of small, four-petalled flowers. *I. amara* 'Giant Hyacinth Flowered' is a popular choice and the flowers are a pure, glistening white which have a greater intensity than most other flowers and makes a dazzling show. *I. umbellata* is a lower, bushy plant with domes of flowers but in a wide range of colours that includes pinks, purple and cherry reds.

Candytufts are ideal for filling gaps in borders or to sow with other hardy annuals such as Nigella (love-in-a-mist) and larkspur. Short varieties, such as *I. umbellata* 'Flash Mixed' and *I. umbellata* 'Fairy Series' can also be

soil	Any reasonable well-drained, moisture-retentive garden soil
site	These plants are happy growing in the full sun. Ideal as border edging
temp	A hardy annual, withstanding temperatures down to -15°C (5°F)
general care	Apart from watering regularly in dry weather, candytufts are relatively easy to care for
pests & diseases	Aphids on new growth may cause some problems. Clubroot may be troublesome on acid soils

Iberis amara 'Giant Hyacinth Flowered'

sown in gaps in paving and gravel. If plants are left to set seed they will usually be followed by a crop of new plants the following year, although you will probably find that the brighter colours in mixtures of plants will gradually disappear over the years.

Candytuft is a hardy annual that should be sown, in spring or early summer, in the position where it is to flower. Alternatively, you can sow two seeds per compartment in cell trays or small pots in the greenhouse in spring for earlier flowers – seedlings dislike being transplanted.

Candytuft is related to cabbages and wallflowers and may suffer from clubroot in acid soils. If this soil-borne disease is present in the border, you should avoid planting candytuft.

	SPRING	SUMMER	AUTUMN	WINTER	height (cm)	spread (cm)	flower colour	
Iberis amara 'Giant Hyacinth Flowered'	🖐🖐🖐	● ● ●	🖐🖐		40	20	⬜	Tall spikes of glistening, white flowers. Good for cutting
I. umbellata 'Appleblossom'	🖐🖐🖐	● ● ●	🖐🖐		30	20	⬜	Neat plants, covered in pastel flowers
I. umbellata 'Flash Mixed'	🖐🖐🖐	● ● ●	🖐🖐		30	20	⬛	Domed plants with vibrant blooms

🖐 planting   ● flowering

Impatiens
Busy Lizzie

Busy Lizzies are a favourite bedding plant, yet just a few decades ago these well-known plants were only grown as windowsill plants. Plant breeders have transformed them into compact, free-flowering plants that can be used throughout the garden. They are ideal for tubs and windowboxes, hanging baskets and borders. Once planted they need little maintenance and, unlike most annuals, they thrive in shady gardens.

Although they are strictly perennials, they flower so quickly from seed they are grown as annuals and are usually bought already in flower in spring.

There are about 850 species of Impatiens in the wild and they get their name from their seed pods. These explode when they are ripe, seemingly 'impatient' to shed their seeds.

Most busy Lizzies are bred from *Impatiens walleriana*, although other species have been used to produce the New Guinea busy Lizzies. These have larger leaves and flowers than the rest, and have a more angular habit. Though originally only available as varieties that had to be propagated from cuttings, there are now seed-raised types such as 'Java Mixed'. The only disadvantage of these is that they do not usually have the dazzling variegated foliage of some of the cuttings-raised plants. 'Tango' is another exciting addition for gardeners

Impatiens walleriana Super Elfin Series

soil	Any reasonable well-drained, moisture-retentive garden soil
site	Grow in the sun or partial shade. Avoid hot, scorching, dry positions
temp	Not frost-hardy plants – only enduring minimum temperature of 5°C (41°F)
general care	Water these plants copiously in dry weather. They are ideal to be grown in containers
pests & diseases	Fungal diseases can kill seedlings in greenhouse. Vine weevil grubs eat roots of container plants

who prefer to plan their colour schemes because all the pants have large, vibrant tangerine flowers.

A neglected group are the varieties of *Impatiens balsamina* (Indian balsam). These are much easier to grow from seed than other Impatiens and are very different in habit. They are fleshy and branch at the base, producing upright stems of flowers. Older types had flowers

Impatiens New Guinea Group 'Java Mixed'

Impatiens New Guinea hybrids

that were rather hidden under the foliage but new varieties have largely eliminated this problem. Even so, they are at their best when grown in containers so they can be seen from the side. You can then really appreciate the double, camellia-like flowers along the stems, in a wide range of colours. They have a shorter flowering season than standard busy Lizzies, but are useful because of their height and ease of cultivation. They perform best in the full sun.

Busy Lizzies will not tolerate any frost and must be planted out only after the last frost is forecast. They grow well in shade and semi-shade, though they may be less compact than when planted in full sun. In addition to traditional bedding uses, try a few among ferns and hostas to add some much-needed colour in the summer.

Busy Lizzies should be sown in spring in a temperature of approximately 20°C (68°F). The seeds require light to germinate so they should be sown on the

I. walleriana 'Mosaic Rose'

surface of the compost and not covered. A very light sprinkling of vermiculite can be used as this allows light through and keeps the seeds

moist. Seedlings are likely to rot if the compost is too wet or the temperature is too low. Seedlings and plug plants are widely available and these are a sensible alternative if you have trouble providing good conditions for sowing.

Grey mould (*Botrytis*) may affect the flower buds if conditions are too damp, and red spider mite is troublesome under glass.

	SPRING	SUMMER	AUTUMN	WINTER	height (cm)	spread (cm)	flower colour	
Impatiens balsamina 'Camellia Flowered Mixed'	🪣 ✂ ✂	❋ ❋ ❋ ❋	❋		60	40	▌	Tall, fleshy plants with columns of vibrant, double blooms
I. balsamina 'Tom Thumb Mixed'	🪣 ✂ ✂	❋ ❋ ❋ ❋	❋		25	25	▌	Compact plants with upright stems of large, double flowers
Impatiens New Guinea Group 'Java Mixed'	🪣 ✂ ✂	❋ ❋ ❋	❋ ❋		35	40	▌	Large flowers on compact plants
I. New Guinea Group 'Spectra'	🪣 ✂ ✂	❋ ❋ ❋	❋ ❋		35	40	▌	Large flowers above deep green leaves
I. New Guinea Group 'Tango'	🪣 ✂ ✂	❋ ❋ ❋	❋ ❋		35	40	▉	A brilliant bedding plant that will brighten up the patio
I. walleriana Accent Series	🪣 ✂	❋ ❋ ❋	❋ ❋		20	25	+	Low, spreading plants with a wide range of colours
I. walleriana 'Bruno'	🪣 ✂	❋ ❋ ❋	❋ ❋		30	30	+	Larger than usual plants and flowers. Plants are vigorous
I. walleriana 'Double Carousel Mixed'	🪣 ✂	❋ ❋ ❋	❋ ❋		25	30	+	Spreading with double flowers. Some blooms are bicoloured
I walleriana Expo Series	🪣 ✂	❋ ❋ ❋	❋ ❋		20	25	+	Compact plants with wide range of colours. Ideal for pots
I. walleriana 'Mosiac Rose'	🪣 ✂	❋ ❋ ❋	❋ ❋		25	30	▉	Each flower pink with white stippling in centre of each petal
I.walleriana 'Safari F2'	🪣 ✂	❋ ❋ ❋	❋ ❋		30	30	+	Useful for large beds as the seed is cheaper than most
I. walleriana 'Starbright'	🪣 ✂	❋ ❋ ❋	❋ ❋		20	25	+	Vibrant mixture of colours, all with white, starry centres

🪣 *sowing*   ✂ *transplanting*   ❋ *flowering*   + *many colours*

Lagurus
Hare's tail

Lagurus ovatus is one of the most popular annual grasses and is one of the most intriguing and tactile of all plants. Although the foliage of young plants is unremarkable and may have visitors wondering why you have planted grass in your flowerbeds, once the flower stems start to appear they will find it impossible not to stroke the oval, fluffy flowerheads, which give the plant its name of Hare's tail.

This grass is Mediterranean in origin and grows best in a sunny spot. It will tolerate dry and poor soil, though it produces more flowerheads if it is grown in more fertile conditions. It can be sown in clumps in gaps in the herbaceous border and looks pretty interspersed with herbaceous plants such as hardy geraniums. Pots of seedlings can be planted to fill gaps left by spring-flowering bulbs. It also looks good when planted with hardy annuals such as cornflower (Centaurea) and Californian

Lagurus ovatus

soil	Prefers light, sandy soils but is happy in anything well drained
site	These plants will perform at their best when situated in the full sun
temp	Hardy annual, withstanding temperatures as low as -15°C (5°F)
general care	Easy to grow if sown in situ. There is very little general care needed as Lagurus tends to look after itself
pests & diseases	Relatively trouble free. Pests and diseases do not usually cause any problems

poppy (Eschscholzia) to create a prairie style border.

Hare's tail grass is a hardy annual and is best sown where it is to flower in the border. Sow the seeds in rows about 20cm (8in) apart and when the seedlings are large enough to handle, thin the seedlings to 15cm (6in) apart to give them room to develop. The tiny 'Nanus' variety can be planted more closely and is useful in paving and as an edging plant. Alternatively, sow a pinch of seeds in small pots in the greenhouse and plant them out into the garden in late spring. Light frosts will not harm the plants.

If you wish to cut and dry the flowerheads for winter decoration, cut them before they are fully developed and before the pollen is produced on the fluffy heads. If cut later they become grey and less fluffy when dry.

	SPRING	SUMMER	AUTUMN	WINTER	height (cm)	spread (cm)	flower colour	
Lagurus ovatus	🌱 🌱 🌱	● ● ● ●	● ●		45	20	▢	Tactile flowerheads. Good for drying
L. ovatus 'Nanus'	🌱 🌱 🌱	● ● ● ●	●		15	15	▢	Tiny, bushy plants with full-sized, fluffy heads

 planting   ● flowering

Laurentia

You may have trouble finding this charming annual in catalogues and it pays to look for it under the alternative names of Isotoma and Solenopsis. Whatever it is called, this unusual relative of lobelia combines colour with a neat habit and intriguing flowers.

It is an Australian plant that naturally has pale blue, starry flowers that cover the mounds of deep green leaves. The foliage is finely toothed and can be completely clothed by the flowers when the plants are at their peak. The plants form neat domes of flowers and are good for edging borders and for containers. The taller types, such as 'Mill Troy', are also loose enough in habit for hanging baskets. In addition to the pretty flowers there is a light scent too.

Although the colour range has been widened to include white and pink, there is usually some variation in plant habit and flower shape among the colours, and the blue kinds are usually much more satisfactory than the rest.

The plants set lots of seed pods. It will help to keep the plants neat and prolong the flowering period if you can go over them periodically and remove faded blooms. Even in cold areas, the plants can self-seed and it

soil	Any reasonable well-drained, moisture-retentive garden soil
site	These plants are happiest growing in a position situated in the full sun
temp	Not frost-hardy plants – only enduring minimum temperature of 5°C (41°F)
general care	Apart from watering regularly in dry weather, these plants require very little specialized care
pests & diseases	Aphids on young plants, especially in dry weather, can be problematic, but otherwise trouble free

is not unusual to find plants appearing the following year in paving and gravel under hanging baskets.

Plants should be raised from seed in late winter to ensure they flower by mid-summer. Sow in a greenhouse at a temperature of 20°C (68°F). The seed and seedlings are very small and should be handled carefully. Prick out into small pots and grow on in gentle heat keeping the compost moist, but not wet. Plant out in late spring after the last frost.

Laurentia axillaris 'Blue Stars Blue'

	SPRING	SUMMER	AUTUMN	WINTER		height (cm)	spread (cm)	flower colour	
Laurentia axillaris 'Blue Stars Blue'	🌱🌱🌱	● ● ● ●	● ●		🪣	20	20		Compact plants, free flowering
L. axillaris 'Mill Troy'	🌱🌱🌱	● ● ● ●	● ●		🪣	30	30		Starry, lavender blue flowers. Good for hanging baskets
L. axillaris 'Star Gazer'	🌱🌱🌱	● ● ● ●	●		🪣	15	15		Masses of starry flowers over feathery foliage

 sowing transplanting ☀ flowering

Lavatera
Mallow

Lavateras are perfect plants for new gardeners to try. These hardy annuals have large seeds and they rapidly grow into bushy, leafy plants that will fill large gaps in borders. They are not fussy about soil and will even grow in areas with some shade as long as they get sun for at least half the day.

The flowers are 10cm (4in) across and although the colour range is not great, the petals have a beautiful, silky sheen and both the glistening white and rose pink varieties will bloom for many months.

soil	Any reasonable, well-drained, moisture-retentive garden soil
site	These plants are happy growing in either full sun or partial shade
temp	Hardy annual, withstanding temperatures as low as -15°C (5°F)
general care	Apart from watering regularly in dry weather, these plants require very little specialized care
pests & diseases	Aphids attacking new foliage and stems can be a problem, but otherwise fairly trouble free

Lavatera trimestris 'Silver Cup'

These are leafy, robust plants and should be given plenty of room. They combine best with other large annuals such as larkspur (Consolida), Amaranthus and cosmos. They can also be planted in the herbaceous border among Michaelmas daisies and late-flowering Japanese anemones.

Lavatera can be sown in the border where they are to flower or sown under glass. In the border you can sow two or three seeds in groups about 20cm (8in) apart. Keep them moist as they germinate and protect against slugs and snails.

Alternatively, you can sow them in pots under glass in late spring. Do not sow them too early because the seedlings grow rapidly and pot-bound plants will flower prematurely and will not develop their full potential.

Lavatera trimestris 'Mont blanc'

	SPRING	SUMMER	AUTUMN	WINTER	height (cm)	spread (cm)	flower colour	
Lavatera trimestris 'Dwarf White Cherub'	planting	flowering			35	25	☐	Compact plants smothered with flowers. Ideal for containers
L. trimestris 'Loveliness'	planting	flowering			90	40	▨	Ideal for filling large borders
L. trimestris 'Mont Blanc'	planting	flowering			50	40	☐	Free-flowering plants with large white flowers
L. trimestris 'Silver Cup'	planting	flowering			60	40	▩	Tough, reliable, grow-anywhere annual; masses of blooms

 planting   flowering

Limnanthes
Poached egg plant

The poached egg plant is one of the easiest of all plants to grow and always delights the gardener with its masses of glistening, saucer-shaped blooms in yellow and white. It grows wild on the west coast of the USA and usually persists for several years in gardens because it self-seeds freely. It is a particular favourite of organic gardeners because the flowers attract bees and hoverflies, the larvae of which eat aphids.

soil	Any reasonable garden soil that retains moisture, but is not waterlogged
site	These plants prefer growing in a position in the full sun
temp	Hardy annual, withstanding temperatures as low as -15°C (5°F)
general care	Apart from watering regularly in dry weather, these plants require very little specialized care
pests & diseases	Aphids can be problematic, but otherwise these plants are rarely troubled by pests and diseases

Limnanthes douglasii

Limnanthes gets its common name from the colour of the flowers, which have a golden centre and white edge. It is a firm favourite with children who also appreciate the fact that plants will flower in just a few months after sowing. However, after a glorious display, the plants quickly collapse and die and should then be pulled up – they do not last as long as most bedding plants.

Limnanthes is a good choice for sowing in gravel and paving, and as an edging to vegetable beds. They can also be sown on rock gardens if there are not delicate plants that might be swamped. In mild areas, self-sown plants often germinate in autumn and these overwintered seedlings will flower in late spring the following year, often overlapping with spring bulbs. In these areas Limnanthes is useful grown under hedges. Here it flowers before the hedge takes the moisture from the soil and makes it too dry in summer – before this happens the Limnanthes will have flowered and died.

An unusual variant, *Limnanthes douglasii* 'Sulphur Yellow', is sometimes available but it is not as attractive as the common variety and the flowers are usually smaller. It is a curious variety but certainly no better than the species.

Sow the seed in late spring where it is to flower. Thin out the seedlings to about 10cm (4in) apart when they are big enough to handle. Alternatively you can sow the seeds under glass in a temperature of approximately 20°C (68°F). Sow into plug trays in late spring and plant them out when they are well established in the tray.

	SPRING	SUMMER	AUTUMN	WINTER	height (cm)	spread (cm)	flower colour	
Limnanthes douglasii	🌱 🌱 🌱	● ● ●			15	20		Spreading plants, lots of blooms. Attracts beneficial insects
L. douglasii 'Sulphur Yellow'	🌱 🌱 🌱	● ● ●			15	20		Unusual variety with pure yellow blooms

🌱 planting   ● flowering

Limonium
Statice

Limonium sinuatum **is a familiar plant, often seen in mixed bunches of cut flowers and as dried flowers. It is incredibly easy to grow and a packet of seed, sown in spring, will produce huge armfuls of flowers. It is also an attractive garden plant and, although not commonly used for bedding, can look quite beautiful, especially if you are able to obtain seeds of a single colour.**

Statice plants are rather odd. They look rather like big dandelions at first, forming great rosettes of deep green leaves and showing little sign of the mass of flowers that will follow. At first, a few green stems appear, each with flaps of green tissue along the sides. The triangular heads of small flowers start to open but soon each plant becomes a huge bouquet of flowers. Each flower is tubular and papery and the flowers are usually in shades of pink, mauve, blue, yellow and white, but some mixtures include salmon and orange shades.

A bonus is that statice attracts hordes of butterflies in summer and the blue and purple shades seem to be favourites with these insects. If you are hoping to cut and dry the flowers, it is important to harvest them as soon as the flowers are fully open.

Limonium sinuatum cultivar

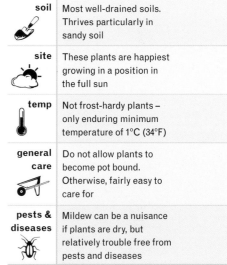

soil	Most well-drained soils. Thrives particularly in sandy soil
site	These plants are happiest growing in a position in the full sun
temp	Not frost-hardy plants – only enduring minimum temperature of 1°C (34°F)
general care	Do not allow plants to become pot bound. Otherwise, fairly easy to care for
pests & diseases	Mildew can be a nuisance if plants are dry, but relatively trouble free from pests and diseases

The colour range and size of statice plants means that they should be combined with large annuals such as Cosmos and Lavatera towards the middle of the border. This is because the flowers tend to be at the top of the plants and the sides look less attractive.

Sow in spring at around 18°C (64°F). The seedlings have long seed leaves and are easy to transplant into trays. Plant them out after the last frosts about 30cm (12in) apart in a sunny spot and keep them watered in the early stages to ensure they form large rosettes of leaves before flowering begins.

	SPRING	SUMMER	AUTUMN	WINTER	height (cm)	spread (cm)	flower colour	
Limonium sinuatum 'Forever Mixed'	🪣 ✂ ✂	❀ ❀ ❀ ❀			50	30	+	Long stems, ideal for cutting and drying
L. sinuatum Supreme Series	🪣 ✂ ✂	❀ ❀ ❀ ❀			50	30	+	Good range of colours, strong stems

 sowing   *transplanting*   *flowering*   [+] *many colours*

Linaria
Toadflax

Toadflax is an old-fashioned favourite that is easy to grow and combines exquisite, dainty flowers with a bright display of flowers in a bewildering array of colours. The blooms vary in colour from red, pink, yellow, purple and white, and each often combines two or more colours.

The plants seem fragile and have thin stems with narrow, grey-green leaves, but it is a hardy annual that can be sown in the position where the plants are to flower. In gardens with light, sandy soil the plants will self-seed and reappear every summer with no effort from you.

It is an ideal annual for dry, sunny spots in the garden and is often sown in banks which are full of gravel and among paving slabs. In rich soil or in partial shade the plants become larger than usual and may flop when they are in bloom, so this is an annual that really does do best in rather poor conditions. *Linaria maroccana* 'Fairy

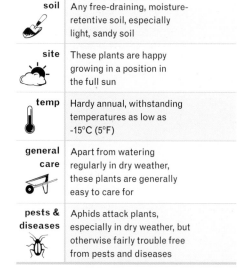

soil	Any free-draining, moisture-retentive soil, especially light, sandy soil
site	These plants are happy growing in a position in the full sun
temp	Hardy annual, withstanding temperatures as low as -15°C (5°F)
general care	Apart from watering regularly in dry weather, these plants are generally easy to care for
pests & diseases	Aphids attack plants, especially in dry weather, but otherwise fairly trouble free from pests and diseases

Linaria maroccana 'Fairy Bouquet'

Bouquet' is the most popular variety, with a wide range of colours and 2cm (¾in) flowers on short plants. 'Northern Lights' is a taller variety and is a good choice if you want to use the plants for cutting for the house.

Because of the multitude of flower colours, this plant combines well with other mixed flowers, such as Californian poppies (Eschscholzia), nemesias and antirrhinums.

Sow the tiny seeds in rows in well-prepared soil that has been raked to a fine structure. The rows should be 15–20cm (6–8in) apart and when the seedlings are large enough to handle, thin them to about 5cm (2in) apart so they have room to grow. The flowering period is rather short but is longer if the plants are grown in average soil, given enough room to flourish and watered when dry.

	SPRING	SUMMER	AUTUMN	WINTER	height (cm)	spread (cm)	flower colour	
Linaria maroccana 'Fairy Bouquet'	🌱🌱🌱	● ● ●			20	15	+	Short plants with masses of small flowers; wide colour range
L. maroccana 'Northern Lights'	🌱🌱🌱	● ● ●			40	20	+	Tall, bushy plants with a long season of flowers

planting	● flowering	+	many colours

Linum

Flax

Flax is often seen as a farm crop, creating shimmering blue fields in the sunshine where it is grown as a source of linseed. But most types are also attractive garden plants and many perennials with blue or yellow flowers are grown. There are also annuals and these include linums with red and blue flowers.

Several cultivars of *Linum grandiflorum* are readily available in seed catalogues that are easy to grow and will produce a good flowering display.

Each bloom is saucer-shaped and measures up to 4cm (1½in) across. The petals have a shiny, silky texture and many have a darker centre. *Linum* 'Magic Circles' has a mixture of sparkling flowers. Some are white with a red centre and others red with a dark eye making a vibrant combination. Among the blue varieties is *L.* 'Blue Dress' with a profusion of soft blue flowers that are very cooling to the eye.

Flax is an elegant, willowy plant with slender stems and fine, thin foliage. It should be combined with other elegant plants and it looks good with ornamental grasses, larkspur and Nigella (love-in-a-mist) and especially annual Gypsophila. It is also suitable for sowing in wildflower mixtures in freshly dug soil and combines well with cornflowers and poppies. The round seedheads on slender stems can also be cut and dried for winter decoration or left for wild birds to feast upon.

The seed should be sown in weed-free soil where the plants are to flower. Sow the seed thinly along rows about 20cm (8in) apart. The seedlings should be thinned to about 10cm (4in) apart and kept weed-free. Flowering is from early summer onwards. Plants will very often self-seed, especially if they are being grown in light, well-drained soils.

soil	Any reasonable well-drained, moisture-retentive garden soil
site	These plants prefer growing in a position in the full sun
temp	Hardy annual, withstanding temperatures as low as -15°C (5°F)
general care	Apart from watering regularly in dry weather, these plants are generally easy to care for
pests & diseases	Aphids can attack new shoots, but otherwise fairly trouble free from pests and diseases

Linum grandiflorum 'Magic Circles'

 planting   flowering

	SPRING	SUMMER	AUTUMN	WINTER	height (cm)	spread (cm)	flower colour	
Linum grandiflorum 'Blue Dress'	🌱🌱🌱	●●●			50	15	▦	Pretty blooms of denim blue
L. grandiflorum 'Magic Circles'	🌱🌱🌱	●●●			45	15	▯	Slender plants with glistening, red-eyed blooms

Lobelia

There are many different types of lobelia that can be grown in the garden, but the ones used as bedding plants are cultivars of *Lobelia erinus*. They are available as low growing bushy plants or as trailing forms for use in containers and hanging baskets.

Lobelia erinus 'Mrs Clibran'

The various colours available include white, pale blue, dark blue, lilac and red. Some are solid colours and others have a white eye in the centre of the flower. Due to its wide range of colours, lobelia can be planted to complement most other bedding plants.

Seed is sown in late winter and early spring under glass, where a germination temperature of 18–20°C (64–68°F) can be maintained. The seed is tiny and sown on the surface of a pot or tray of levelled compost and not covered. Keep the surface of the compost moist until the seeds start to germinate which can take a couple of weeks.

Once the seedlings are roughly 1cm (⅜in) tall they should be pricked out and grown on in trays. Because the seedlings are so small, prick them out into small clumps of six to eight seedlings. Care needs to be taken when handling the seedlings as they are prone to fungal diseases at this stage. When pricked out, maintain a night temperature of 13°C (54°F) and do not overwater.

Alternatively, small pinches of seed can be sown into plug trays and germinated in the same way. When the seedlings have filled the cells, they can be transplanted into trays and grown on.

When hardening off, some cultivars such as 'Crystal Palace' may change colour. The green leaves turn bronze, which is normal.

Lobelia erinus 'Crystal Palace'

Lobelia erinus 'Cascade Mixed'

soil	Grows in most garden soils or multipurpose compost in containers
site	Like a sunny position in the garden, but will grow in partial shade
temp	Half-hardy plants, withstanding temperatures down to 1°C (34°F)
general care	Dead flowers can be trimmed off. Liquid feed in mid-summer to keep flowering
pests & diseases	Generally trouble free from pests and diseases, although slugs and snails sometimes attack

	SPRING	SUMMER	AUTUMN	WINTER	height (cm)	spread (cm)	flower colour	
Lobelia erinus 'Cambridge Blue'	🪣 ✂ ✂	● ● ● ●	●		🪣	15	15		Compact habit, light green foliage
L. erinus 'Cascade Mixed'	🪣 ✂ ✂	● ● ● ●	●		🪣	15	35	+	Trailing habit. Good in containers and baskets
L. erinus 'Crystal Palace'	🪣 ✂ ✂	● ● ● ●	●		🪣	15	15		Dark foliage, with bronze tint
L. erinus 'Mrs Clibran'	🪣 ✂ ✂	● ● ● ●	●		🪣	15	15		Compact, bushy plants
L. erinus 'Rosamund'	🪣 ✂ ✂	● ● ● ●	●		🪣	15	15		Compact habit
L. erinus Riviera Series	🪣 ✂ ✂	● ● ● ●			🪣	15	10	+	Compact habit and early flowering
L. 'White Lady'	🪣 ✂ ✂	● ● ● ●	●		🪣	15	15		Compact habit. Occasional blue flower

 sowing   *transplanting*   *flowering*   *many colours*

Lobularia

Sweet alyssum
or Sweet Alison

In some catalogues this well-known annual may be listed under Alyssum. It is a hardy annual that comes from Europe and western Asia. The fragrant flowers have a sweet scent rather like honey and are mainly white, although other cultivars are available with pink and purple shades.

Traditionally, sweet alyssum was grown with lobelias as an edging plant, but it can be planted in containers or in blocks between low growing perennials. It is easy to grow and

	soil	Will grow in most garden soils, but avoid very dry sites
	site	Prefers a sunny spot but will also grow reasonably well in partial shade
	temp	Lobularia are hardy, withstanding temperatures down to -15°C (5°F)
	general care	Water plants regularly in dry weather and trim off any old flowers when they occur
	pests & diseases	Slugs and snails can attack. Powdery mildew can also be a problem, so water in dry weather

Lobularia maritima 'Carpet of Snow'

is suitable for sowing directly into the garden. In fact it often self-seeds and naturalizes itself in cracks in paving.

For bedding, sow in early to mid-spring in trays of compost. Avoid sowing too early in the season as the plant is fast growing. Only gentle heat is required for germination. Once the seedlings have been pricked out, provide frost protection. Pinch out the growing tips of young plants to produce bushier plants. From mid-spring onwards, the plants can be kept in a cold frame, which also helps to keep them bushy and compact until they are planted out. Keep the plants just moist to prevent excessive growth and help control powdery mildew, which can sometimes be a problem in wet, warm conditions.

When established in the garden, occasional liquid feeding will help to keep the plants flowering all summer long.

Lobularia maritima 'Snow Crystals'

	SPRING	SUMMER	AUTUMN	WINTER	height (cm)	spread (cm)	flower colour	
Lobularia maritima 'Aphrodite'	🪣 ✂ ✂	● ● ● ●	●		10	20	+	Compact, uniform plants. Very good colour mix
L. maritima 'Carpet of Snow'	🪣 ✂ ✂	● ● ● ●	●		10	30	☐	Dense, spreading habit
L. maritima 'Easter Bonnet Mixed'	🪣 ✂ ✂	● ● ● ●	●		10	20	+	Compact habit, early flowering
L. maritima 'Rosie O'Day'	🪣 ✂ ✂	● ● ● ●	●		10	20	▦	Compact plants
L. maritima 'Snow Crystals'	🪣 ✂ ✂	● ● ● ●	●		20	30	☐	Taller growing with larger flowers

 sowing   *transplanting*   *flowering*   *many colours*

Lupinus
Lupin

Lupins are often grown as part of a perennial border for their tall, colourful spikes of flowers, but there are also several annual types that make a showy display over the summer months. These hardy annual types are easy to raise and are ideal for growing in an area of poor soil where other plants struggle to establish. They are also good for filling gaps between shrubs and perennials.

Lupinus 'Blue Bonnet'

The plants make open, bushy plants with spikes of pea-shaped flowers. The colours tend to be shades of blue, pink, mauve and red, with many of the flowers bi-coloured. One cultivar, 'Sunrise', has interesting flowers that are a combination of white, gold, bronze and azure on each bloom.

Although they can be grown in pots or trays in a greenhouse, they grow easily sown directly into the garden, which is how most people grow them. Sow thinly along shallow drills in spring. To aid germination, soak the seed in water for 24 hours before sowing. The seed can be sown in early autumn, but as the plants grow quickly,

there is little advantage to be gained by sowing then – other than encouraging early flowering.

Once the seedlings are 5cm (2in) tall, thin them out to allow the plants plenty of space to bush out, and keep them weed-free.

Once established, very little maintenance is needed, although removal of the faded flower spike will encourage new side branches to develop with more flowers.

The taller varieties can also be used very effectively as cut flowers.

Lupinus 'Blue Bonnet'

soil	Prefers to be grown in a light, well-drained garden soil
site	Best results occur when grown in a sunny position in the garden
temp	Hardy plants, withstanding temperatures as low as -15°C (5°F)
general care	Soak seeds before sowing. Thin seedlings out to allow the plants room to develop
pests & diseases	Slugs, snails and aphids can all cause problems, so try and provide protection from these pests

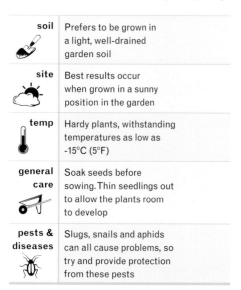

	SPRING	SUMMER	AUTUMN	WINTER	height (cm)	spread (cm)	flower colour	
Lupinus 'Blue Bonnet'	🌱 🌱 🌱	● ● ● ●			35	20		Originally from Texas, USA
L. nanus 'Pixie Delight'	🌱 🌱 🌱	● ● ● ●			45	25		Bushy plants
L. 'Summer Spires'	🌱 🌱 🌱	● ● ● ●			90	45		Tall spikes of bi-coloured flowers
L. 'Sunrise'	🌱 🌱 🌱	● ● ● ●			90	45		Good for cutting. Each flower has four colours

🌱 *planting*   ● *flowering*

Matthiola
Stocks

Compared to many other bedding plants, stocks have a much shorter flowering season, but they are well worth growing for their double scented flowers. They can be used in containers or mixed borders and the taller cultivars can be used as cut flowers.

Brompton stocks are grown as biennials and sown in early to mid-summer. The plants flower the following year from mid-spring onwards. Other cultivars such as the Cinderella Series and 'Appleblossom' are grown as annuals and are sown in early spring to flower during summer. Although fairly hardy, this group is best treated as half-hardy annuals.

The biennials are sown in trays in a cold frame in the summer and pricked out into pots or trays. The plants require no heat, but in cold areas the young plants will benefit from the protection of a cold greenhouse or cold frame over winter. This also prevents the

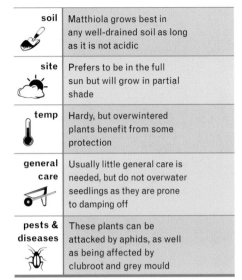

soil	Matthiola grows best in any well-drained soil as long as it is not acidic
site	Prefers to be in the full sun but will grow in partial shade
temp	Hardy, but overwintered plants benefit from some protection
general care	Usually little general care is needed, but do not overwater seedlings as they are prone to damping off
pests & diseases	These plants can be attacked by aphids, as well as being affected by clubroot and grey mould

plants from getting too wet which can cause rots to form. In early spring, strong plants can be planted into containers or the garden.

The annuals are sown in early spring in a temperature of 16°C (64°F) and grown on in cool conditions after being pricked out. They can be planted into the garden in late spring.

Most cultivars naturally have a high percentage of double flowers, but some cultivars are 'selectable'. This means you can tell at the seedling stage which will be single or double flowering. To select double plants, the seedlings need to be below 10°C (50°F) for a week before pricking out. Seedlings that produce double flowers will be yellow/green in colour, whereas the dark green seedlings will produce single flowers. 'Cinderella' and 'Brompton' are both selectable; the seed packet will state whether other cultivars are.

Matthiola incana Cinderella Series

M

Bedding Plants

	SPRING	SUMMER	AUTUMN	WINTER	height (cm)	spread (cm)	flower colour	
Matthiola incana 'Appleblossom'					30	15		Dwarf plants, double scented flowers
M. incana Brompton Mixed					45	30	+	Early double or single fragrant flowers
M. incana Cinderella Series					25	20	+	Compact plants with double flowers
M. incana Ten Weeks Mixed					30	20	+	Scented flowers with lots of doubles

 sowing   transplanting   flowering   many colours

Mimulus
Monkey flower

This is a group of attractive, brightly coloured flowers that are suitable for the garden or containers. Despite their exotic looking blooms, monkey flowers are hardy, although young plants can be nipped by late frosts if they have not been hardened off properly.

The plants will grow quite happily in shaded areas or where the soil is too moist for other types of bedding plants. In fact, hot, dry areas should be avoided as the plants will not grow well in those conditions and flowering will end prematurely.

The funnel-shaped flowers are produced early in the season in many shades of cream, yellow, red, pink and orange. Many of the flowers have attractive blotches or spots on them to add to the interest. The cultivars available are hybrids of *Mimulus guttatus* and *M. luteus*, which originate from North America and Chile respectively. Both are perennials, although the cultivars are grown as half-hardy annuals.

Sow the seed in early spring in a greenhouse at around 16–18°C (61–64°F).

The seed is very small and care needs to be taken to ensure it is sown thinly and evenly over the surface of the compost. Do not cover the seed and make sure the compost is kept constantly moist.

When the seedlings are large enough to be handled, prick out into cell trays and grow on in cool conditions. Mimulus dislikes warm growing conditions. If too warm, the plants will quickly grow tall and spoil. Once the seedlings have established, they can be grown on in a cold frame or sheltered part of the garden and covered over with fleece if frost is forecast. Plant out in late spring.

soil	Likes a moist garden soil that does not dry out in summer
site	These plants are happy growing in either full sun or partial shade
temp	Although hardy, treat as a half-hardy annual. Can cope down to -5°C (41°F)
general care	Do not allow to dry out and remove dead flowerheads regularly. Otherwise little general care is needed
pests & diseases	Monkey flowers can be affected by powdery mildew, as well as attacks from slugs and snails

Mimulus x hybridus 'Viva'

Mimulus x hybridus 'Magic Mixed'

	SPRING	SUMMER	AUTUMN	WINTER	height (cm)	spread (cm)	flower colour	
Mimulus x hybridus 'Calypso'	🪴	✂	✺ ✺ ✺			20	25	+	Wide colour range, mainly spotted or bi-coloured
M. x hybridus 'Magic Mixed'	🪴	✂	✺ ✺ ✺			20	25	+	Compact habit, early flowering
M. x hybridus Mystic Series	🪴	✂	✺ ✺ ✺			20	25	+	Flowers have no markings
M. x hybridus 'Viva'	🪴	✂	✺ ✺ ✺			25	30	+	Taller growing, blotched flowers

 sowing   *transplanting*   ✺ *flowering*   + *many colours*

Mirabilis

Four o'clock
flower *or*
Marvel of Peru

Mirabilis is guaranteed to be a talking point when seen by visitors, not only for its very showy trumpet-like flowers, but for the fact that they do not open until late afternoon or early evening – hence its common name. By the following morning the fragrant flowers have died, to be replaced by new ones later in the day.

Mirabilis jalapa comes from Peru and other parts of South America where it grows as a bushy perennial. In a garden situation they are mostly grown as half-hardy annuals, although in mild areas the plants will often survive the winter and regrow the following summer. They also produce a tuber that can be lifted in the autumn, stored over winter and potted to start into growth in spring. Large tubers of established plants can be divided to make several new plants.

When growing from seed, sow in late winter or early spring, as the plants take several months to reach flowering size. A temperature of approximately 18°C (64°F) is needed for germination. Grow on the seedlings in small pots, keeping them in gentle heat and moist at all times. The plant grows fairly fast and it may be necessary to pot on into large pots if they outgrow the smaller ones. In late spring, harden off and plant into the garden or into large containers.

Flowering starts around mid-summer and will continue until early autumn. The flowers can be plain in colour or marked. It is not unusual to have several different coloured flowers on one plant. *Mirabilis* 'Broken Colours' is a good example of this and the flowers look

soil	Any reasonable garden soil that retains moisture, but which drains freely
site	A position in the garden with as much sun as possible is preferred
temp	Fairly hardy. Can withstand temperatures down to -5°C (23°F)
general care	Water and liquid feed in dry weather. Otherwise, little general care is necessary
pests & diseases	Slugs and aphids can be a problem, but relatively trouble free from pests and diseases

as though different colours have been painted on them.

The plants are harmful if eaten, so keep them away from young children.

Mirabilis jalapa

M

Bedding Plants

	SPRING	SUMMER	AUTUMN	WINTER	height (cm)	spread (cm)	flower colour	
Mirabilis jalapa 'Broken Colours'	🪣	✂	● ● ●	🪣	50	50	+	Unusual flowers with bright markings
M. jalapa 'Red Glow'	🪣	✂	● ● ●	🪣	50	50	▨	Masses of flowers

 sowing   *transplanting*   🌼 *flowering*   + *many colours*

Moluccella

Bells of Ireland

This is an unusual plant that is not often grown as a summer bedding plant. However, it can be mixed with other plants with great effect for something a little different. It looks good when planted with the white tobacco plant (Nicotiana), Californian poppies (Eschscholzia), love-in-a mist (Nigella) and dwarf ornamental grasses. Its stiff, upright habit contrasts well with feathery and moving plants.

Moluccella can also be used as part of a mixed border between herbaceous perennials, shrubs and roses, and the green is very good at toning down bright colours.

Moluccella is a half-hardy annual with light-green rounded leaves on tall stems. Between the leaves, small white fragrant flowers are produced in whorls, which are surrounded by a large,

shell-like green calyx. The calyces turn brown and papery as seed forms in late summer. They will remain like this until well into the autumn, when the changing weather eventually damages them.

Moluccella laevis 'Bells of Ireland'

soil	Moluccella likes a fertile, well-drained soil that retains moisture
site	Ideally prefers a sunny position but will grow in partial shade
temp	Half-hardy, withstanding temperatures down to 0°C (32°F)
general care	Keep watered in dry weather, but otherwise does not require any specialized general care
pests & diseases	Generally trouble free. These plants are usually not affected by pests and diseases

To grow Moluccella, sow the seeds in a tray or pot in a greenhouse in early spring and when the seedlings are large enough to handle, prick them out into trays and grow on. A temperature of around 16–18°C (61–64°F) is all that is needed for germination. For growing on, the temperature can then be lowered. In late spring, harden off the plants and plant out.

Alternatively, the seed can be sown directly into the flowering position in late spring when the soil has warmed up. The plants will grow well enough when sown outside, but flowering will be later than greenhouse raised plants.

Moluccella can also be used while still green for cut flowers and looks very good mixed with other summer flowers. The dry stems can also be cut in autumn and used in flower arrangements.

Myosotis
Forget-me-not

Forget-me-nots are pretty, spring flowering biennials that produce masses of tiny flowers. They can be used in spring bedding schemes or as part of a mixed border where they mix well with other spring plants such as wallflowers (Erysimum), double daisies (Bellis) and tulips. They also look stunning in containers and windowboxes, and will provide a colourful display for several months in spring.

The main colour is blue, of which there are several shades, but you can also get pink and white forget-me-nots either as single colours or as a mixture. The leaves are grey-green and slightly hairy.

Traditionally, seed was sown outside in a seedbed, and the seedlings transplanted out and grown on in rows before being planted into their permanent position in autumn. However, to prevent root disturbance, it is better to raise the seedlings in a tray. Sow mid-summer in a cold greenhouse or cold frame and when the seedlings are large enough prick out into seed trays. The plants need to be grown on somewhere cool or outside, with plenty of ventilation. By mid-autumn the plants will be large enough to transplant into the garden or containers.

Although the plants are hardy, in severe winters the foliage can be damaged, but as soon as the weather starts to warm up in early spring new foliage will grow, followed shortly by flowers. The plants also dislike very wet soil and these areas should be avoided to prevent the plants from rotting off.

Occasionally, the plants will survive as short-lived perennials, but it is better to remove them after flowering in early summer. Otherwise, when left in the borders, they tend to get powdery mildew.

Myosotis sylvatica 'Blue Ball'

soil	Grows in most reasonable garden soils, but avoid waterlogged areas
site	These plants are happy growing in either full sun or partial shade
temp	Fully hardy plants, withstanding temperatures down to -15°C (23°F)
general care	Plant out in autumn to establish before winter. Otherwise, little general care is necessary
pests & diseases	Slugs, snails and powdery mildew can all have an affect on forget-me-nots

M

Bedding Plants

	SPRING	SUMMER	AUTUMN	WINTER	height (cm)	spread (cm)	flower colour	
Myosotis sylvatica 'Blue Ball'	● ● ●	● 🪣 ✂	✂ ✂		15	15	■	Compact plants, good flowering
M. sylvatica 'Royal Blue'	● ● ●	● 🪣 ✂	✂ ✂		30	20	■	Taller growing and early flowering
M. sylvatica 'Sylva Mixed'	● ● ●	● 🪣 ✂	✂ ✂		20	15	+	Good mixture of colours
M. sylvatica Victoria Series	● ● ●	● 🪣 ✂	✂ ✂		15	15	+	Dwarf and compact habit

 sowing   *transplanting*   *flowering* | + | *many colours*

Nemesia

The flowers of Nemesia are very cheery, which is one of the reasons it has been a popular bedding plant over the years. It is a fast-growing annual that flowers just a couple of months after sowing to provide masses of brightly coloured flowers in a wide selection of colours. These range from straight colours, such as yellow, orange, cream and pink, to pastel shades and interesting bi-coloured flowers.

soil	Enjoys any reasonable moist but well-drained soil. Does not tolerate dry soil
site	Prefers to be situated in a sunny position in the garden
temp	Half-hardy annual, withstanding temperatures down to 1°C (34°F)
general care	Avoid sowing too early in the spring and deadhead regularly to prolong flowering period
pests & diseases	Aphids can affect these plants in a greenhouse. Root rots can be a problem in wet seasons

Nemesia strumosa originate from South Africa and to grow well and flourish they require a sunny spot. What they do not like, however, is dry soil. They should always be grown in a moisture-retentive soil or watered in dry weather. In poor, dry soils the plants will mature too early and stop flowering.

Unfortunately, nemesias do not flower for very long, unlike many other bedding plants, and for this reason they are best grown on their own in a border or container. They can then be removed or changed without disturbing other plants. Regular watering in dry weather and the removal of dead flowers will help to extend the flowering season. *Nemesia* 'Sundrops', an award winning cultivar, does have a slightly longer flowering season and can be grown in both a container or garden border.

The seed is sown in a greenhouse in a temperature of around 16–18°C (61–64°F) and the seedlings pricked out into trays or cell trays as soon as possible. Grow the young plants on in gentle heat and harden-off before planting out in late spring. This process might cause a few of the lower leaves to take on a bronze appearance, but this is perfectly normal.

The best time to sow is mid-spring onwards as sowings made very early in the season will have finished flowering by mid-summer.

Nemesia 'Sundrops Mixed'

	SPRING	SUMMER	AUTUMN	WINTER	height (cm)	spread (cm)	flower colour	
Nemesia strumosa 'Carnival'	sowing transplanting	flowering flowering flowering			20	15		Compact plants with large flowers
N. strumosa 'KLM'	sowing transplanting	flowering flowering			25	15		Masses of small flowers. Blue top and white lower petal
N. strumosa 'National Ensign'	sowing transplanting	flowering flowering			25	15		Bi-coloured flowers with red upper and white lower petal
N. strumosa 'Prince of Orange'	sowing transplanting	flowering flowering			20	15		Compact plants with bright flowers
N. strumosa 'Sundrops Mixed'	sowing transplanting	flowering flowering flowering			20	15	+	Mound forming plants ideal for bedding or containers

 sowing   *transplanting*   *flowering* | + *many colours*

Nemophila

This easy-to-grow group of plants originates from California, where they produce low spreading plants. *Nemophila maculata* has many saucer-shaped flowers that have a dark blotch on each petal. Cultivars of this species also have unusual flowers. *N. menziesii* is commonly known as baby blue-eyes because of its sky-blue flowers with white centres.

The plants are hardy annuals and are usually sown in spring where they are to flower. They can be sown in autumn and the young plants will overwinter without too many problems. Autumn sown plants will usually flower earlier in the season than spring sown plants. Seed should be sown in shallow drills roughly 20cm (8in) apart and the seedlings thinned to around 15cm (6in). This allows room for the plants to develop and spread.

In dry weather it may be necessary to water the plants to keep them flowering, as they tend to produce fewer flowers in dry conditions. Nemophila often self-seed

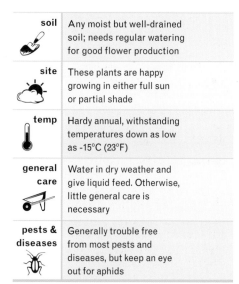

soil	Any moist but well-drained soil; needs regular watering for good flower production
site	These plants are happy growing in either full sun or partial shade
temp	Hardy annual, withstanding temperatures down as low as -15°C (23°F)
general care	Water in dry weather and give liquid feed. Otherwise, little general care is necessary
pests & diseases	Generally trouble free from most pests and diseases, but keep an eye out for aphids

Nemophila menziesii 'Snow Storm'

around the garden and will naturalize in beds and borders quite happily.

For best results, grow nemophilas on their own at the front of borders, along paths or in containers. They are very versatile and will grow quite happily in full sun or against a shady wall, where they will add a splash of colour. They also look very good when grown in containers and windowboxes, always attracting attention because of their distinctive flowers.

For growing in containers it is possible to raise the plants in spring by sowing a few seeds into each cell of a plug tray filled with multipurpose compost. Stand the tray outside in a sheltered position and keep moist. When seedlings are 5cm (2in) tall, they can be transplanted into the container.

	SPRING	SUMMER	AUTUMN	WINTER	height (cm)	spread (cm)	flower colour	
Nemophila maculata 'Five Spot'	transplant sow	flower flower flower flower	sow		20	20		Each flower has a purple spot at the tip of each petal
N. maculata 'Penny Black'	transplant sow	flower flower flower	sow		15	20		Very dark flowers with a white rim
N. menziesii 'Snow Storm'	transplant sow	flower flower flower flower	sow		20	20		Slightly off-white flowers

 sowing   transplanting   flowering

Nicotiana
Tobacco plant

Nicotiana is a popular bedding plant, flowering all summer long. Many new cultivars are readily available as plants from garden centres or as seed. Shorter types are ideal for containers and the slightly taller ones are excellent when bedded out. The colours tend to be shades of, pink, red, purple and white, although interesting pale green flowering forms are available.

Nicotiana sylvestris is a much taller growing plant and in good soil will reach 1.5m (5ft). It is ideal for use as a dot plant or mixed with other tall growing, open-headed flowers such as *Verbena bonariensis* and Cleome. It has large leaves and tall spikes of white fragrant flowers that do not open in full sun, making it ideal for semi-shade or the evening.

Nicotiana is reasonably easy to grow from seed sown from early spring to mid-spring. Later sowings can be made, but they will not start to flower until mid-summer.

Sow the small seeds thinly onto the surface of multipurpose compost and cover lightly with compost or vermiculite. Keep the compost moist, at 18–20°C (64–68°F) until the seeds germinate. Prick out into cell trays and grow on in gentle heat, keeping them moist.

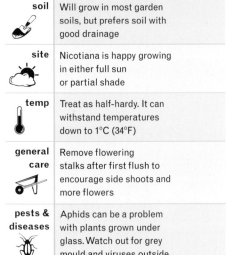

soil	Will grow in most garden soils, but prefers soil with good drainage
site	Nicotiana is happy growing in either full sun or partial shade
temp	Treat as half-hardy. It can withstand temperatures down to 1°C (34°F)
general care	Remove flowering stalks after first flush to encourage side shoots and more flowers
pests & diseases	Aphids can be a problem with plants grown under glass. Watch out for grey mould and viruses outside

Low light levels and cool, fluctuating temperatures can induce chlorosis (yellowing) in the leaves occasionally in some colours. However, this does not seem to have any effect on the plant's flowering ability at a later stage.

After hardening off young plants, bed out into the garden or containers in late spring.

Nicotiana x *sanderae* 'Avalon Bright Pink'

	SPRING	SUMMER	AUTUMN	WINTER	height (cm)	spread (cm)	flower colour	
Nicotiana 'Lime Green'	🪣 ⚒ ⚒	● ● ● ●	●		🪣	60	30	▨	Unusual coloured flowers
N. x *sanderae* 'Avalon Bright Pink'	🪣 ⚒ ⚒	● ● ● ●	●		🪣	20	15	▨	Dwarf plants, ideal for containers
N. x *sanderae* 'Avalon White'	🪣 ⚒ ⚒	● ● ● ●	●		🪣	20	15	☐	Part of the Avalon Series. Naturally compact plants
N. x *sanderae* Domino Series	🪣 ⚒ ⚒	● ● ● ●	●		🪣	40	30	⊞	Sturdy plants and good colour range
N. x *sanderae* 'Havana Appleblossom'	🪣 ⚒ ⚒	● ● ● ●	●		🪣	35	20	▨	Pale pink flowers with a darker reverse
N. x *sanderae* Merlin Series	🪣 ⚒ ⚒	● ● ● ●	●		🪣	30	20	⊞	Compact plants. Good for containers
N. sylvestris	🪣 ⚒ ⚒	● ● ● ●	●		🪣	150	60	☐	Large leaves, scented flowers

🪣 *sowing*　⚒ *transplanting* *flowering*　⊞ *many colours*

Nigella
Love-in-a-mist

If you are trying to create a cottage-style border this plant is a must. Nigella is easy to grow, and its attractive flowers and feathery green foliage mix extremely well with other plants.

Nigella is a native of southern Europe and is a hardy annual. The seeds can be sown in autumn or spring, but in cold areas you will get better results from spring sowings. Sow the seeds along shallow drills where the plants are to flower. Thin the seedlings to approximately 10–15cm (4–6in) apart and allow them to develop.

The flattish flowers with a 'ruff' of fine foliage are mainly blue. This is the colour most people associate with love-in-a-mist and is still the most popular colour. Several shades of blue are available, but white and pink flowers are also included in mixed packets of seed. These look good in a mixed border, and the pastel shades blend in easily with other colours.

Love-in-a-mist is ideal for growing between perennials to fill gaps or they can be mixed with other hardy annuals such as English marigold (Calendula), Clarkia and larkspur (Consolida). Fine, feathery grasses such as *Stipa tennuissima* also work well when planted with Nigella.

soil	Will grow in any reasonable well-drained garden soil
site	Prefers to be situated in a sunny position in the garden
temp	A hardy annual, withstanding temperatures as low as -15°C (23°F)
general care	Remove seed pods regularly to encourage more flowers to develop for a longer period
pests & diseases	Relatively trouble free. Pests and diseases do not usually cause any problems

Nigella also makes excellent cut flowers. The feathery foliage and flowers can be used on their own or mixed with other summer flowers from the garden. Flower arrangers also dry the large round seed pods and use them in winter arrangements.

If you do not intend to save the seed pods, they should be removed to encourage and prolong flowering. If a few seed pods are left on in late summer, the plants will self-seed and the following spring a batch of healthy seedlings will appear.

Nigella damascena 'Persian Jewels'

	SPRING	SUMMER	AUTUMN	WINTER	height (cm)	spread (cm)	flower colour	
Nigella damascena 'Miss Jekyll'	planting	flowering			45	20		Old favourite with semi-double flowers
N. damascena 'Oxford Blue'	planting	flowering			75	40		Tall growing plant with dark blue double flowers
N. damascena 'Persian Jewels'	planting	flowering			40	20	+	Good cut flowers and good colour mixture

 planting ● *flowering* + *many colours*

Nolana

Nolana is an extremely attractive summer flowering plant that for some reason is not as popluar as many other summer bedding plants. It originates from semi-desert and coastal areas in South America and is treated as a half-hardy annual.

It produces a semi-trailing plant with succulent green foliage and trumpet-shaped blooms that can be up to 5cm (2in) in diameter. These can be shades of blue or white and the flowers mostly have a yellow centre, although *Nolana* 'Shooting Star' has dark veining in the centre of the light blue flowers.

The flowers look a little similar to petunias and Nolana can be used instead of these plants in some situations. Nolana makes an excellent container plant and looks extremely good when planted in windowboxes and hanging baskets. Its spreading habit also makes it ideal for planting in borders where you want to create a summer ground cover effect.

The plants are raised from seed sown in early spring in a greenhouse at a temperature of at least 16–18°C (61–64°F). An earlier sowing in late winter will ensure the plants will flower in early summer, whereas the early spring sown plants may not actually start to flower until mid-summer.

Once the seedlings have germinated, they can be pricked out into small pots and grown on in cooler conditions. Too much heat causes the plants to grow tall and leggy. Pinching out the growing point while the plants are growing will make them form bushier plants. Plant out into a sunny position in late spring after the danger of frost has passed.

Nolana will flower until the first frosts of the autumn, especially if the dead flowerheads are removed on a regular basis and the plants are fed with a high potash fertilizer.

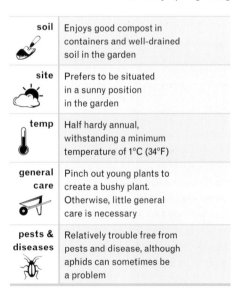

soil	Enjoys good compost in containers and well-drained soil in the garden
site	Prefers to be situated in a sunny position in the garden
temp	Half hardy annual, withstanding a minimum temperature of 1°C (34°F)
general care	Pinch out young plants to create a bushy plant. Otherwise, little general care is necessary
pests & diseases	Relatively trouble free from pests and disease, although aphids can sometimes be a problem

Nolana paradoxa 'Blue Bird'

	SPRING	SUMMER	AUTUMN	WINTER	height (cm)	spread (cm)	flower colour	
Nolana paradoxa 'Blue Bird'					25	30		Semi-trailing, good for containers and baskets
N. paradoxa 'Shooting Star'					20	25		Delicate blue flowers, dark centre. Good for containers
N. paradoxa 'Snowbird'					30	35		Dazzling white flowers and strong growing plants

 sowing   *transplanting*   *flowering*

Osteospermum

Osteospermums are closely related to Dimorphotheca (*see page 79*), which are grown as summer flowering half-hardy annuals from seed each year. Both come from South Africa and produce daisy-like flowers.

Recent plant breeding has produced many new and interesting cultivars of this mainly shrubby perennial. All have attractive daisy-like flowers that open in the sun, and so need a warm, sunny position to grow well. The colour range is large and includes various shades of pink, yellow, purple, mauve and white. Some cultivars such as *Osteospermum* 'Whirlygig' have unusual flowers where the petals are crimped or spoon-shaped.

For bedding, the plants can be grown in containers or the border where they mix with plants such as argyranthemums, gazanias, pelargoniums and cannas to give a tropical feel. Although some plants will grow to be quite large, when used as annuals for the summer this will not be the case.

Osteospermums will flower well into autumn; many cultivars are able to withstand some frost. In mild areas the plants will often

Osteospermum 'Sunny Alex'

soil	Any reasonable well-drained light garden soil is best for osteospermums
site	These plants are happiest situated in a position in the garden in the full sun
temp	Treat as half-hardy. They withstand temperatures down to 1°C (34°F)
general care	Deadhead regularly to encourage more flowers. They are best grown fresh each year
pests & diseases	Relatively trouble free from pests and diseases, but watch out for attacks from aphids

survive the winter, especially in well-drained soil and shelter. Take short cuttings in late summer and when rooted, put into small pots over winter. Keep the plant quite dry and frost-free until spring, when they will start to grow. Young, fresh plants are much better for bedding out and will produce more flowers than old, woody plants.

Osteospermum 'Pink whirls'

O

Bedding Plants

		SPRING	SUMMER	AUTUMN	WINTER	height (cm)	spread (cm)	flower colour	
Osteospurmum 'Buttermilk'	🌱 🌱	● ●	● ● ●	● ●		60	60		Bronze reverse to petals and mauve centre
O. 'Pink whirls'	🌱 🌱	● ●	● ● ●	● ●		15	90		Low, spreading plant
O. 'Sunny Alex'	🌱 🌱	● ●	● ● ●	● ●		50	60		Bushy plant with golden-yellow daisy flowers
O. 'Whirligig'	🌱 🌱	● ●	● ● ●	● ●		60	60		Unusual flowers with spoon-shaped petals. Blue on reverse

 planting   *flowering*

Papaver

Poppy

The brilliant, silky petals of poppies make them among the most popular garden flowers, whether you prefer the gigantic blooms of perennial oriental poppies or the more delicate flowers of the annuals. There are 70 species of poppies, from around the world, but the corn poppy (*Papaver rhoeas*) remains a favourite because of its delicate flowers and its ease of cultivation.

Papaver somniferum 'Irish Velvet'

It was Reverend Wilks in 1879 who first noticed a plant in a cornfield with white edges to its petals and from this he bred his *Papaver rhoeas* 'Shirley Series', which included pastel colours with no central black blotch and no harsh colours.

P. r. 'Angel's Choir' has double flowers in a bewildering range of colours – no two are the same. An advantage of double flowers is that they last a little longer than single flowers and may also have more impact in the border.

One of the most popular varieties of the opium poppy (*Papaver somniferum*) is 'Peony Black', which has double flowers packed with petals in a rich blackcurrant colour. The opium poppy also has dramatic seedpods

soil	Any reasonable garden soil that retains moisture, but which drains freely
site	These plants are happiest growing in a position in the full sun
temp	These plants are hardy as both annuals and biennials
general care	Water in dry weather. Remove dead flowers regularly to prolong flowering
pests & diseases	Can be problems with aphids on leaves and flower stems. Mildew can also affect some plants

Papaver croceum 'Meadow Pastels'

and 'Hens and Chickens' is a strange variety with single flowers. Each seedpod is surrounded by a ring of tiny pods. It is an excellent choice for drying and winter decorations.

The Iceland poppy (*Papaver croceum*) is a biennial or perennial but 'Meadow Pastels' can be sown under glass in a temperature of 20°C (68°F) and planted out in late spring. It will then produce its graceful flowers in citrus shades all summer.

Hardy annual poppies should be sown where they are to flower, in spring and thinned out to 10–15cm (4–6in) apart. Wider spacing will produce stronger, bigger plants.

	SPRING	SUMMER	AUTUMN	WINTER	height (cm)	spread (cm)	flower colour	
Papaver croceum 'Meadow Pastels'	🪣 ⟋	● ● ●			35	20		Biennial Iceland poppy but will flower the first year
P. rhoeas 'Angel's Choir'	⟋ ⟋ ⟋	● ● ●			75	30	+	Wonderful mixture of double flowers, wide range of colours
P. rhoeas Shirley Series	⟋ ⟋ ⟋	● ● ●			75	30		Single and semi-double flowers in pastel colours
P. somniferum 'Hens & Chickens'	⟋ ⟋ ⟋	● ● ●			70	30		Large flowers are followed by large, ornamental seed pods
P. somniferum 'Irish Velvet'	⟋ ⟋ ⟋	● ● ●			90	30		Huge, fully double, almost black or white flowers

 sowing   *transplanting*   ● *flowering*   + *many colours*

Pelargonium

Geranium

Pelargoniums are usually called geraniums, a confusing state of affairs since true geraniums are hardy. But bedding geraniums (pelargoniums) will not tolerate frost and are tender shrubs, often with flowers of scarlet red, a colour never seen in the hardy, true geraniums.

Traditionally, pelargoniums were raised from cuttings, usually taken in late summer and kept in frost-free conditions over the winter. The disadvantage of this method is that heating is required in cold climates. But many gardeners still use this method because it is the only way to maintain stock of some of the finest varieties, including those with variegated and coloured foliage. These include the sumptuous *Pelargonium* 'Mrs Pollock', with green, yellow-edged leaves, zoned with red and *P.* 'Frank Headley', which combines a good show of salmon flowers with bright, white-edged leaves. Ivy-leaved or trailing pelargoniums are now available from seed but most are still grown from cuttings. Traditional types had large, double flowers such as *P.* 'Amethyst', but the Continental types with thinner stems and single flowers are rapidly becoming popular. This is because they bloom profusely. *P.* PAC 'Evka', with variegated leaves and red flowers on a compact plant, makes a super basket plant.

Plant breeders have worked wonders and there are now many series of pelargonium that flower freely the first year from seed, something that was unthinkable 30 years ago. Most have been developed to be compact, free-flowering plants that give a colourful display in borders and containers. Until recently these were mostly in plain colours, but the Ripple Series has flowers that are attractively speckled and stippled in two tones of pink and the Maverick Series includes single colours and 'Maverick Star' which is pale pink with a deep pink centre.

This is a group of plants that is constantly changing, so look through your catalogues to see what is new each year.

soil	Any reasonable garden soil that retains moisture, but which drains freely
site	These plants are happiest growing in a position in the full sun
temp	These are not frost hardy, withstanding only down to 1°C (34°F)
general care	Remove old flower stems and water regularly in dry weather. Otherwise, easy to care for
pests & diseases	Aphids and other pests can be troublesome but outside plants are generally free from problems in summer

Bedding Plants

'Mixed fancy leaved pelargoniums

Pelargonium 'Vista Deep Rose'

Pelargonium seed is expensive because the flowers have to be pollinated by hand Most are F1 hybrids but a few are F2 hybrids. This seed is less expensive but should still give good results. The seed is not difficult to germinate, but it should be sown in late winter if the plants are to produce flowers early in summer. Cover the seeds with a little compost and keep in a temperature of 21°C (70°F). Germination should take about seven to ten days and the seedlings need good light to grow on. Take care not to

Pelargonium Horizon Series

Pelargonium 'Sensation Scarlet'

overwater them when they are small. Red-flushed foliage is a sign that the plants are overwatered or too cold.

Cuttings of coloured leaved and ivy-leaved pelargoniums are taken in late summer. Overwinter the young plants in light, frost-free conditions and keep the compost on the dry side.

Pelargoniums also make excellent conservatory plants over the winter or house plants where you have a sunny windowsill. Plants will live for many years in a large pot and grow to be tall. Flowering will often continue throughout the winter where the temperature is kept at 10°C (50°F) or above.

	SPRING	SUMMER	AUTUMN	WINTER	height (cm)	spread (cm)	flower colour	
Pelargonium 'Amethyst' (Ivy leaved)	transplanting	flowering	flowering		30	25		Trailing, compact plant with clusters of double flowers
P. Avanti Series (Multiflora seed-raised)	transplanting	flowering	flowering	sowing	30	25		Compact plants with many stems of bright flowers
P. 'Blanche Roche' (Ivy leaved)	transplanting	flowering	flowering		30	25		Double flowers with a lilac tint
P. 'Caroline Schmidt' (Fancy leaved)	transplanting	flowering	flowering		60	45		Strong-growing with white-edged leaves and double flowers
P. 'Frank Headley' (Fancy leaved)	transplanting	flowering	flowering		45	30		Brightly variegated leaves and attractive flowers
P. 'Happy Thought' (Fancy leaved)	transplanting	flowering	flowering		60	45		Bright red flowers above foliage with central gold splash
P. Horizon Series (Zonal, seed-raised)	transplanting	flowering	flowering	sowing	35	25		Compact plants with weather-resistant blooms
P. Maverick Series (Zonal, seed-raised)	transplanting	flowering	flowering	sowing	35	25		Well-branched plants with large heads of single flowers
P. 'Moulin Rouge' (Zonal, seed-raised)	transplanting	flowering	flowering	sowing	35	25		Vigorous plants with masses of flowers. Ideal for bedding
P. 'Mrs Pollock' (Fancy leaved)	transplanting	flowering	flowering		30	25		Flowers unimportant; grown for its golden, patterned leaves
P. PAC 'Evka' (Mini ivy leaved)	transplanting	flowering	flowering		25	20		Compact trailer; single, red flowers and white-edged foliage
P. Ripple Series (Zonal, seed-raised)	transplanting	flowering	flowering	sowing	30	25		Delicately striped and spotted flowers in two tones of pink
P. 'Tango Orange' (Zonal, seed-raised)	transplanting	flowering	flowering	sowing	38	25		Dazzling flowers above light green foliage

 sowing   *transplanting*   flowering

Perilla

Beefsteak plant

Not many gardeners have discovered Perilla as a garden plant but it has long been revered in its home in the warm parts of Asia. Here, it is a valuable herb that is used to flavour pickles and other foods. It is especially popular in Japan where it is used in the preparation of sashimi (raw fish). In the West it is usually called Perilla or beefsteak plant.

Perilla is a tall, robust plant with leaves rather like a coleus (Solenostemon) and a spicy fragrance and taste. Towards the end of the season, plants produce flowers, but these are small and insignificant and it is best to remove them to encourage more leaves to be produced. The typical plant has green leaves and is rather dull to look at, though there is usually some purple spotting and striping on the leaves. The most decorative plants are those with deep purple leaves and are usually called *Perilla frutescens* var. *crispa*. In addition to the wonderful, rich purple colour, these plants have attractively curled and deeply cut foliage, and make superb 'dot' plants to liven up bedding displays. They combine well with orange and red flowers, such as dahlias and marigolds, but also look spectacular with white and pink flowers and silver foliage.

Perilla grows best in good soil that is moist in summer. It will thrive in either sun or partial shade. Sow in spring in a greenhouse at around 20°C (68°F). Germination is often poor and only about half the seeds will grow. Transplant the seedlings into trays when they are large enough to handle, and take care to ensure they are not overwatered when they are small or they will rot. As soon as temperatures start to rise in late spring they can be planted out when the danger of frost has passed.

soil	Any reasonable garden soil that retains moisture, but which drains freely
site	These plants are happy growing in a sunny site but with shelter provided
temp	These are not frost hardy, withstanding only down to 5°C (41°F)
general care	Pinch out growing tips and water regularly during spells of persistent dry weather
pests & diseases	Relatively trouble free. Pests and diseases do not usually cause any problems

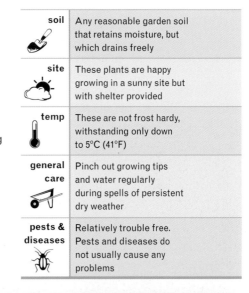

Perilla frutescens var. *crispa*

	SPRING	SUMMER	AUTUMN	WINTER	height (cm)	spread (cm)	flower colour	
Perilla frutescens 'Red and Green'	🪣 ⚒ ⚒	● ● ● ●			90	30	☐	Fragrant, spicy foliage, sometimes flecked with purple
P. frutescens var. crispa	🪣 ⚒ ⚒	● ● ● ●			90	30	☐	Fragrant, curly, deep purple foliage

🪣 sowing ⚒ transplanting ● flowering

Petunia

Petunias are stalwarts of the summer garden. Their trumpet-shaped flowers can obscure the leaves and, with good weather, feeding and watering, they can continue flowering until the first frost of autumn. This is because they are strictly perennials, but we treat them as annuals because they are so easy to raise from seed and modern varieties flower so rapidly.

The perennial nature of petunias has led to the development of new types, such as the Surfinia Series. These rarely set seed, so flower profusely all summer, and are propagated from cuttings. They are usually bought as plug-plants or young potted plants in spring. Just three plants will fill a large basket and trail 1m (3ft) or more in summer. They can also be used to fill flower beds and, planted 60cm (2ft) apart they are a cost-effective way to provide colour. As if to confuse matters, trailing petunias can now be raised from seed and the Explorer and Wave series have a similar habit to Surfinias but their seeds are more expensive than most other types.

Million Bells Series is another perennial type that is raised from cuttings and has tiny flowers studding the bushy mounds of narrow leaves.

Seed-raised petunias are classified according to the size of the flowers.

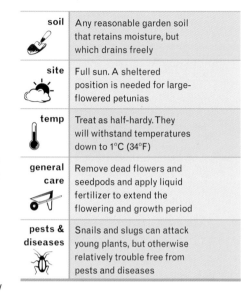

soil	Any reasonable garden soil that retains moisture, but which drains freely
site	Full sun. A sheltered position is needed for large-flowered petunias
temp	Treat as half-hardy. They will withstand temperatures down to 1°C (34°F)
general care	Remove dead flowers and seedpods and apply liquid fertilizer to extend the flowering and growth period
pests & diseases	Snails and slugs can attack young plants, but otherwise relatively trouble free from pests and diseases

Grandifloras have large flowers, up to 13cm (5in) across and are the most spectacular. But these large flowers are the most

Petunia 'Prism Sunshine'

susceptible to damage in wet and windy weather so they should be planted in sheltered gardens and in containers on the patio. Multifloras have flowers about 8cm (3in) across, but they make up for the small size in the large number of flowers they produce. The colour range is the same as the Grandifloras and they are the best choice for borders because they are more resistant to wet and cold weather.

A recent development is the Milliflora type. These are compact plants with small, upward-facing flowers and are good for containers.

The colour range of petunias has always been enormous and there are varieties that are striped with white, edged with white and veined in contrasting colours. But yellow petunias are now becoming more popular and 'Prism Sunshine' holds its colour well, though it does fade in hot, dry conditions.

An overlooked virtue of petunias is their scent. Some have no fragrance but the blue and purple flowers have a sweet, heavy fragrance that is most pronounced in the evening and these should be planted by the patio so the scent can be

Petunia Million Bells Series 'Cherry'

Petunia Surfinia Series 'Blue Vein'

appreciated on warm summer evenings.

Petunia seed is expensive and very small, so great care should be taken when sowing. Sow the seed in early spring in a temperature of 21°C (70°F). Do not cover the seed with compost. Use vermiculite to allow light to reach the seeds. Take care not to overwater the compost, but ensure the surface does not dry out.

Garden centres sell pots of seedlings, and plug plants are also available, which are useful if you have trouble getting petunias to germinate.

After pricking out the petunia seedlings, grow them on in cool conditions to keep the plants bushy and compost. Plant out in late spring.

	SPRING	SUMMER	AUTUMN	WINTER	height (cm)	spread (cm)	flower colour	
Petunia 'Chiffon Morn' (Grandiflora)	sowing transplanting transplanting	flowering flowering flowering	flowering flowering		30	30		Large, pastel pink flowers with cream centres
P. Daddy Series (Grandiflora)	sowing transplanting transplanting	flowering flowering flowering	flowering flowering		30	30		Large flowers with distinct, attractive veining
P. 'Double Delight Mixed' (Grandiflora)	sowing transplanting transplanting	flowering flowering flowering	flowering flowering		30	30	+	Fully double flowers, some striped with white
P. 'Fantasy Mixed' (Milliflora)	sowing transplanting transplanting	flowering flowering flowering	flowering flowering		25	25	+	Small plants with miniature, trumpet-shaped flowers
P. Million Bells Series (Milliflora)	transplanting transplanting transplanting	flowering flowering flowering	flowering flowering		20	40	+	Tiny flowers on spreading plants. Raised from cuttings
P. Mirage Series (Multiflora)	sowing transplanting transplanting	flowering flowering flowering	flowering flowering		30	30	+	Masses of small flowers. Wide range of colours and patterns
P. 'Prism Sunshine' (Grandiflora)	sowing transplanting transplanting	flowering flowering flowering	flowering flowering		30	30		Unusual colour. Fades to cream in hot weather, yellow veins
P. Storm Series (Grandiflora)	sowing transplanting transplanting	flowering flowering flowering	flowering flowering		35	30	+	Large, wavy flowers. Bred to withstand wet weather
P. Surfinia Series (Grandiflora trailing)	transplanting transplanting transplanting	flowering flowering flowering	flowering flowering		20	100	+	Long stems that cascade or spread. Raised from cuttings

 sowing   transplanting   flowering + many colours

Phacelia
California desert bluebell

Phacelias form great carpets of blue in their home in the western states of the USA, flowering after spring rains and often setting seed rapidly before drought kills them. Their blue flowers are very attractive to bees and butterflies, and organic gardeners often use them to edge their gardens to attract pollinators and hoverflies.

They are among the easiest annuals to grow and because they are hardy annuals they can be sown, where they are to flower, in spring.

There are about 150 species of Phacelia but very few are available from seed companies. They often self-seed but none are invasive. 'Lavender Lass' is unusual because of its large flowers, up to 2.5cm (1in) across, in a pretty shade of pale lavender with a cream centre to each bloom.

soil	Any reasonable garden soil that retains moisture, but which drains freely
site	These plants prefer growing in a position in the full sun
temp	Hardy annual, withstanding temperatures down to -15°C (5°F)
general care	Water regularly in dry weather. Otherwise, little general care is needed for these plants
pests & diseases	Aphids may infect young plants. Apart from this, relatively trouble free from pests and diseases

Phacelia campanularia 'Ocean Waves'

The delicate colouring of most phacelias makes them ideal to mix with other pastel annuals such as Gypsophila, love-in-a-mist (Nigella) and larkspur, but remember that phacelias are all quite low growing, so should be sown in front of taller plants.

Sow the seeds in late spring in weed-free soil in shallow drills and thin the seedlings to 15cm (6in) when large enough to handle. In mild areas, seed can be sown in early autumn and the plants will grow through the winter and bloom the following year.

All phacelias thrive on heavy soils, but they do not like to be waterlogged over winter. Autumn sown plants should be covered with a cloche on heavy soils to prevent them from rotting off, or better still sow in spring as the soil warms up and dries out.

	SPRING	SUMMER	AUTUMN	WINTER	height (cm)	spread (cm)	flower colour	
Phacelia 'Blue Wonder'	🪴	● ● ●	🪴		30	20		Valuable for the bright blue flowers in summer
P. campanularia 'Lavender Lass'	🪴	● ● ●	🪴		30	20		Attractive, scented blooms that attract beneficial insects
P campanularia 'Ocean Waves'	🪴	● ● ●	🪴		30	20		Masses of pastel flowers in midsummer

🪴 *sowing*   ● *flowering*

Phlox

Many gardeners are surprised to find that annual Phlox exists. They are familiar with the perennial, herbaceous types and even alpine phlox that brighten rock gardens in late spring. *Phlox* x *drummondii*, a Texan native, was one of the most popular annuals in the 19th Century.

The number of varieties, however, gradually dwindled until the 1990s when several new varieties, with intriguing names, such as 'Phlox of Sheep' rekindled interest in them and there is now a wide choice of varieties.

They are easy to grow and bloom over a long season so long as they are not allowed to dry out and are deadheaded. Though the individual flowers are not large, they are carried in small domes. Simply cut off the flower clusters when the last flower has died.

The range of colours is extraordinary and most varieties are mixtures. If you need a real kaleidoscope of colours choose 'Tapestry'. This is a tall variety, excellent for cutting, with flowers in every shade of pink and purple, as well as creamy yellow; most flowers have a contrasting eye or picotee edge. If you want a more restrained display, 'Lord Chancellor' is a good choice because it is a blend of deep, rich colours including crimson, plum and red. 'Twinkles' and 'Twinkle Stars Mixed' have star-shaped flowers in a wide range of shades, most with white petal edges or centres to create a sparkling show.

Most modern varieties have been bred to be small and compact, and are excellent for containers where they benefit from the extra moisture and liquid feeding. If deadheaded and watered in dry weather, phlox are among the longest-flowering annuals.

Sow the seeds under glass at around 20°C (68°F) and protect the plants from frost.

Phlox Pink and White Series

Phlox x *drummondii* 'Lord Chancellor'

soil	Any reasonable garden soil that retains moisture, but which drains freely
site	These plants are happy growing in either full sun or partial shade
temp	Half-hardy plants, withstanding temperatures down to 1°C (34°F)
general care	Regularly remove faded flower clusters. The tall varieties may need some support
pests & diseases	Protect young plants from slugs and snails. Mildew can affect plants late in summer

P

Bedding Plants

	SPRING	SUMMER	AUTUMN	WINTER	height (cm)	spread (cm)	flower colour	
Phlox drummondii 'Crème Brulee'	🪣 🥄 ✂	✹ ✹ ✹ ✹			25	20		Interesting mixture of colours
P. drummondii 'Lord Chancellor'	🪣 🥄 ✂	✹ ✹ ✹ ✹			20	20		Rich blend of colours
P. drummondii 'Mount Hampden'	🪣 🥄 ✂	✹ ✹ ✹ ✹			20	20		Compact plants with semi-double flowers
P. drummondii Pink and White Series	🪣 🥄 ✂	✹ ✹ ✹ ✹			35	20		Shades of pink, with subtle white markings
P. drummondii 'Tapestry'	🪣 🥄 ✂	✹ ✹ ✹ ✹			50	25	+	Tall plants with blooms in a wide range of colours
P. drummondii 'Twinkles'	🪣 🥄 ✂	✹ ✹ ✹ ✹			20	20	+	Dazzling, star-shaped flowers, often edged with white

 sowing   transplanting   ✹ flowering   + many colours

Portulaca
Sun plant

Without flowers, portulacas are rather dull plants. The red stems and the cylindrical leaves are fleshy, making the plant look heavy for its size. But when the flowers open you would be forgiven for thinking they are the most beautiful plants in the world.

The flowers, which are usually double, have a satin sheen and the colours are intense, in a variety of pinks, magenta, red, yellow, orange and white. The flowers open wide in the sunshine, which gives them an added brilliance. Traditional varieties had the disadvantage that the flowers remained closed in dull weather but *Portulaca grandiflora* 'Sundial Mixed' and others stay partially open under cloudy skies, though they are best when the sun shines. 'Sundial Peppermint' is a curiosity with pale pink flowers that are speckled in deep pink. 'Warm Gold' makes a bright splash of colour with its light orange flowers, enhanced by the bright red centre to the blooms.

Portulacas have a low, spreading habit and are suitable for rock gardens and for edging, as well as containers. Because they are succulent, they will survive dry soils and drought, though they benefit from watering in summer. They must be watered carefully as young seedlings, though, or they will rot. It is an advantage to add some grit to the compost when sowing to help reduce the risk of overwatering.

Portulacas have tiny seeds and these should be sown on the surface of the compost and germinated in a temperature of 20°C (68°F). They require plenty of light and should be watered sparingly once the seedlings have germinated. Prick out the delicate seedlings and grow on in gentle heat.

soil	Any reasonable garden soil that retains moisture, but which drains freely
site	Full sun. The flowers do not open in dull weather or when grown in shade
temp	These are not frost-hardy plants. Minimum temperature of 5°C (41°F)
general care	Seedlings must not be overwatered when young – use gritty compost for good drainage
pests & diseases	Aphids can attack young plants. Seedlings are also prone to fungal diseases

Portulaca grandiflora 'Sundial Mixed'

	SPRING	SUMMER	AUTUMN	WINTER	height (cm)	spread (cm)	flower colour	
Portulaca grandiflora 'Sundial Mixed'	🪴 ✂ ✂	● ● ● ●	●		15	20		Bred to flower well in cool climates
P. grandiflora 'Sundial Peppermint'	🪴 ✂ ✂	● ● ● ●	●		15	20		Double flowers are pale pink, speckled with deep pink
P. grandiflora 'Warm Gold'	🪴 ✂ ✂	● ● ● ●	●		15	20		Glowing blooms with red centres

🪴 sowing   ✂ transplanting   ● flowering

Primula

The first flowers of primroses and polyanthus are a sure sign that spring has arrived. From the pale yellow blooms of the wild primrose (*Primula vulgaris*), a kaleidoscope of colours has been achieved and modern varieties have large flowers in shades of pink, red, blue, yellow and peach. Many also have contrasting eye zones that add to their charm.

The plants of the Primrose group have rosettes of foliage and a dome of flowers on individual flower stems among the leaves. The Polyanthus group differ only in that the flowers are all attached to a tall stem to create a bunch on a stalk. But this division is not absolute and intermediate forms occur in many varieties.

Mixed bedding primulas

Primroses and polyanthus are usually treated as biennials and are sown in summer and planted out into their flowering positions in autumn to bloom the following spring. Seeds need light to germinate, so they should be sown on the compost surface and not covered. Seeds also germinate best in cool conditions. Keep the temperature below 18°C (64°F), which may be a problem in summer. Cover the seed tray or pot with a piece of glass to prevent the seeds from drying out and place in a shady spot in the garden.

Primroses and polyanthus can be planted in the garden or in a variety of containers. Although a few flowers may open in autumn, most appear in spring after the worst of the winter weather.

soil	Any reasonable garden soil that retains moisture, but which drains freely
site	These plants are happy growing in either full sun or partial shade
temp	These are hardy plants, withstanding temperatures as low as -15°C
general care	Keep plants moist. Good plants can be divided after flowering and retained for several years.
pests & diseases	Aphids on leaves and flower stems. Vine weevil grubs eat the roots of plants in containers

P

Bedding Plants

	SPRING	SUMMER	AUTUMN	WINTER	height (cm)	spread (cm)	flower colour	
Primula 'Arctic Mixed' (Primrose group)	● ● ●	🪣 🪣	✎ ✎ ✎		15	15	+	Large flowers and good weather-resistance
P. Crescendo Series (Polyanthus group)	● ● ●	🪣 🪣	✎ ✎ ✎		20	15	+	Large flowers in a wide range of colours
P. 'Dreamer' (Primrose group)	● ● ●	🪣 🪣	✎ ✎ ✎		15	15	+	Large flowers with contrasting eyes on compact plants
P. 'Gold Lace' (Polyanthus group)	● ● ●	🪣 🪣	✎ ✎ ✎		20	15	■	Heritage variety with small, black flowers edged with gold
P. 'Pacific Giants' (Polyanthus group)	● ● ●	🪣 🪣	✎ ✎ ✎		20	15	+	Huge flowers on robust plants. Best in sheltered sites
P. vulgaris (Primrose group)	● ● ●	🪣 🪣	✎ ✎ ✎		15	15	▦	Usually yellow flowers above scalloped, green leaves

🪣 sowing   ✎ transplanting   ● flowering   + many colours

Ricinus
Castor oil plant

The castor oil plant is a popular foliage plant for summer displays and makes a very impressive dot plant. It is found throughout subtropical areas of the world. In frost-free areas it forms a large spreading shrub, but in a bedding display it will normally only grow to around 1.2m (4ft) over the summer.

Ricinus communis

It is grown for its large, boldly lobed leaves and is ideal for tropical-looking bedding schemes where it can be planted alongside cannas, bananas, tree ferns, tithonias and amaranthus.

Although the wild species has green leaves, most varieties have foliage flushed with bronze or maroon. The flowers are insignificant but they are followed by showy, prickly seedpods that are often brightly coloured and contain three large seeds.

soil	Any reasonable garden soil that retains moisture, but which drains freely
site	These plants are happy growing in a sunny, sheltered position if possible
temp	Half-hardy plants, withstanding temperatures down to 1°C (34°F)
general care	Plants grow best when planted in moist, rich soil. Young plants may need staking
pests & diseases	Fairly trouble free. These plants are generally not affected by pests and diseases, particularly outside

Ricinus communis

These are easy to collect and save for the following year. They are toxic if ingested.

Ricinus communis 'Impala' has particularly attractive leaves that are bronze when mature but maroon when young. The fruits are bright scarlet and very showy.

Ricinus is a strong-growing, shrubby plant and will branch as the plant matures, but young plants have one main stem. It can be grown in containers, but because of the plant's root system it needs a large pot and rich compost. It benefits from watering in dry weather and regular liquid feeding.

The seeds are large and attractively mottled and should be sown individually, in spring. Sow one in each pot or in compartments of large cell trays. Keep the pots at around 20°C (68°F) to germinate. The seedlings are large and grow quickly but must be kept free from frost.

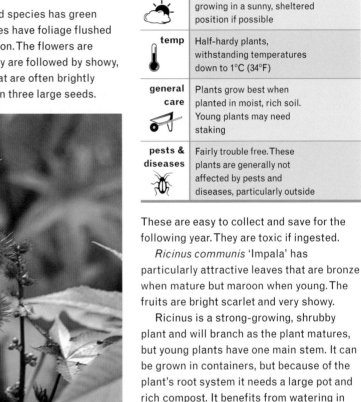

	SPRING	SUMMER	AUTUMN	WINTER	height (cm)	spread (cm)	foliage colour	
Ricinus communis 'Carmencita'	🪴 ✂ ✂	● ● ●	● ● ●		150	90		Dark brown foliage with red flowers and fruit
R. communis 'Carmentica Pink'	🪴 ✂ ✂	● ● ●	● ● ●		150	90		Green leaves on red stalks
R. communis 'Impala'	🪴 ✂ ✂	● ● ●	● ● ●		120	90		Large, bronze leaves, maroon when young and red fruits

🪴 *sowing*　　✂ *transplanting*　　● *flowering*　　 *harvesting*

R

Bedding Plants

Rudbeckia

Black-eyed
Susan *or*
Coneflower

Rudbeckias are bold plants with simple daisy-shaped flowers in various shades of orange, yellow or red petals around the central dark cone. The plants form a tuft of large, bristly leaves at first and then send up branching stems of blooms. The taller kinds have a slightly unruly character.

The tall varieties are perfect for mixing with herbaceous plants or for combining with less formal annuals such as calendulas and cosmos.

The short varieties are neat enough to be used in formal bedding with salvias and marigolds. Rudbeckias are among the last annuals to flower and are useful to extend the season of flowers into autumn.

Rudbeckia hirta 'Rustic Dwarfs Mixed' is a traditional mixture and has all the colours you would expect from rudbeckias. These include gold, orange, mahogany and brown. The plants have a useful, medium height and the plants are well-branched, with masses of flowers. 'Toto' is shorter and the flowers are orange with a brown centre but they are smaller than most and in perfect proportion. 'Prairie Sun' is taller than most and a great border filler. The flowers are bright yellow and each petal is deep gold at the base, contrasting with the bright green centre.

Rudbeckias are easy to grow and the seeds are large and easy to handle. Sow in spring in trays at around 20°C (68°F). Prick out into cell trays or small pots and grow on in cool conditions. Protect young plants from frost, but they are hardier than most half-hardy annuals and are the first plants to be put in the coldframe in spring.

Rudbeckia hirta 'Rustic Dwarfs Mixed'

Rudbeckia hirta 'Prarie Sun'

soil	Any reasonable garden soil that retains moisture, but which drains freely
site	These plants are happy growing in a sunny position in the garden
temp	Treat as a half-hardy annual. Withstands temperatures down to 1°C (34°F)
general care	Water regularly during spells of dry weather. Remove faded flowers to keep plants tidy
pests & diseases	Slugs and snails attack young plants, but otherwise relatively trouble free from pests and diseases

	SPRING	SUMMER	AUTUMN	WINTER	height (cm)	spread (cm)	flower colour	
Rudbeckia hirta 'Becky Mixed'	🪣🪣✂	● ● ●	● ●		20	20	▨	Dwarf plants with large flowers
R. hirta 'Prairie Sun'	🪣🪣✂	● ● ●	● ●		90	45	▨	Bold plants with sunny flowers in all weathers
R. hirta 'Rustic Dwarfs Mixed'	🪣🪣✂	● ● ●	● ●		45	30	▨	Reliable variety with large flowers, ideal for cutting
R. hirta 'Toto'	🪣🪣✂	● ● ●	● ●		30	25	▨	Neat habit and flowers of just the right size

 sowing   *transplanting*   *flowering*

Salpiglossis

Salpiglossis are closely related to petunias but are far more exotic. They share the same trumpet-shaped flowers but the flowers of Salpiglossis can be red, bright yellow, violet, deep blue, pink or brown and they are usually veined or flushed with gold.

Natives of Peru and Argentina, they are ideal for adding a touch of the exotic to the garden. They are upright in habit and carry the flowers in clusters at the top of the branched stems. While older varieties needed staking and were rather straggly, modern varieties such as *Salpiglossis sinuata* 'Casino Mixed' are compact and branch at the base. There is a wide range of colours but some of the most popular are grown due to their weird shades, almost unknown in other plants. 'Kew Blue' is a tall variety with inky blue flowers that deserve to be placed next to white flowers to show off their intensity. 'Chocolate Pot' is more compact but the brown, velvety flowers, veined with black and lit by golden stamens in the centre, contrasts with orange flowers and the dusky foliage of red coleus or Perilla.

Salpiglossis need rich soil and a sunny, sheltered position. In cold summers they will not grow well and are likely to rot if the weather is cold when they are planted out. In hot, dry positions they become stunted, so they should be watered in dry weather and given liquid fertilizer. They are most suited to sheltered patios where they thrive in containers.

Sow the seeds in late winter or early spring in the greenhouse at around 20°C (68°F). The seed is fine and the seedlings are delicate and prone to overwatering. Avoid putting them into large pots before they are ready and grow them on in warm conditions to prevent them suffering from fungal diseases such as grey mould.

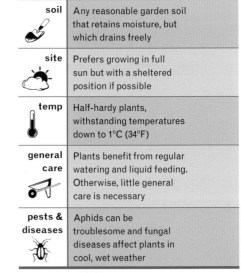

soil	Any reasonable garden soil that retains moisture, but which drains freely
site	Prefers growing in full sun but with a sheltered position if possible
temp	Half-hardy plants, withstanding temperatures down to 1°C (34°F)
general care	Plants benefit from regular watering and liquid feeding. Otherwise, little general care is necessary
pests & diseases	Aphids can be troublesome and fungal diseases affect plants in cool, wet weather

Salpiglossis sinuata 'Kings and Queens' (left caption, vertical)

Salpiglosis sinuata 'Casino Mixed' (right caption, vertical)

	SPRING	SUMMER	AUTUMN	WINTER	height (cm)	spread (cm)	flower colour	
Salpiglosis sinuata 'Casino Mixed'	🪣 🔧 🔧	✹ ✹ ✹ ✹		🪣	50	20	+	Compact, well-branched plants. Good for containers
S. sinuata 'Kew Blue'	🪣 🔧 🔧	✹ ✹ ✹ ✹		🪣	70	20	■	Exotic, sultry flowers for a special place in the garden
S. sinuata 'Kings and Queens'	🪣 🔧 🔧	✹ ✹ ✹ ✹		🪣	50	20	+	Upright, sturdy habit. Good colour mix

 sowing   transplanting   ✹ flowering   + many colours

Salvia
Sage

There are almost one thousand species of Salvia and they include shrubs, such as sage (*Salvia officinalis*), as well as the more familiar bedding plants. Only a few species are common in gardens and only two are used as bedding plants, with another that is an essential component of the traditional cottage garden.

Since the middle of the 19th century, when the idea of bedding was invented, *Salvia splendens* has provided much of the bright red in our summer gardens. The red flowers and red buds on conical spikes above the deep green leaves have a formality and neatness that suits small borders. The traditional partners planted alongside Salvia includes white alyssum and blue lobelia, although marigolds and petunias are also obvious companions.

Salvias have a tidy habit and the old flower spikes usually disappear as the new growth and flowers engulf them.

Salvia splendens 'Blaze of Fire' is the traditional variety, however *Salvia splendens* 'Red Arrow' has been bred to cope with cooler and wetter summer weather.

New colours have been added to salvias and the *Salvia splendens* Phoenix Series is available as single colours and mixtures, and includes a wonderful violet-purple that is especially effective with yellow marigolds and calceolarias. The *Salvia splendens* Sizzler Series also features a mixture of colours including pastel colours. *Salvia splendens* 'Sizzler Red Stripe' has

Salvia farinacea 'Strata'

soil	Any reasonable garden soil that retains moisture, but which drains freely
site	Prefers a position in the garden which receives full sun
temp	Treat as half-hardy, down to 1°C (34°F). *S. viridis* down to -15°C (5°F)
general care	Water regularly during spells of dry weather. Otherwise, little general care is necessary
pests & diseases	Slugs and snails attack young plants. Apart from this, not prone to pests and diseases

Salvia splendens 'Blaze of Fire'

Salvia splendens 'Red Arrow'

fascinating flowers streaked with bright red and white.

Over recent years, *Salvia farinacea* has become very popular again with gardeners. It forms upright, compact, bushy plants with attractive, deep green leaves that are white underneath. The small flowers are carried above the leaves on slender, vertical, deep blue stems and a mass planting is a sea of blue and bees. *Salvia farinacea* 'Strata' is especially attractive because the flower stems are silver, creating a two-coloured, blue and silver effect.

Both these salvias are treated as half-hardy annuals and should be sown in the greenhouse in early spring in a temperature of 21°C (70°F). Prick the seedlings out into cell trays and grow on in gentle heat. In late spring after hardening off, the young plants can be bedded out or used in containers.

However, *Salvia viridis* (also known as clary) is a hardy annual and is sown outdoors in spring, in the position where it is to flower. It is an aromatic, fast-growing plant and the flowers are small, pink and hardly worth a second glance. But the bracts at the top of the stems, among which the flowers appear, are very showy and either pink, purple or white.

This colouring is not present on young plants, which look decidedly weedy, but once it appears the plants are pretty for a long time. It is best sown with other hardy annuals when the bracts will blend with other flowers in the pink and purple colour range. Try planting Nigella, larkspur (Consolida), Godetia, Clarkia and Lavatera alongside.

The stems of clary can be cut and hung upside down to dry and used in winter, dried arrangements.

Try to protect young plants especially from slug and snail attack.

	SPRING	SUMMER	AUTUMN	WINTER	height (cm)	spread (cm)	flower colour	
Salvia farinacea 'Strata'					40	25		Bushy plants with deep green leaves
S. farinacea 'Victoria'					45	25		Useful as 'dot' plants among flower bedding plants
S. splendens 'Blaze of Fire'					30	20		Traditional, bright red bedding salvia
S. splendens 'Phoenix Purple'					25	20		Unusual variation on common bedding salvia. Other colours
S. splendens 'Red Arrow'					28	20		Weather-resistant variety. Good for bedding
S. splendens 'Sizzler Mixed'					30	20		Makes an interesting change from usual salvias
S. splendens 'Sizzler Red Stripe'					30	20		Bright spikes of flowers that are striped with red and white
S. viridis 'Bouquet'					45	25		Colour produced by bracts around the small flowers
S. viridis 'Claryssas'					40	30		Sow with annual poppies and Nigella for dried flowers

 sowing   transplanting   flowering

S

Bedding Plants

Scabiosa

Pincushion flower *or* Scabious

Scabiosa is usually considered a perennial, but the annual types offer gardeners some fascinating plants in a wider range of colours. While perennial types, such as *Scabiosa caucasica*, are lilac, blue or white, a packet of mixed annual scabious will provide flowers in deep blue, maroon, rose pink, salmon pink, cream, yellow and white. Another attraction is the fragrance of the flowers, which is light and sweet.

Dwarf varieties are the most popular but the taller scabious are worth growing because they make long-lasting cut flowers. *Scabiosa atropurpurea* 'Salmon Queen' is especially lovely because of its unusual pink colour.

Even when the flowers have faded, the round seedheads are pretty. *Scabiosa stellata* is grown specifically for its seedheads. The pale blue or lilac blooms are attractive but the spherical seedheads, which can be cut and dried for winter decoration, are the main reason for growing the plant.

Scabious are easy to grow, either by sowing them where they are to flower, as hardy annuals or by sowing them under glass. They prefer a sunny position in the garden and thrive in neutral or alkaline soils. Because the plants have feathery leaves and slender stems, they mix well with

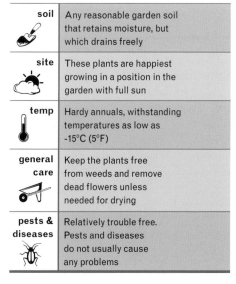

Scabiosa stellata 'Paper Moon'

Scabiosa atropurpurea 'Dwarf Mixed'

annual grasses, which also give the scabious some support.

If sowing under glass, wait until late spring when a little extra heat will be necessary. A temperature of about 12°C (54°F) is all that is needed. Alternatively, sow the seeds in the border in clumps or rows in late spring, and thin the seedlings to about 15cm (6in) apart when all have germinated. Avoid leaving all the strongest seedlings or you may find that when the plants come through, most will be the same colour.

soil	Any reasonable garden soil that retains moisture, but which drains freely
site	These plants are happiest growing in a position in the garden with full sun
temp	Hardy annuals, withstanding temperatures as low as -15°C (5°F)
general care	Keep the plants free from weeds and remove dead flowers unless needed for drying
pests & diseases	Relatively trouble free. Pests and diseases do not usually cause any problems

S

Bedding Plants

	SPRING	SUMMER	AUTUMN	WINTER	height (cm)	spread (cm)	flower colour	
Scabiosa atropurpurea 'Dwarf Mixed'	🌱 🌱	● ● ●	●		45	20	+	Fragrant flowers; lots of colours. Popular with butterflies
S. atropurpurea 'Salmon Queen'	🌱 🌱	● ● ●	●		90	25		Fragrant flowers on tall plants. Good for cutting
S. stellata 'Paper Moon'	🌱 🌱	● ● ●	●		45	25		Flowers are followed by pretty, dried seedheads

 planting   *flowering*   + *many colours*

Scaevola
Fan flower

This Australian plant has become a popular addition to baskets, containers and windowboxes in recent years. What it offers gardeners is a long succession of pretty, fan-shaped flowers on trailing stems. The plants have rather fleshy, narrow leaves but soon become covered in masses of flowers. As the stems elongate, they carry a succession of flowers that does not stop until the first frost of autumn.

Most varieties have flowers in shades of lilac or lavender blue with a white eye, but *Scaevola aemula* 'Zig Zag' is interesting because the flowers are striped in blue and white.

When planted in borders, the plants form low mounds of blooms, but Scaevola is usually planted in containers where it will trail over the edges. Because the growth is sprawling and the young stems can be rather vigorous, it is best planted in large containers where its spread does not look

soil	Any reasonable garden soil that retains moisture, but which drains freely
site	Best grown in a sunny, sheltered position – usually grown in containers
temp	Not frost-hardy plants, only withstanding temperatures of minimum 5°C (41°F)
general care	Water copiously during spells of dry weather. Otherwise, little general care is necessary
pests & diseases	Aphids can attack new foliage and stems. Apart from this, fairly trouble free

out of place. However, this vigour means that it can be planted alongside other large plants such as petunias, verbenas and *Helichrysum petiolare*. Its colouring looks good with most plants, but especially those with white, pink and purple flowers and silver foliage.

Scaevola is a tender perennial and is propagated by cuttings, although it is often difficult to find non-flowering shoots for this purpose. Cuttings can be taken in spring or summer, or old plants can be kept frost-free over winter and cuttings taken from these in spring, using new shoots. Root the cuttings in a propagator where a temperature of around 20°C (68°F) is maintained. Plants can also usually be bought in small pots in the spring from garden centres.

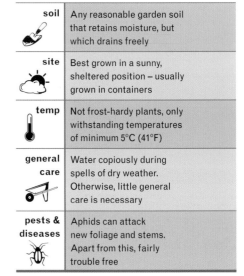

Scaevola aemula 'Blue Wonder'

S

Bedding Plants

	SPRING	SUMMER	AUTUMN	WINTER	height (cm)	spread (cm)	flower colour	
Scaevola aemula 'Blue Wonder'	planting	flowering			20	40		Long, trailing stems with masses of fan-shaped flowers
S. aemula 'Diamond Blue'	planting	flowering			20	40		Flowers cover foliage of this long-flowering basket plant
S aemula 'Zig Zag'	planting	flowering			20	40		Blooms prettily striped in blue and white

planting   flowering

Senecio
Cineraria

Where bright, silvery foliage is required to complement bright, summer flowers, _Senecio cineraria_, often known under the name of _Cineraria maritima_, is the most popular choice. It is easy to grow from seed, widely available as plants in spring and will thrive in any sunny position.

Although it is usually grown as an annual and discarded at the end of autumn, it is a short-lived shrub and will survive for several years in coastal gardens or where the soil is not waterlogged in winter. It will then produce masses of bright yellow flowers. However, these are usually removed by gardeners before they open so that the plants put all their energy into producing more, fresh foliage. Old plants should be cut back in spring to keep them compact. The leaves are covered with a white felt that reflects the light, helping them cope with strong sun in the wild and giving them a bright, silvery appearance.

soil	Any reasonable garden soil that retains moisture, but which drains freely
site	Best grown in the full sun – ideal plants for coastal gardens
temp	Frost hardy when mature but raised under glass from seed in frost-free conditions
general care	Plants can live for several years in well-drained soils and coastal gardens. The flowers are usually removed
pests & diseases	Relatively trouble free. Pests and diseases do not usually cause any problems

Senecio cineraria 'Sliver Dust'

This Mediterranean plant is a good contrast to most summer flowers but especially with pink and purple flowers such as heliotrope, verbenas and petunias. It can be grown in borders but is compact enough, in the first year, for patio containers, too.

There are two main varieties: _Senecio cineraria_ 'Silver Dust' is the most popular and has lacy leaves. _Senecio cineraria_ 'Cirrus' has bolder leaves that are rounded at first and lobed as the plants mature; it also tends to be more compact.

Sow the seeds in spring in a greenhouse or on a windowsill at around 18–21°C (64–70°F) and ensure the seedlings have plenty of light. The seedlings are large and easy to handle, and can be transplanted into trays. Young plants will survive light frost, but they must not be overwatered when small or they may rot.

Bedding Plants

	SPRING	SUMMER	AUTUMN	WINTER	height (cm)	spread (cm)	flower colour	
Senecio cineraria 'Cirrus'					30	30		Grown for its bold, rounded, silver leaves
S. cineraria 'Sliver Dust'					30	45		The most popular variety, with frilly, silver leaves

 sowing   transplanting   flowering

Solenostemon

Coleus *or* Flame nettle

Solenostemon are better known as coleus and their common name, flame nettle, is descriptive as the large leaves of most kinds are brightly coloured in red, gold and orange. But there is a large number of varieties, some with deeply dissected foliage, and the range of colours includes deep purple and remarkable combinations and patterns.

It is worth buying good seed mixtures, such as *Solenostemon scutellarioides* 'Flame Dancers', to avoid raising plants that are predominantly green. Some mixtures are balanced combinations of different colours and others, such as 'Black Dragon' with frilly leaves and 'Wizard Red', will produce similar, ornamental plants.

All seed-raised coleus have a tendency to produce flowers at the ends of the shoots. Pinch out the shoot tips as the flowers form to encourage plenty of fresh foliage.

It is easy to raise coleus from seed, but they are difficult to keep over winter and you need to grow new seedlings each spring. An alternative is to grow the tender perennial types that are raised from cuttings. These named varieties often have better leaf colour and are less likely to flower. They can thus be trained as standards and grow into larger

S. scutellarioides 'Winsome'

S. scutellarioides 'Speckles'

soil	Any reasonable garden soil that retains moisture, but which drains freely
site	Sun or partial shade. Best in sheltered sites and in containers
temp	Not frost hardy, only withstanding temperatures down to 5°C (41°F)
general care	Pinch out shoot tips to prevent flowers forming. Otherwise, little general care is necessary
pests & diseases	Relatively trouble free when grown outside. Pests and diseases do not usually cause any problems

plants than the annuals. 'Pineapple Beauty' is the most popular and has leaves that are golden yellow with a deep crimson blotch at the base. Keep in a bright place in winter in a minimum temperature of 5°C (41°F).

Solenostemon scutellarioides 'Dazzler'

	SPRING	SUMMER	AUTUMN	WINTER	height (cm)	spread (cm)	flower colour	
Solenostemon scutellarioides 'Dazzler'		● ● ● ●			40	30		Maroon, green and white, long, frilled leaves
S. scutellarioides 'Flame Dancers'		● ● ● ●			30	30		Red, pink and gold foliage
S. scutellarioides 'Palisandra'		● ● ● ●			45	30		Deep purple, velvety foliage
S. scutellarioides 'Rainbow Mixed'		● ● ● ●			40	30		Wide range of colours and patterns
S. scutellarioides 'Speckles'		● ● ● ●			45	30		Bright light golden leaves with brown splashes
S. scutellarioides 'Winsome'		● ● ● ●			30	30		Reddish foliage with mottled green patterns on edges
S. scutellarioides 'Wizard Red'		● ● ● ●			25	30		Dwarf, compact plant with bright red leaves

 sowing transplanting ● flowering

Stipa
Pony-tail grass

Of the many ornamental grasses that can be added to gardens, *Stipa tenuissima*, the pony-tail grass, is one of the most decorative and endearing. It gets its common name from the foliage and flowering stems that are as fine as hair and are held in upright bunches.

Although it is a hardy perennial, if seed is sown in early spring the plants will produce their flowers in the first year and they make a delicate addition to the flower border. Because of its whispery outline, pony-tail grass looks best when planted with less formal annuals such as many of the hardy annuals. Californian poppies (Eschscholzia), English marigolds (Calendula), swan river daisies (Brachyscome), cornflowers, tickseed (Coreopsis) and love-in-a-mist (Nigella) all make good companions, along with other annual grasses.

soil	Any reasonable garden soil that retains moisture, but which drains freely
site	These plants are happy growing in a position in the garden in the full sun
temp	These are hardy perennials, withstanding temperatures down to -15°C (5°F)
general care	Easy plants to grow. Will flower in the first year from seed. Can be trimmed down in winter
pests & diseases	Relatively trouble free. Pests and diseases do not usually cause any problems

Stipa tenuissima

Sow the seed in spring in a temperature of 20°C (68°F). The seedlings are very thin and wispy, and may be difficult to transplant at first. It is easiest to transplant them in small clusters into small pots. An easy way around this is to sow a pinch of seed into each cell of a plug-tray and when they have filled the cell, transplant into small pots. The plants do not need high temperatures to grow on and they can be placed outside in a coldframe, but take care not to overwater them when they are small. Once they have filled their pots with roots, they can be planted out into the garden.

They grow best in a site in full sun where they will not be swamped by larger plants. Although they can be used as 'dot' plants among lower plants, they look best when planted in informal 'drifts' of three or more.

At first the plants look like ordinary grass but they then produce a long succession of silky, feathery flower spikes that most find irresistible to touch and stroke. They are pale green at first but as they ripen they turn pale gold. Stipa will also self-seed, but spare seedlings can easily be hoed off.

Sutera
syn. Bacopa

Sutera is a South African plant that has become popular as a hanging basket and container plant because of its delicate flowers and rampant growth. It has small, mid-green foliage and a creeping habit. If planted into borders, a single plant can cover an area 60 sq cm (24 sq in).

When planted in hanging baskets, windowboxes and containers it will cascade over the sides to form a sheet of flowers and foliage at least 30cm(12in) long. Its growth is so dense that it sometimes crowds out weaker plants, such as busy Lizzies, so give it room to grow. The small flowers have five petals, but produced in profusion all summer. They are usually white, but pink varieties have recently become available. All can be used as a substitute for lobelia and have the advantage that they have a longer season of flowers.

In addition to their use in mixed containers of bedding plants, Sutera is

soil	Any reasonable garden soil that retains moisture, but which drains freely
site	Sun or partial shade. Popular for hanging baskets and containers
temp	Not frost hardy, only withstanding temperatures down to a minimum 5°C (41°F)
general care	Easy to grow – may swamp delicate plants in baskets. Benefits from regular watering and feeding
pests & diseases	Relatively trouble free. Pests and diseases do not usually cause any problems

useful as a carpeting plant in pots of shrubs to cover the soil in summer. Feed regularly with liquid fertilizer.

Plants sometimes lose vigour towards the end of the season, but this is usually because they require more fertilizer. Liberal liquid feeding and watering will boost their growth and the production of flowers. Deadheading is unnecessary.

Although seed is sometimes available, plants are almost always grown from cuttings and bought as young plants in spring. These grow rapidly and it is easy to produce more plants by taking tip cuttings of shoots throughout spring and summer. These cuttings root quickly and will be big enough to plant into baskets in a few months. If you have a frost-free greenhouse, cuttings can be taken in late summer and overwintered for use the following year.

Sutera cordata 'Snowflake'

	SPRING	SUMMER	AUTUMN	WINTER	height (cm)	spread (cm)	flower colour	
Sutera cordata 'Pink Domino'	🌱🌱🌱	●●●●●	●●●		10	30	▨	Trailing stems dotted with delicate flowers
S. cordata 'Snowflake'	🌱🌱🌱	●●●●	●● ●		10	30	☐	Vigorous plant for hanging baskets

 🌱 planting   ● flowering

Tagetes

French marigolds *or* African marigolds

French marigolds may have been overtaken by busy Lizzies as the most popular summer bedding plants, but they are unbeatable when you need a splash of bright colour in a sunny spot. In addition to French marigolds (*Tagetes patula*) which are usually short plants, there are African marigolds (*Tagetes erecta*), which have larger flowers and are usually taller. Modern varieties, however, are dwarf and some are even shorter than certain French marigolds, but their flowers are always larger.

The two have been crossed to produce intermediate types called Afro-French marigolds, which usually do not set seeds so do not require deadheading. All these have quite large flowers, but *Tagetes signata*, usually called just tagetes, have small, single flowers produced in vast numbers. The bushy plants have fine, feathery foliage.

All these marigolds have rather pungent foliage, but some modern varieties, such as *Tagetes* 'Vanilla' have less scent, which some people may find an advantage.

French marigolds are ideal for containers, borders and edging, and there is a wide variety of flower types. The singles, such as *T.* 'Naughty Marietta', have bold flowers and have the advantage that, in late summer, the flowers are less prone to fill with rainwater and become mouldy – a problem with African marigolds in wet

Tagetes 'Safari Mixed'

soil	Any reasonable garden soil that retains moisture, but which drains freely
site	Tagetes are happiest planted in a position in the full sun
temp	Not frost hardy, only withstanding minimum temperatures of 5°C (41°F)
general care	Water regularly during spells of dry weather. Remove dead flowers to keep plants tidy
pests & diseases	Slugs and snails can attack young plants. Otherwise these plants are trouble free

Tagetes 'Golden Gem'

seasons. There are fully double varieties such as *T.* 'Juliette' and also crested marigolds with a raised centre, such as *T.* 'Honeycomb'. The colour range includes all shades of yellow, as well as orange, brick red and mahogany, and the flowers are often bicoloured. *T.* 'Mr Majestic' has bold flowers that are striped in dark red and yellow.

Bedding Plants

African marigolds are grown for their ball-shaped, double flowers. The colour range is narrower, comprising orange, gold and lemon yellow. Traditional types such as *T.* 'Crackerjack' are tall, bushy plants, but there are now short varieties such as *T.* 'Sahara Mixed' which have large flowers on plants that are shorter than most French marigolds.

Tagetes 'Safari Yellow'

Tagetes 'Safari Tangerine'

Tagetes (*Tagetes signata*) are less common, but they are vibrant plants covered in a profusion of small flowers. Use them in containers, borders and for edging. Their simple, single flowers are popular with bees and butterflies.

Marigolds are easy to raise from seed in spring and should be sown in a temperature of 20°C (68°F). The seedlings are large and easy to transplant. Grow on in gentle heat where the plants will quickly develop. The young plants are prone to frost damage and should only be planted out after the last frost has passed.

Bedding Plants

	SPRING	SUMMER	AUTUMN	WINTER	height (cm)	spread (cm)	flower colour	
Tagetes 'Crackerjack' (African)					60	45		Old-fashioned, tall mixture. Easy and reliable
T. 'Durango Red' (French)					25	25		Bushy plants with sizzling, deep red blooms
T. 'Golden Gem' (T. signata)					20	20		Bushy plants with feathery foliage and small blooms
T. 'Honeycomb' (French)					25	20		Large red flowers, edged with orange
T. Inca Series (African)					30	35		Compact plants with large, double flowers
T. 'Juliette' (Afro-French)					30	25		Large, double, gold blooms flushed with orange
T. 'Lemon Gem' (T. signata)					20	20		Vibrant, sunny flowers – superb with purple verbena
T. 'Mr Majestic' (French)					30	25		Striping of large, single flowers varies with the weather
T. 'Naughty Marietta' (French)					30	30		The single flowers have a deep red centre
T. 'Red Gem' (T. signata)					20	20		Each flower is edged with gold, with a golden centre
T. 'Safari Mixed' (French)					25	25		Large, semi-double blooms
T. Sahara Mixed (African)					20	25		Dwarf plants with large flowers
T. 'Starfire Mixed' (T. signata)					20	20		Exciting mixture of single and bicoloured blooms
T. 'Sunspot Yellow' (African)					30	30		Economical, compact, and early-flowering
T. 'Trinity Mixed' (Afro-French)					30	25		Relatively large flowers
T. 'Vanilla' (African)					40	30		Unusual, pale flowers
T. Zenith Series (Afro-French)					30	25		Large flowers in a wide range of colours

 sowing   transplanting   flowering

Tanacetum

Tanacetum is often listed as Pyrethrum in seed catalogues, so it is sometimes difficult to find. *Tanacetum parthenium*, the most common species, however, will be familiar to many as feverfew and is sometimes seen for sale in herb sections at garden centres. It is a short-lived, slightly woody perennial that usually seeds itself in the garden, but it is so easy to grow from seed that it is also grown as an annual.

The plant usually grows to about 40cm (16in) high but it will be shorter in the first season. *Tanacetum parthenium* 'Golden Moss' never gets taller than 10cm (4in). It is grown mainly for its frilly, curled, bright yellow leaves, though it also produces white, daisy flowers with yellow centres. It is usually grown as an edging plant around borders, but can also be planted in containers. It is a traditional ingredient of carpet bedding, usually in parks where it is combined with echeverias, sedums and other foliage plants. It thrives in sun but can scorch in a hot summer if the soil is dry.

T. p. 'White Gem' is a taller variety that is grown for its pretty flowers. It is a good cut flower and can be used to fill in borders around contrasting plants. It grows best in full sun or a lightly shaded spot where the soil does not get too dry in summer.

Tanacetum parthenium 'White Gem'

soil	Any reasonable garden soil that retains moisture, but which drains freely
site	These plants are happy growing in full sun. Short types are ideal for edging
temp	Frost hardy when mature, withstanding temperatures down to -15°C (5°F)
general care	Deadhead regularly to encourage more flowers. Otherwise, little general care is necessary
pests & diseases	Leaf miner can cause some problems, but apart from this, relatively trouble free from pests and diseases

T. ptarmiciflorum, often called silver feather, is a much more spectacular plant and needs a sunny spot and well-drained soil. It forms a clump of stems set with leaves that look as though they have been cut from aluminium and are intricately divided. The flowers, which do not appear until the second year, are daisy-like and usually removed.

All tanacetums should be sown in spring at around 20°C (68°F). *T. parthenium* is easy to grow and needs only light protection from frost in spring. *T. ptarmiciflorum* is prone to overwatering when small, so water seedlings with care.

If plants are retained for a second year, prune them hard in spring to boost vigorous growth and to remove old, dead stems.

Bedding Plants

	SPRING	SUMMER	AUTUMN	WINTER	height (cm)	spread (cm)	flower colour	
Tanacetum parthenium 'Golden Moss'					10	15		Bright, golden ferny, foliage
T. parthenium 'White Gem'					30	25		Pretty flowers on dense, bushy plants
T. ptarmiciflorum 'Silver Feather'					30	30		Finely-divided, bright silver foliage

 sowing   transplanting   flowering

Tithonia

Mexican sunflower

If marigolds and busy lizzies seem boring or too domesticated for your garden and you want something distinctive and different, tithonias could be right for you. Sometimes called Mexican sunflower, *Tithonia rotundifolia* is a tall, sparsely branched plant with upright-facing orange or yellow flowers about 8cm (3in) across. The leaves and stems are covered in velvety hairs, and the leaves are lobed and bold in shape.

Bedding Plants

soil	Any reasonable garden soil that retains moisture, but which drains freely
site	These plants are happiest growing in a sunny, sheltered position if possible
temp	Not frost hardy, only withstanding minimum temperatures of 5°C (41°F)
general care	Water regularly during spells of dry weather and remove any dead flowers
pests & diseases	Slugs and snails can attack young plants. Otherwise, fairly free from pests and diseases

Tithonia rotundifolia

The plant in the wild is tall and can reach 1.5m (5ft) in height. Newer varieties are shorter, but still have large flowers. Even so, they are no substitute for French marigolds. They are better suited for planting in herbaceous borders and among taller annuals. They are too tall and sparse in habit for small containers.

Tithonias have simple daisy flowers, but because of their large size, striking colours and bold foliage, they can be mixed with sub-tropical foliage plants to create a sumptuous border. Try mixing them with purple-leaved cannas, brugmansias and ricinus.

They begin to flower in midsummer and then continue until autumn, reaching their peak after most other bedding plants are looking tired.

Tithonias are sun lovers and they flower best in hot summers. In cold, wet weather the foliage is prone to fungal diseases and the lower leaves frequently die as the plants grow taller, so place them behind shorter plants.

The seedlings are particularly prone to fungal diseases when they are small and great care must be taken not to keep the compost too damp. For this reason it is best to delay sowing until mid or late spring when temperatures are higher and there are better light levels than in early spring.

Sow the large seeds in a temperature of around 20°C (68°F). Transplant the seedlings into small-cell trays and then pot the plants into individual pots before planting out in early summer when there is no risk of frost.

	SPRING	SUMMER	AUTUMN	WINTER	height (cm)	spread (cm)	flower colour	
Tithonia rotundifolia 'Arcadian Blend'	🪣 ✂	✂ ● ●	● ●	●	70	40		More compact than most; good range of colours
T. rotundifolia 'Goldfinger'	🪣 ✂	✂ ● ●	● ●	●	90	40		Bright flowers on tall plants

 sowing   *transplanting*   ✿ *flowering*

Tropaeolum
Nasturtium

Nasturtiums are found wild in South America but are an integral part of the summer cottage garden and are one of the easiest plants to grow. Their bright flowers, in all shades of red, yellow and orange, appear just above the foliage over a long period and the plants thrive in dry, hot soils.

Nasturtiums, in fact, tend to produce lush leaves that cover the flowers if the plants are grown in rich soil and given too much water and fertilizer, so they are the obvious choice for dry, poor soils.

However, they can be ruined by several pests. The most important are blackfly, which infest the leaves and shoots, and the caterpillars of cabbage white butterflies, attracted by the scent of the mustard oils that the plants contain. It is these oils that give the give the leaves and flowers an added value; they are a tasty addition to salads with their peppery, cress-like taste.

One of the most popular varieties is *Tropaeolum majus* Alaska Series. This has the usual range of bright flower colours, but the leaves are heavily marbled and splashed with white, making the plants attractive even before they have started to bloom. The Gleam Series have large,

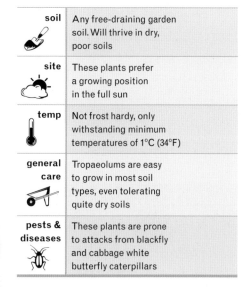

soil	Any free-draining garden soil. Will thrive in dry, poor soils
site	These plants prefer a growing position in the full sun
temp	Not frost hardy, only withstanding minimum temperatures of 1°C (34°F)
general care	Tropaeolums are easy to grow in most soil types, even tolerating quite dry soils
pests & diseases	These plants are prone to attacks from blackfly and cabbage white butterfly caterpillars

semi-double flowers and the plants are spreading, making them suitable for hanging baskets.

Sow two seeds, about 20cm (8in) apart in the open garden in late spring. Let both grow if they all germinate. Nasturtiums often self seed in the garden, but seedlings that germinate in the autumn are killed by winter frosts.

Tropaeolum majus Alaska Series

	SPRING	SUMMER	AUTUMN	WINTER	height (cm)	spread (cm)	flower colour	
Tropaeolum majus Alaska Series	🌱🌱🌱	●●●●	●●		20	20	+	Bright coloured flowers and white-variegated leaves
T. majus Gleam Series	🌱🌱🌱	●●●●	●●		30	40	+	Semi-double flowers on spreading plants
T. majus Jewel Series	🌱🌱🌱	●●●●	●●		23	25	+	Semi-double flowers on dwarf plants
T. majus 'Mahogany Jewel'	🌱🌱🌱	●●●●	●●		30	30	■	Compact plants with vibrant blooms
T. majus 'Strawberries & Cream'	🌱🌱🌱	●●●●	●●		25	25	□	Creamy yellow flowers with red blotches
T. majus Tom Thumb Series	🌱🌱🌱	●●●●	●●		20	25	+	Free-flowering mixture

 planting   *flowering*   + *many colours*

T

Bedding Plants

Verbena

Although there are more than 200 species of Verbena throughout the Americas, only a few have made an impact on our gardens. They are long-established bedding plants, loved for their bright flowers that are produced throughout summer. The most common types are raised from seed and are bushy plants with rounded heads of small blooms in shades of white, pink, purple and blue, often with contrasting white centres.

Verbena x *hybrida* Quartz Series has rather large heads of flowers that almost smother the leaves. They are available in attractive mixtures such as 'Waterfall Mixed', which is a blend of blues and purples with white. It is also more resistant to mildew than most.

These bedding verbenas are ideal for borders and containers.

'Imagination' has a different habit to most, with finely-divided foliage and a wiry, spreading habit. It is ideal for baskets and cascading out of containers on the patio.

An increasing number of cuttings-raised verbenas are available and these have the advantage of uniformity and the

Verbena 'Quartz Burgandy'

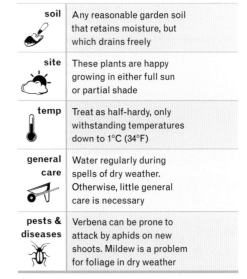

soil	Any reasonable garden soil that retains moisture, but which drains freely
site	These plants are happy growing in either full sun or partial shade
temp	Treat as half-hardy, only withstanding temperatures down to 1°C (34°F)
general care	Water regularly during spells of dry weather. Otherwise, little general care is necessary
pests & diseases	Verbena can be prone to attack by aphids on new shoots. Mildew is a problem for foliage in dry weather

length of flowering period. The Tapien Series has fine foliage and is popular for baskets and windowboxes.

Verbena rigida is an old favourite. It is an upright plant with rough stems and leaves, and clusters of small lilac flowers throughout summer. It is a traditional companion for yellow calceolarias, marigolds and heliotrope.

Some verbenas have a light fragrance and most attract moths in the evening.

Seed should be sown in a greenhouse at around 20°C (68°F). It often germinates slowly and erratically. Seedlings suffer if the compost is too wet so water sparingly, but do not allow the seeds to dry out.

Verbena x *hybrida* 'Peaches & Cream'

	SPRING	SUMMER	AUTUMN	WINTER	height (cm)	spread (cm)	flower colour	
Verbena x *hybrida* 'Imagination'	🪣 ✂ ✂	● ● ●	● ● ●		30	45	▨	Spreading plants – ideal for baskets
V. x *hybrida* 'Novalis Mixed'	🪣 ✂ ✂	● ● ●	● ● ●		25	25	+	Rounded heads of white-eyed flowers on bushy plants
V. x *hybrida* 'Peaches & Cream'	🪣 ✂ ✂	● ● ●	● ● ●		20	20	▨	Pretty, pastel flowers – prone to mildew
V. x *hybrida* Tapien Series	✂ ✂ ✂	● ● ●	● ● ●		20	30	▥	Cuttings-raised verbenas. Foliage and spreading habit
V. x *hybrida* Quartz Series	🪣 ✂ ✂	● ● ●	● ● ●		25	25	+	Compact plants with large flowers
V. rigida	🪣 ✂ ✂	● ● ●	● ● ●		30	20	▨	Upright, slender plants with small, vibrant flowers

🪣 *sowing*   ✂ *transplanting*   ● *flowering*   + *many colours*

Vinca rosea
Madagascan periwinkle

The Madagascan periwinkle, also known as *Catharanthus roseus*, has hit the headlines recently as a source of drugs for the treatment of some types of cancer, but gardeners value it for its pretty flowers that are produced over a long period.

Vinca rosea mixed

In frost-free areas, it can be grown outside all year and forms a pretty, small shrub with beautiful, glossy foliage and pink or white flowers in every month of the year. In colder gardens it is grown as a potplant or for summer bedding. It is at its best in containers on the patio or in borders in sheltered sites, where it will benefit from good soil and plenty of water during the summer.

Most varieties produce flowers in a range of pink shades from deep crimson to pale, shell pink as well as white, and many have contrasting, deep red eyes.

Vinca rosea

They are ideal container plants and grow best in urban, sheltered areas where nights are not cold and they are protected from chilling winds.

soil	Any reasonable rich, well-drained, moist garden soil
site	A sunny position but sheltered from cold winds
temp	Not frost hardy, only withstanding minimum temperatures of 5°C (41°F)
general care	Keep plants well watered and fertilized in summer, especially during particularly dry spells
pests & diseases	Relatively trouble free from pests and diseases outside. Whitefly are a problem under glass

Although related to the hardy, garden periwinkle, the Madagascan periwinkle is not at all invasive. In fact, it is one of the more challenging annuals to grow in temperate climates, but the pretty flowers are extremely rewarding when seen at their best.

Sow the seed in spring in a greenhouse at a temperature of approximately 20°C (68°F) and transplant the seedlings when they are large enough to handle into cell trays. Keep the seedlings as warm as possible while they are young to prevent a check in growth. Do not plant them outside until it is warm at night, as the plants are very sensitive to cold. Plants can also be propagated by cuttings taken in summer and overwintered in frost-free conditions.

Whitefly and red spider mites may be a problem for Madagascan periwinkles grown under glass, but outdoors they are reasonably trouble free.

All parts are poisonous if eaten, so consider where to plant them if small children are around.

	SPRING	SUMMER	AUTUMN	WINTER	height (cm)	spread (cm)	flower colour	
Vinca rosea 'Pretty in Mixed'	🪣 ✂ ✂	✂ ✸ ✸	✸		30	30	▢	Long-flowering but needs sheltered site
V. rosea Victory Series	🪣 ✂ ✂	✂ ✸ ✸	✸		25	25	+	Compact, well branched plants and good colour range

🪣 sowing   ✂ transplanting   ✸ flowering   + many colours

Viola

Pansy *or* Violet

Violas are one of the most popular flowering plants for both the garden and containers. By growing several different types you can have flowers all year round. Pansies generally have larger flowers than violas. Although violas have smaller blooms, they have them in larger quantities. Both pansies and violas are hardy, short-lived perennials that are grown as annuals or biennials.

A huge range of colours is available from single colours with no markings to flowers with a dark blotch in the centre of the flower. Other flowers are bi-coloured or even tri-coloured with dark veins radiating from the centre that look like whiskers on a kitten's face. The flower sizes range from delicate 2.5cm (1in) flowers to larger 10cm (4in) blooms that look like velvet.

Seed can be sown in early spring for plants to flower during summer and early autumn, and in late summer for winter and spring flowering.

The winter-flowering types have been bred to flower during the cold short days of winter, although the best flowers are produced from late winter into spring. Towards late spring when the weather warms up, winter-flowering types will grow tall and leggy and should be removed to make way for summer-flowering types. Likewise, the summer types do not flower very well after late autumn.

To grow violas the seed should be sown thinly in pots or trays of compost and lightly covered with compost or vermiculite. The

soil	Any reasonable garden soil that retains moisture, but drains freely
site	These plants are happy growing in either full sun or partial shade
temp	Violas are frost hardy. They will withstand winter temperatures to -15°C (5°F)
general care	Deadhead regularly to encourage more flowers. Otherwise, little general care is necessary
pests & diseases	Aphids, slugs and snails, leaf spots, powdery mildew, foot rot and mosaic virus all afflict Viola

Viola Ultima Series

seed germinates best in cool conditions and ideally the temperatures should be around 15°C. Very high temperatures will greatly reduce the germination rate. When sowing in the summer months, place the seed tray outside in a cool shady position to aid germination.

Pansies and violas can be planted out into borders or used in baskets and containers with great effect. They look very good planted en masse, whether in single or mixed colours. They can also be used as an edging plant to taller spring-flowering plants, such as wallflowers.

Viola Ultima Blue

Viola 'Molly's Sister'

The winter- and spring-flowering kinds are effectively combined with certain spring-flowering bulbs, such as hyacinths, early dwarf tulips or early Cyclamineus Narcissus (daffodils).

Regularly deadhead pansies and violas to ensure continuous flowering. Otherwise, little special care is necessary.

Pansies and violas have more than their fair share of pests and diseases and are prone to aphids, foot rot, leaf spot, powdery mildew, rust, slugs, snails and viruses, particularly mosaic virus.

	height (cm)	spread (cm)	flower colour	
Viola 'Blue Moon' (Viola)	15	20		Semi-trailing – good in baskets
V. 'Little Rascals' (Viola)	10	15		Masses of small multicoloured flowers
V. 'Molly's Sister' (Viola)	20	15		Unusual flower colour – long flowering period
V. Penny Series (Viola)	15	20	+	Compact mound, small flowers
V. 'Sorbet Mixed' (Viola)	15	15		Early flowering. Whiskered faces
V. 'Tiger Eye' (Viola)	15	20		Flowers have a network of veins
V. 'Velour Mixed' (Viola)	20	20	+	Early and long flowering
V. 'Chalon Improved' (Summer pansy)	20	20	+	Beautifully frilled, seven-ruffled flowers
V. 'Clear Crystal Mixed' (Summer pansy)	15	20	+	Large, bright flowers without blotches
V. 'Joker Light Blue' (Summer pansy)	20	20		Light blue with white faces
V. 'Swiss Giants Mixed' (Summer pansy)	20	20	+	Large flowers with dark blotches
V. Dynamite series (Winter pansy)	15	20	+	Large flowers; very hardy; ideal for containers
V. 'Floral Dance Mixed' (Winter pansy)	20	20	+	Free flowering, early flowering
V. Ultima Series (Winter pansy)	15	20	+	Wide range of colours, with clear and blotched flowers
V. 'Universal Mixed' (Winter pansy)	15	20	+	Medium sized flowers and uniform growth
V. 'Voodoo' (Winter pansy)	15	15		Striking mix of velvety black and orange flowers
V. 'Panola'	15	15	+	Cross between pansy and viola. Long flowering period

Seasons across the table are headed SPRING, SUMMER, AUTUMN, WINTER.

 sowing   transplanting   flowering   + many colours

Zea
Ornamental maize

If people are growing maize in their garden, it is normally the edible sweet corn. However, the ornamental types make excellent dot plants as part of a bedding display or just to add extra interest to a mixed border. A few multi-coloured leaved zeas in a mixed border will add height and interest all summer long.

Zea mays japonica has striking foliage with cream, pink and deep red variegation. 'Baby Fingers' has green leaves, but produces an assortment of golden, red, brown and almost black corns that can be dyed and used as indoor decorations. In fact, they create a stunning effect when used in conjunction with ornamental grasses. The colourful foliage can also be used in dried flower or floral arrangements around the house.

Outdoors, Zea can be planted to create a natural screen in a garden. As dot plants, ornamental maize is usually planted in the centre of the bed. It also looks good when planted next to other tall plants such as the castor oil plant (Ricinus), the tall, white flowering *Nicotiana sylvestris* and the dark leaved, red flowering *Dahlia* 'Bishop of Llandaff'.

Unlike the edible form, which is often sown directly into the vegetable garden, decorative maize is best started into growth in a greenhouse. Sow the large seed individually into a small pot filled with multipurpose compost. Keep the seeds in a temperature of approximately 16°C (64°F) and grow the plants on in gentle heat. If the plants outgrow their small pots, move them into a slightly larger one to keep them growing, as a check in growth can stunt the plants.

Plant out decorative maize in late spring when the danger of frost has passed and be sure to keep the plants well watered until they become established and start to make new growth.

In a good summer, the plants will produce several cobs of corn, which can be dried in the autumn and used as seed for the following year.

Occasionally, Zea can be attacked by aphids, so check for infestations.

soil	Grows in most garden soils that retain moisture in summer
site	These plants are happy when grown in a position in full sun
temp	Half-hardy, withstanding temperatures down to 1°C (34°F)
general care	Water regularly during spells of dry weather. Otherwise, little general care is necessary
pests & diseases	Relatively trouble free. There are few problems from pests and diseases, apart from possible aphid attack

Zea mays japonica

Zea mays japonica

	SPRING	SUMMER	AUTUMN	WINTER	height (cm)	spread (cm)	flower colour	
Zea mays 'Baby Fingers'	🪣 ✂	● ● ●	●		180	45	☐	Produces miniature corns in many colours
Z. mays japonica	🪣 ✂	● ● ●	●		120	30	☐	Multi-coloured leaves

 🪣 *sowing*   ✂ *transplanting*   ● *flowering*

Zinnia

Once a very popular summer bedding plant, zinnias are now regaining much of their popularity and making a comeback. The reason they fell out of favour was because they were not reliable in poor summers. They like warm, dry weather and in cool damp weather the older varieties never used to flower.

Fortunately, several new cultivars have been introduced that are more tolerant of cooler weather. The Profusion Series is one of the leading types grown by both commercial growers and home gardeners. The plants are dwarf and produce single flowers in cherry-red, white and orange. *Zinnia haageana* 'Persian Carpet' is also a good performer in wet weather as the smaller flowers continue to develop and open. Both these dwarf cultivars are suitable for planting in the garden or in containers.

Taller types such as *Z. elegans* 'Allsorts of Zinnia', 'Candy Cane' and 'Envy' have large, double, colourful flowers. They are ideal for a sunny border and as cut flowers.

All zinnias are sensitive to frost and cold weather and should never be planted out

Zinnia haageana 'Persian Carpet'

soil	Any reasonable, fertile garden soil that retains moisture
site	These plants are happiest grown in a position in the full sun
temp	Frost-tender plants, only withstanding temperatures down to 5°C (41°F)
general care	Water regularly in spells of dry weather and deadhead to keep the plants flowering for as long as possible
pests & diseases	Grey mould can be a problem in damp conditions, but otherwise fairly trouble free

until the danger of frost has passed. Sow seeds from mid-spring onwards. Some catalogues may recommend sowing directly into the soil, but the best plants are the ones raised in a greenhouse at 18–20°C (64–68°F).

Zinnia Profusion Series Mixed

	SPRING	SUMMER	AUTUMN	WINTER	height (cm)	spread (cm)	flower colour	
Zinnia elegans 'Allsorts of Zinnia'	🪴 ✂	● ● ●	●		75	75	▢	Small, large, single and double flowers
Z. elegans 'Candy Cane'	🪴 ✂	● ● ●	●		60	60	▢	Double flowers with flecked petals
Z. elegans 'Envy'	🪴 ✂	● ● ●	●		60	60	▢	Large, double flowers with an unusual colour
Z. haageana 'Persian Carpet'	🪴 ✂	● ● ●	●		40	40	▢	Maroon, purple, bi-coloured flowers. Rain-resistant
Z. Profusion Series Mixed	🪴 ✂	● ● ●			30	30	▢	Single flowers, dwarf habit and good weather tolerance

 sowing   transplanting   ● flowering

Troubleshooting

Growing a varied range of bedding plants attracts an equally varied selection of pests, diseases and other problems. The following diagram is designed to help you diagnose conditions suffered by your plants from the symptoms you can observe. Starting with the part of the plant that appears to be the most affected, by answering successive questions 'yes' [✓] or 'no' [✗] you will quickly arrive at a probable cause. Once you have identified the cause, turn to the relevant entry in the directory of pests and diseases for details of how to treat the problem.

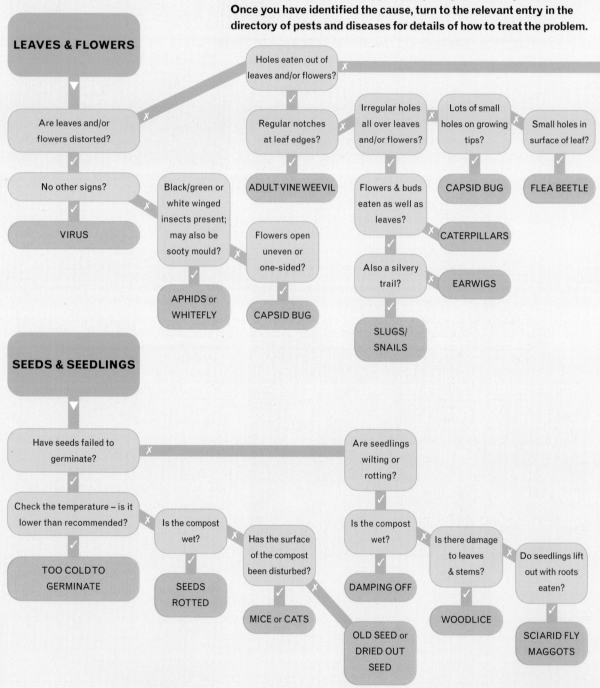

LEAVES & FLOWERS

Holes eaten out of leaves and/or flowers?

Are leaves and/or flowers distorted?

Regular notches at leaf edges?

Irregular holes all over leaves and/or flowers?

Lots of small holes on growing tips?

Small holes in surface of leaf?

No other signs?

Black/green or white winged insects present; may also be sooty mould?

ADULT VINE WEEVIL

Flowers & buds eaten as well as leaves?

CAPSID BUG

FLEA BEETLE

VIRUS

Flowers open uneven or one-sided?

CATERPILLARS

APHIDS or WHITEFLY

CAPSID BUG

Also a silvery trail?

EARWIGS

SLUGS/ SNAILS

SEEDS & SEEDLINGS

Have seeds failed to germinate?

Are seedlings wilting or rotting?

Check the temperature – is it lower than recommended?

Is the compost wet?

Is the compost wet?

Is there damage to leaves & stems?

Do seedlings lift out with roots eaten?

TOO COLD TO GERMINATE

Has the surface of the compost been disturbed?

SEEDS ROTTED

DAMPING OFF

WOODLICE

SCIARID FLY MAGGOTS

MICE or CATS

OLD SEED or DRIED OUT SEED

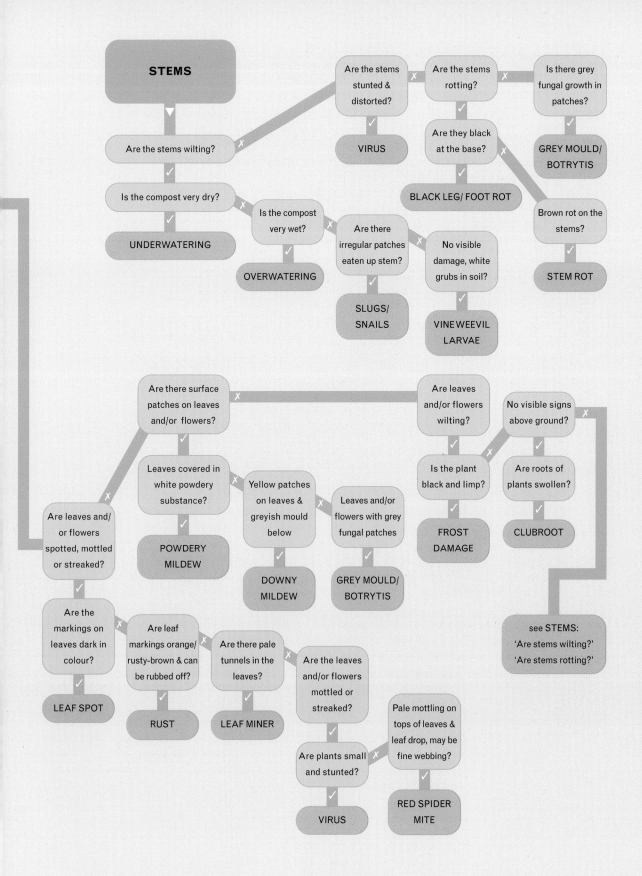

STEMS

Are the stems wilting?

Are the stems stunted & distorted? → VIRUS

Are the stems rotting?

Is there grey fungal growth in patches? → GREY MOULD/ BOTRYTIS

Are they black at the base? → BLACK LEG/ FOOT ROT

Brown rot on the stems? → STEM ROT

Is the compost very dry? → UNDERWATERING

Is the compost very wet? → OVERWATERING

Are there irregular patches eaten up stem? → SLUGS/ SNAILS

No visible damage, white grubs in soil? → VINE WEEVIL LARVAE

Are there surface patches on leaves and/or flowers?

Are leaves and/or flowers wilting?

No visible signs above ground?

Leaves covered in white powdery substance? → POWDERY MILDEW

Yellow patches on leaves & greyish mould below → DOWNY MILDEW

Leaves and/or flowers with grey fungal patches → GREY MOULD/ BOTRYTIS

Is the plant black and limp? → FROST DAMAGE

Are roots of plants swollen? → CLUBROOT

Are leaves and/ or flowers spotted, mottled or streaked?

see STEMS:
'Are stems wilting?'
'Are stems rotting?'

Are the markings on leaves dark in colour? → LEAF SPOT

Are leaf markings orange/ rusty-brown & can be rubbed off? → RUST

Are there pale tunnels in the leaves? → LEAF MINER

Are the leaves and/or flowers mottled or streaked?

Pale mottling on tops of leaves & leaf drop, may be fine webbing? → RED SPIDER MITE

Are plants small and stunted? → VIRUS

Pests & Diseases

Bedding plants are generally easy to grow, hence their popularity. However, like all plants they can occasionally be prone to attack from pests and diseases. Although there are many problems that can affect your plants, they will normally only suffer a few. In many cases, problems can be avoided by growing the plants in the correct conditions and, if the plants are affected, the pests and diseases can usually be controlled.

Slugs & snails

These are serious pests in many gardens and can very quickly cause a great deal of damage by eating holes in leaves or, in the case of seedlings, the entire plant. There are many controls that can be attempted, including: sprinkling slug pellets thinly around affected plants; hand-picking the pests off plants individually; spreading an absorbent gritting aggregate around affected plants; biological control (nematodes); and beer traps and garlic water, which both attract slugs and snails. The secret is to start early before the damage is done.

Rabbits

In rural areas, rabbits will enter gardens and graze bedding plants to ground level. The most effective way of preventing damage is to make the garden rabbit-proof with wire mesh. Certain plants are also less attractive to hungry rabbits, such as dahlias, African and French marigolds, Verbena and Impatiens.

Deer

Deer are becoming more and more of a problem in many areas, and the only effective control is to secure the garden against them. They will cause damage to most plants, including trees and shrubs.

Birds

In spring, some flowers – especially yellow polyanthus – can be pecked by birds. Control of this problem is difficult to effect, although old CDs suspended around the plants do help to deter the birds.

Aphids

There are many species of aphid that will attack plants, both in the garden and in the greenhouse. Aphids are often referred to as greenfly and blackfly, and they feed by sucking the sap from the young stems, leaves and flowerbuds. This weakens affected plants, distorts their growth and can spread viruses. The aphids also excrete a sticky substance called honeydew, that encourages sooty mould to grow. Control is with an insecticide or organic spray such as Derris.

Whitefly

These small winged insects also feed by sucking sap from plants. They tend to be more of a problem in greenhouses, where the conditions are warmer – especially on plants such as Abutilon, Brugmansia and fuchsias. Control by using insecticides containing imidacloprid or bifenthrin. Organic fatty acids will also have some effect. The introduction of a biological control in the form of a tiny parasitic wasp is also effective.

Red spider mite

This is a microscopic spider-like mite that feeds by sucking sap from the leaves of plants, particularly under glass or out doors in hot, dry weather. The foliage of the affected plant takes on a pale mottling and, in severe infestations, silk webbing between the leaves. Insecticides will have some effect on the pests. Biological control with a predatory mite is also very effective, as is keeping the plants misted with water, as red spider mites dislike cool, damp conditions. This pest should be thoroughly dealt with as soon as it is identified anywhere in the garden or greenhouse.

Mice

Mice are mainly a problem in spring, when seeds are being sown in a greenhouse. They scratch the surface of the compost in search of seeds for food. Set traps or use mouse bait.

Cats

Although they are domestic pets, cats can cause damage outside in the garden where hardy annuals have been sown by scratching holes to bury their droppings. Their urine can also scorch the flowers and foliage of plants. There are various repellent sprays and powders available, or gadgets that emit an ultrasonic sound which is supposed to frighten the cat away, but their effectiveness is not always guaranteed.

Woodlice

Woodlice are present in most gardens, but fortunately they feed mainly off dead plant material rather than living plants. They occasionally eat the base of seedlings, but established plants are generally not harmed. Control of woodlice is difficult, although good garden hygiene will help to control their numbers.

Vine weevil

There are several types of weevil, but the vine weevil is the most troublesome. Small, cream-coloured grubs with brown heads feed on the roots of many plants, especially when grown in containers. Particular favourites include Impatiens, Begonia and Fuchsia. The plants will suddenly collapse and die and, when you remove them from their container, you will see that the fine roots will have been eaten. In bedding plants the adults (pictured) do little damage, but small notches eaten from the edge of a leaf are a tell-tale sign that they are about. Control is by drenching the compost with imidacloprid, or by using a biological control in the form of a pathogenic nematode, that is watered into the compost or soil in late summer.

Caterpillars

There are many different moth and butterfly caterpillars that eat holes in the leaves of plants. Many of these creatures are nocturnal feeders, which makes it difficult to find them on or around plants during the day. Spraying with rotenone (Derris) is very effective, or you can pick off the caterpillars individually. As with most forms of pest control discussed in these pages, the earlier the better!

Cutworms

The cutworm is a moth caterpillar that lives in the soil surrounding plants and feeds by eating roots and the base of the stem, resulting in the plant suddenly dying. The caterpillars are up to 4cm (1¼in) in length and usually a dark, greenish-brown in colour. They are less of a problem in ground that is well cultivated. Unfortunately, no insecticides for control are available.

Capsid bugs

Capsid bugs are pale green insects that suck sap from the tips of shoots on plants such as fuchsias and dahlias, resulting in many small holes. They also feed on the flower buds, causing them to become misshapen and to open un-evenly, if at all. These pests insert a toxic saliva into the plants they attack that causes areas of the expanding leaves to be killed. In fuchsias, sometimes the problem can be so serious that it can lead to the failure of flowering altogether. Control of this pest is not easy, although an insecticide spray applied as soon as damage is spotted will help.

Earwigs

These brown creatures are easily recognized by their large pincers at the rear and can be found in most gardens. They chew ragged holes in young leaves and flowers, especially dahlias. Earwigs can easily be caught in traps made from small plant pots filled with straw or shredded paper and positioned on canes at flower height. The earwigs will hide in them during the day and can be removed and destroyed.

Sciarid flies

These are small flies that can be found on the surface of compost in plant pots or seed trays in a greenhouse. Generally they do not cause much damage and are often a sign that you are over-watering, as they prefer wet conditions. Allowing the surface of the compost to dry out before watering will help to get rid of them.

Flea beetles

These are tiny, metallically shiny beetles which will jump from plants when disturbed. They eat small holes in the upper surface of leaves. Flea beetles are often found on wallflowers, stock and alyssum. Derris dust can be used to control them on seedlings.

Viruses

Viruses can affect many plants in several ways, but the most common symptoms are distorted and stunted growth and mottling or streaking on leaves and flowers. They are mainly spread from infected to healthy plants by sap-sucking insects such as aphids and whitefly. No virus control is available, but good pest control will help to contain the disease in most bedding plants.

Damping off

A fungal disease that attacks seedlings and causes them to collapse and die. The disease can spread quickly in warm, moist conditions, causing a great deal of damage. Use clean pots and trays and avoid sowing the seeds too thickly. Water seedlings only with mains water, as the spores may infect a garden water butt. Water compost after sowing with copper-based fungicide and again after pricking out.

Foot rot/Root rot/Black leg

These three common plant diseases are all very similar and attack tissue at the base of the plant or the roots, causing the leaves to yellow and wilt. The fungal disease responsible for these three conditions is similar to damping off (see above) and tends to be more of a problem in young plants when they are grown in un-hygienic conditions. To avoid all three problems, always grow your plants in clean pots and use fresh compost.

Powdery mildew

White powdery mould develops on the surface of the leaves and stems, and the plant may yellow and look distorted. There are many different types of mildew, but each one is specific and usually only attacks a single genus of plants. Keep the plants watered and well fed, as powdery mildew is worse in hot, dry weather. At the first sign of attack, spray with a fungicide containing mycobutanil.

Downy mildew

This fungal disease shows as yellow blotches on the upper surface of the leaf followed by greyish or purplish fungal growth below the leaf. It is more of a problem on young plants growing in moist conditions. Give young plants adequate ventilation in a greenhouse and avoid watering over the foliage.

Rust

The tell-tale signs of this disease are orange or rust-coloured raised spots on the leaves and stems. Rust is more of a problem in wet summers. Remove affected leaves and spray with a fungicide that contains mycobutanil. If rust has been a problem in your garden in the past, look out for disease-resistant cultivars.

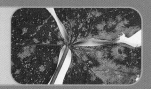

Wilting

There are many reasons that cause plants to wilt. Dry soil or compost around the plants' roots is perhaps the most common reason. Plants growing in very wet conditions can also wilt as a result of the fibrous roots rotting. Young, tender plants that have not been hardened off properly may also wilt when planted out, especially in warm or windy conditions. Wilting can also be a disease, such as in the case of asters.

Leaf spots

Leaf spots can be caused by many different diseases. The spots can vary in shape, colour and size, depending on the disease. Any damaged leaves should be removed and, if the problem persists, spray with a fungicide. Watering over foliage in bright weather can also cause spots or scorch marks.

Frost damage

This is usually a problem in spring when bedding plants are first planted out. Symptoms are black, withered foliage. In severe cases the whole plant will be affected. Ideally, only plant after the danger of frost has passed, or cover plants with horticultural fleece for protection if a late frost is forecast.

Leaf miners

Leaf miners eat the centre of leaves, leaving dead or discoloured patches, but they cause little actual damage. However, the tracks that they leave behind on leaves as they burrow through them can be unsightly, so you might want to bring them under control. These pests are difficult to get at, so the best method of dealing with them is to use a systemic insecticide. Plants likely to be attacked include chrysanthemums and Calendula. Pick off and dispose of damaged leaves.

Club root

This disease is usually associated with cabbages in a vegetable garden, but it affects all members of the Brassica family, including wallflowers and stocks. It is a soil-borne fungal disease that affects the roots, causing them to swell and distort. Eventually the plant will collapse and die. Control is very difficult, but adding lime to the soil will help, as the disease prefers acid conditions. It is also advisable to grow the plants in containers, using sterile compost.

Tuber/Corm rot

Various fungal and bacterial diseases can cause rots on bulbs, tubers and corms. They usually show as a soft area that turns brown and rotten, especially when the plants are in storage. If caught early, the affected area can be cut off back to healthy flesh and the wound dusted with sulphur. Always store bulbs, tubers and corms in cool, dry conditions to avoid rot.

Stem rot

Stem rot is a fungal disease which, as its name suggests, causes the stem of the affected plant to rot. Both the base or the whole stem can suffer from the condition. The plant will wilt and eventually die. The disease has the worst effects in cold, wet weather. Remove and dispose of affected plants.

Index of Plants

General Index

Acknowledgements

The author and publishers would like to thank Coolings Nurseries for their cooperation and assistance with the photography in this book, including the loan of tools and much specialist equipment. Special thanks go to Sandra Gratwick. Coolings Nurseries Ltd., Rushmore Hill, Knockholt, Kent, TN14 7NN. Tel: 00 44 1959 532269; Email: coolings@coolings.co.uk; Website: www.coolings.co.uk.

The author would also like to thank Nottingham City Council, Kindergarten Plants and Ball Colgrave Ltd. The publishers would also like to thank Thompson & Morgan (UK) Ltd for a number of the plant portraits that appear throughout the A–Z sections of this book.